IRISH FLOUR MILLING

Oil painting of Shackleton's mill, on the Liffey near Lucan, Dublin, by Kevin McNamara.
(Reproduced by kind permission of Messums, London)

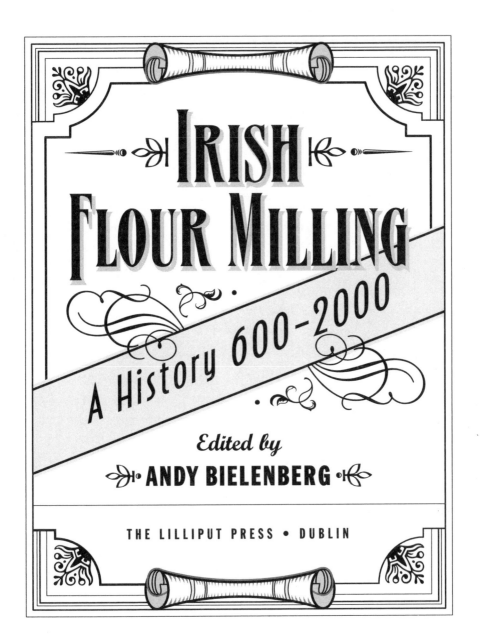

IRISH FLOUR MILLING

A History 600–2000

Edited by

ANDY BIELENBERG

THE LILLIPUT PRESS • DUBLIN

First published 2003 by
THE LILLIPUT PRESS LTD
62-63 Sitric Road, Arbour Hill, Dublin 7, Ireland

A CIP record is available from the British Library.

ISBN 1 84351 019 7 (pbk)
1 84351 020 0 (hbk)

Set in 11.5 on 14.5 point Jensen
Designed and typeset by Anú Design, Tara
Printed by Creative Print and Design Group, Middlesex

Contents

Acknowledgments

The idea to write this history originated with Edward Hallinan, whose family were significant flour millers in various parts of Co. Cork. His motivation and historical connections within the industry were critical in bringing the book to press, and he deserves special credit for its completion.

We would like to thank our sponsors Andrews Milling Belfast, Barnetts Belfast, Dock Milling, Flavahans (Kilmacthomas), IAWS Plc, Odlum Group Ltd and Rank's, and the following: Bill Alton (ex Rank's), Robert Barnett (Barnetts Belfast), Ken Brisbane (ex Rank's and Glynn's), Lynett Brown, Gordon Bull (Rank's), David Carroll (ex Bolands), Bill Cleland (Neill's), James Davidson, Dr Brian Donnelly (National Archives), Alex Findlater, permission from Fingal County Council to use Shackleton's mill, John Flahavan (Flahavans), John Flynn (ex Bolands and Odlums), Stuart Freeman, Seamus Funge (Rank's), Sandy Gallie (ex Robinsons), Chris Graham (ex Robinson Milling Systems), Mrs Caroline Hamilton, Dr Fred Hamond, Nora Harty (ex IFMA), Pam Nicol (Mercier), Plunkett Hayes (Croom Mills), Niall Higgins (Dock Milling), Stuart Holohan, William Hogg (Mills & Millers of Ireland), Joe Humpheries (ex Bolands), The Industrial Heritage Association of Ireland, David Johnstone, Arthur Jones (Rank's), Alan Keegan, Canice Kelly (Rank's), Peter Lyons, John K. Lynch (Mills & Millers of Ireland), Philip Lynch (chairman of IAWS), Walter McDonagh (Going & Smith and Shackleton's), Brian McGee, John McInerney (IAWS), Hughie McSweeney, Dawson Moreland (Andrews Milling Belfast), Michael Moreland (Andrews Milling Belfast), Patrick J. Murphy (ex Bolands), Claire O'Callaghan (Odlum Group), Dan O'Donoghue (ex Bolands), Loftus Odlum (ex Odlum Group), Norman Odlum (last president of the IFMA), Philip Odlum (Odlum Group), Stephen Odlum (Odlum Group), Tim Odlum (Odlum Group), Dick Roberts, Mark Robinson (ex Bolands), Jeromy Shiels, George Spillane (ex

Rank's), Canon Troy P.P., Tom Tynan (IAWS) and Declan Wallace (Rank's), and many others interested in the industry.

We would like to acknowledge the research of John McHugh, the trade figures of Peter Solar, and the special assistance of Mary Shackleton. Brian Donnelly of the National Archives was particularly helpful in providing access to some of the surviving business records of the industry. Finally, we would like to thank Marsha Swan and The Lilliput Press for taking on a difficult text.

Foreword

Flour milling is one of the oldest and most essential of industries known to man, who needs to have cereals broken down before utilizing them as a food source. The story of Irish flour milling – and its significant role in the development of the commercial, industrial and social life of Ireland – comes at a most appropriate time following a major transition in the industry since the Second World War.

We congratulate Edward Hallinan, whose family has played a major role in the industry, on his inspiration in bringing together an outstanding team of contributors. They were greatly assisted in their efforts by many friends in the industry.

This is a fascinating tale, moving from the country millers, whose radius of distribution was limited by the distance a horse could travel, right through to 2003 when only five major mills service the needs of the 32 counties. The dramatic new developments in milling technology from the 1870s onwards were quickly adopted in Ireland, with our own company Bolands pioneering them in 1880. The remarkable role of the Odlum family, from their first water-mill in 1834 near Portlaoise to their continued presence in the industry today, proves that the incorporation of the Wise Owl symbol in the family crest is not inappropriate.

This book is a tribute to the many generations who contributed to the development of one of Ireland's greatest industries. They varied from the man who pushed the sack truck, to the millers, whose enterprise and foresight made it all possible. We are pleased to be involved with the Irish flour-milling industry both as suppliers, participants and supporters of *Irish Flour Milling*.

Philip Lynch,
Chairman, IAWS
November 2003

IRISH
FLOUR MILLING

1

The Development of
Milling Technology in Ireland
c. 600–1875

COLIN RYNNE

THIS ESSAY IS primarily concerned with the development of grain-milling technology in Ireland from the earliest water-powered mills to the period immediately preceding the introduction of roller milling. To the surprise of many, the archaeology of mills and milling in Ireland has shed more light on the development of one of humankind's most basic technologies than that of any region of post-Roman Europe or, indeed, of Asia. Long seen as being on the periphery of European technological development, Ireland has confounded many by producing the earliest evidence of water-powered grain mills in the post-Roman world. Ireland, it is clear, was not a sleepy technological backwater prior to the establishment of the Anglo-Norman colony in the late twelfth century. Throughout the later medieval period and in the post-medieval period, contact with England ensured that Ireland remained in the mainstream of such developments. Closer integration with the economy of Britain from the seventeenth century onwards also strengthened these links. But in a country where large and often internationally significant food-processing industries were to develop in the eighteenth century, the advance of native industry perhaps inevitably involved both technology transfer and local innovation. The development of large mills during the second half of the eighteenth century, for example, led to the first significant evolution of multi-storey power transmission for industrial buildings anywhere in Europe. Adaptation and innovation, therefore, are key features of the evolution of grain-milling technology in Ireland.

Milling in Early Medieval Ireland, 600–1200

The introduction of water-powered mills into Ireland, in either the late sixth or early seventh century, is likely to have brought about important changes in the way in which cereal crops were processed for human consumption. Up to this period, the milling of cereals involved the use of the rotary quern, which required great physical effort for relatively small returns but by no means did the advent of water-powered mills completely replace the use of the rotary quern in many parts of Europe. The use of the quern was always associated with small-scale domestic production, as it continues to be in many Asian countries such as Iran, while its use in Ireland was recorded as late as the 1970s in Co. Kilkenny for *práipín* making.[1] The frequency with which disc querns are found on Irish early Christian sites indicates that they were very common, a fact which is also borne out by their frequent mention in both the law tracts and the contemporary hagiographical literature. As in Graeco-Roman antiquity and, indeed, in more recent practice in Ireland and elsewhere, the laborious task of turning the quern in early Irish society was performed by women. It is clear from the early Irish sources that such work was a special task of the *cumal* or bondmaiden, and in *Cormac's Glossary*, *cumal* is defined as a 'woman that is grinding at a quern; for this was the business of bondswomen before (water)mills were made'.[2] The author of the twelfth-century *Cogadh Gaedhel re Gallaibh* provides partial confirmation of this when he boasts that Brian Boru made 'quern maids' of his Norse female captives.[3] An analogous situation was found in contemporary Anglo-Saxon England, where the existence of a special class of female slave, *grindende peowan*, is indicated in Aethelbert's law code.[4]

The use of water-mills and grain-drying kilns in the early historic period is indicative of two important developments: a growing need to ensure regular supplies of grain for a rapidly increasing rural population, and its corollary, the expansion of tillage. Indeed, the increased use of both kilns and water-mills in the processing of extra cereal crops may well have accelerated the expansion of tillage, whilst in their absence no such expansion could have been sustained with any degree of consistency. Yet the relative frequency with which rotary

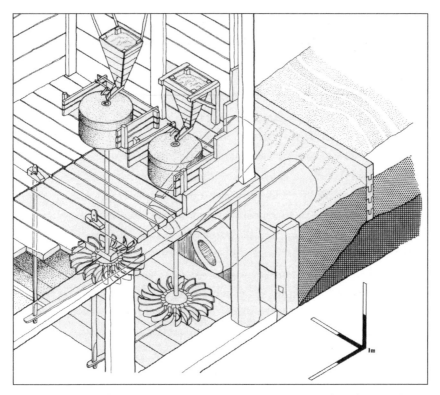

Reconstruction of two-flume horizontal mill at Little Island, Co. Cork, c. 630. This is the earliest known example of its type in the world. (All reconstructions drawn by Colin Rynne.)

querns are recovered from early medieval Irish settlement sites would also seem to indicate that small-scale domestic production was not interrupted by the introduction of the water-mill.

The horizontal- and vertical-wheeled water-mills are both known to have been used in early medieval Ireland, though of these the horizontal-wheeled variety was by far the most common.[5] In most cases a small, fast-flowing stream was impounded by the simple expedient of constructing a dam of earth, stones or clay to create a small reservoir, from which a shallow feeder channel or mill-race led to the millhouse. Incoming water was directed into a hollowed-out wooden trough, splayed internally so as to develop a concentrated water jet, which was then discharged against the dished vanes of the waterwheel. The drive from the waterwheel to the upper millstone was direct, and so the latter rotated with every corresponding revolution of the waterwheel.

Where the production of flour and meal are concerned, the essential differences between the rotary quern and any water-powered variety are that in the former, the grain is fed into the stones by hand, and the finished product, owing to the fact that there is no provision for adjusting the distance between the upper and lower stones, is of much coarser quality. A further important difference involves the drying of the cereal grains prior to their reduction to either meal or flour. In the relatively damp climate of north-western Europe, the use of grain-drying kilns was generally necessary (after short drying seasons or wet harvests) to dry or ripen the crop in the ear in order to facilitate milling and threshing: while kiln drying was not always necessary to facilitate threshing, some form of elementary parching or kilning of the cereal grains was obligatory before milling. For as experiments with rotary querns have indicated, undried grain is not easily milled, and the amount of time needed to process it, in contrast to that taken to process kiln-dried grain, is considerably increased. Corn-drying kilns were already in use in Britain during the late Roman period, and the appearance of water-mills around the same period is hardly coincidental.[6] There is also a close correlation between centres of Roman population and Romano-British water-mill sites. In relation to the post-Roman kilns at Poundbury in Dorset, Michael Monk has noted that the appearance of corn dryers in later Roman Britain is likely to be related to an increased demand for cereal crops. On present evidence, it would appear that similar considerations existed in early medieval Ireland.

The millstone assembly in early Irish horizontal-wheeled mills consisted of an upper revolving stone (the 'runnerstone', O.Ir. *lia*) between 24–40" in diameter, and a lower stationary stone (the 'bedstone', O.Ir. *indeoin*), 22–c. 40" in diameter. The vast majority of the recorded examples were carved out of some variety of sandstone. The underside of the runnerstone and the upper surface of the bedstone were, in addition, carefully dressed so as to ensure the most effective passage of the cereal grains through the stones. The 'zoning' of the millstone surfaces survived on both the runnerstone fragment from Cloontycarthy, Co. Cork (c. 833) and on the working surfaces of the Mashanaglass millstones. This latter mill was believed by its excavator to be seventeenth-century, but the dendrochronology dates for more recently investigated sites, whose surviving components are very similar to those recovered from Mashanaglass, would suggest that the Mashanaglass mill was an early medieval structure.[7]

Milling was essentially a two-stage process, which involved the separation of the husks from the grains and then the reduction of the kernels to either flour or meal. Both of these processes were facilitated by fine adjustment of the millstones with a tentering device, upon whose lower horizontal arm the entire waterwheel assembly rotated. From this a vertical arm extended upwards to the grinding-room floor. An upward movement of the vertical arm produced a corresponding movement of the entire waterwheel assembly, and as the drive-shaft was connected directly to the runnerstone it was possible to lift or lower the latter as required. To remove the husks, the millstones were first set at a distance equivalent to the width of one cereal grain apart, and when the grain had been fed through the stones, it was then removed from the mill and winnowed to separate the unwanted husks. The hopper was then refilled and the arms of the tentering device were finely adjusted so that the stones were now

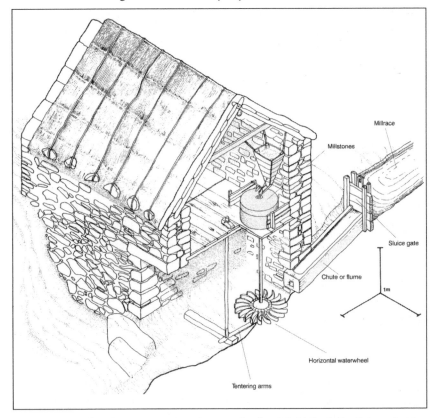

Reconstruction of ninth-century monastic horizontal mill on High Island, Co. Galway, showing main components.

set at a distance of half the width of a cereal grain apart. The finished product was then sieved to remove impurities.

Ireland in the early medieval period shows a remarkable precocity with regard to the development of water-powered grain mills, a phenomenon that has no parallel anywhere in medieval Europe. There are, indeed, more scientifically dated mill sites of the first millennium in the province of Munster alone than there are from the rest of Europe. Two varieties of water-powered grain mill were used in Ireland from the early decades of the seventh century. The first of these was the horizontal-wheeled mill, in which the waterwheel rotated in a horizontal plane and whose movement was communicated to the millstones. These include the earliest-known tide mills, the earliest close association of vertical- and horizontal-wheeled mills in post-Roman Europe and the earliest European twin-flume horizontal-wheeled mills.[8] But most surprisingly of all, the earliest examples of certain varieties of water-mill that are documented throughout Asia and Europe have been found in Ireland; while the earliest known vernacular technical terms in any European language for the component parts of the horizontal-wheeled mill are in Old Irish.

Over thirty Irish mill sites have been dated by dendrochronology and have produced dates which fall between the early seventh and thirteenth centuries. A further seven sites have been dated by radio carbon dating, although up until quite recently the determinations produced for the Irish mills using this technique can at best provide the outline date of 'early medieval'.[9] At least three of the sites dated by dendrochronology were clearly vertical-wheeled mills. There are also a large number of sites discovered during the nineteenth century which, on the basis of their morphology, are also likely to date from the early medieval period, including Mashanaglass, Co. Cork.

The vertical-wheeled water-mill in Ireland is at least as old as the horizontal-wheeled variety. Three early medieval sites employed vertical waterwheels: Little Island, Co. Cork (630); Morett, Co. Laois (770); and Ardcloyne, Co. Cork (787), which produced the first identifiable vertical waterwheel component from an Irish site. But while the Little Island example was contemporary with the twin-flume horizontal-wheeled mill on the same site, the overall relationships between both varieties of mill in early medieval Ireland are still not clearly understood.[10]

The water-powered mill was probably introduced into Ireland sometime before 600 from Mediterranean Europe. By the tenth century, on the basis of

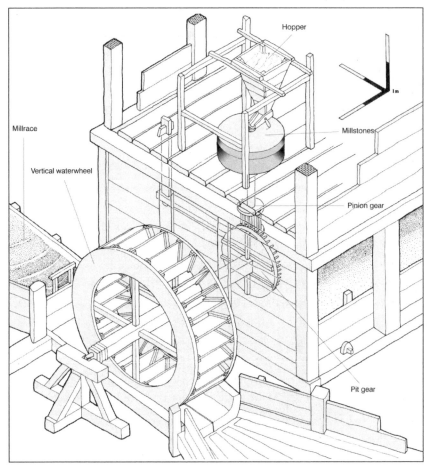

Reconstruction of vertical-wheeled mill at Little Island, Co. Cork, *c.* 630. This is, on present evidence, the earliest known example of its type in Ireland.

the archaeological and documentary evidence, the millwrights' trade had developed as an individual craft in Ireland, while regional millwrighting styles (as evident from the different types of waterwheels in use) had already evolved throughout the entire island. These developments have no satisfactory analogues elsewhere in post-Roman Europe, and attest to the advanced nature of the agrarian economy of early medieval Ireland.[11]

The Later Medieval Period

The landscape of Ireland would have contained a large number of water-mills on the eve of the Anglo-Norman conquest. Water-mills and related features such as dams, millponds and mill-races, were clearly common features of the early historic Irish landscape, so much so that early Irish jurists went to great lengths to provide a legal framework for the water rights pertaining to them, which is evident from the law tract *Coibnes Uisci Thairidne* (Kinship of Conducted Water). By the later medieval period millponds were common features of the landscape, the maintenance of which, along with related features such as a mill-races and sluices, often proved to be a heavy financial burden on both monastic and manorial estates.

As in many parts of Europe, horizontal-wheeled mills in Ireland were gradually replaced by vertical-wheeled mills. In the aftermath of the Anglo-Norman conquest and settlement of Ireland in the late twelfth century, new customs and technology were introduced. Indeed the vertical waterwheel, and other industrial processes and power transmission systems associated with it, are likely to have been used on Anglo-Norman manors and on the monastic estates of the Cistercian and Augustinian houses established in Ireland. Nonetheless, the horizontal-wheeled mill survived in Ireland throughout the medieval period, and in certain parts of Ireland (particularly on the western seaboard) it was still relatively common in the middle of the nineteenth century. Until quite recently the cluster of early medieval dates for Irish horizontal-wheeled sites, and the apparent absence of high medieval sites from the archaeological record, led to the suggestion that a shortage of timber for building purposes seriously curtailed mill-building activity. However, there are unambiguous references to horizontal-wheeled mills in Irish documentary sources dating to the period after the first millennium. In the eleventh-century text of *Togail Bruidne Da Derga* there is a clear-cut reference to a *sciatha* or horizontal waterwheel paddle. There is at least one twelfth-century horizontal-wheeled mill site at Clonlonan, Co. Westmeath (*c.* 1145), and a thirteenth-century example from Corcannon, Co. Wexford (*c.* 1228).

The use of water-powered corn mills in Ireland from the Anglo-Norman period onwards is reasonably well-documented in contemporary sources. However, until quite recently the archaeological evidence was somewhat limited, particularly for mills in urban environments. Many of Ireland's principal coastal towns such as Dublin, Cork and Waterford developed from Viking trading ports, and for the most part, the beginnings of urban development in Ireland date to the latter part of the first millennium. The development of urban centres in Ireland led to the establishment of water-mills within their immediate environs, and the consequent adaptation of the water supply of these mills to different hydrological conditions. In medieval Dublin and Cork, for example, which were both established on tidal rivers, water-powered mills tended to avoid their tidal reaches. For the most part, water-mills were constructed on tributaries that traversed the higher ground overlooking the towns before discharging into the tidal stretches of the main river. This basic locational pattern continued well into the nineteenth century and was only really modified when the introduction of steam-powered prime movers enabled industries to become established directly on the quaysides of Ireland's main ports. In Dublin and Cork these non-tidal tributary streams tended to become extensively regularized from the Anglo-Norman period onwards. For example, the River Poddle in Dublin, a tributary of the Liffey, had already become effectively canalized for industrial and domestic water supply purposes by the thirteenth century.

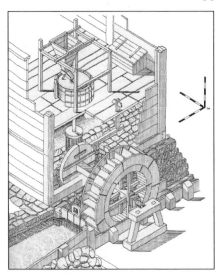

Reconstruction of fourteenth-century vertical mill at Patrick Street, Dublin.

The vast majority of the water-mills erected during the Anglo-Norman period in Munster and indeed, throughout Ireland, were involved in the processing of cereal crops. In 1990 the remains of an Anglo-Norman vertical undershot grain mill were excavated at Patrick Street in Dublin. The mill had been built early in the thirteenth century, and almost entirely rebuilt in the fourteenth. Its waterwheel was positioned directly over a canalized section of the River Poddle. Similar mills would have been quite common throughout the Anglo-Norman lordship, particularly on rivers in low-lying areas. There is little difference between the Patrick Street mill and the undershot water-mills known from early medieval Ireland in terms of both likely power and output. However, there is currently no evidence for the use of either breast-shot or over-shot waterwheels in early medieval Ireland, although if they were never used in this period they would almost certainly have been introduced in the Anglo-Norman period.

Water supply was, of course, an important locational consideration for Europe's larger monastic orders, and no less so when they established houses in Ireland during the twelfth century. Fifty-one out of the fifty-six Augustinian and eighteen of the twenty-five Cistercian houses in Ireland were sited on the banks of rivers. Water was needed for the domestic offices of the abbey as well as for powering the abbey's mill, and in many cases great effort was expended in procuring an adequate supply. At the Augustinian abbey of Athassel, Co. Tipperary, a mill-race was cut across a meander loop on the River Suir over a mile wide in amplitude. This was no mean feat when one considers that the completed channel was over 2000 ft long, and was wide enough to require a bridge over 40 ft wide to span it. At Holy Cross Abbey, Co. Tipperary, a series of islands in the River Suir, which effectively created a narrow water channel, enabled the monks to cut a short mill-race from it for the abbey mill.

However, sites which had a small tributary flowing down a steep slope in a river valley, thus providing a low-volume, fast-flowing water source, were prized. Such sites were exploited by Cistercian abbeys such as at Monasternenagh, Co. Limerick; and Augustinian sites such as Bridgetown, Co. Cork, Rathkeale, Co. Limerick, and Cahir, Co. Tipperary.[12]

The introduction of the wind-powered mill into Ireland is unquestionably an Anglo-Norman development, although the first recorded instance of such a mill occurs almost 100 years after the first recorded English windmill of 1185.

Postmill from treatise by Agostino Ramelli. (*Le Diverse et Artificiose Machine* [1588], pl. 133)

The earliest documented windmill in Ireland was at work at Kilscanlan, near Old Ross, Co. Wexford, in 1281. This is most likely to have been a postmill, in which the actual mill building is rotated about a central wooden pivot in order that the wind sails can face into the prevailing wind. The entire structure could be rotated through 360 degrees by means of a 'tail pole', which enabled the miller to adjust the position of his sails to accommodate changes in wind direction by the simple expedient of rotating the mill building. The mill machinery was contained within a wooden framework, and the entire structure was usually erected on high ground, often on a specially prepared mound adjacent to a township. A number of possible medieval windmill mounds have been identified at Diamor, Bartramstown, Derrypatrick, Hurdlestown, and Agher in Co. Meath, but there is no other published evidence of examples from the rest of Ireland.[13] A small number of windmills are likely to have been used in medieval Munster, especially on the west coast, while from the Anglo-Norman period onwards, the introduction of the windmill was an important technological innovation on the east coast of Ireland. On present evidence it would appear that postmills were no longer built in Ireland after the seventeenth century, and there are no surviving examples.

The rapid expansion of tillage in Ireland during the Anglo-Norman period meant that by the late thirteenth century, the island was a net exporter of cereals. Many religious orders, principally in Britain but also a number in France, obtained supplies from Ireland. The development of more complex distributive networks for cereals in the Munster area can be gleaned from archaeobotanical evidence from the medieval town of Waterford. With the exception of oats, which were brought up in sheaves, all of the cereals brought into the town for consumption were fully processed in the countryside prior to being milled within the town or in water-powered mills within its immediate environs. Anglo-Norman corn-drying kilns, in which the grain was dried to facilitate milling, have been recorded in Waterford and Cork, which clearly indicates that this essential pre-milling process was also conducted within walled towns.[14]

The archaeological evidence for water-powered grain mills in Anglo-Norman Ireland is somewhat sparse. Indeed, to date there is only one excavated example from Patrick Street in Dublin that can be firmly dated to this period, although a second site at Ballyine, Co. Limerick, is likely to date to the high medieval period. At Ballyine the remains of a stone-built mill house and wheelrace for a vertical breast-shot waterwheel were investigated, along with a millpond about 10,000 ft^2 in extent.[15] No date more specific than pre-1857 (i.e. before the first edition of the Ordnance Survey of the area) has been advanced for the site, but the remains of the machinery associated with it clearly indicate that it is medieval. The fragmentary remains of some ten 'pivot stones', which would have formed the lower part of a footstep upon which the pinion gear rotated, were found in the tail race of the mill, into which they were discarded when they wore out. Very similar stones were recovered from an eighth-century undershot water-mill at Morett, Co. Laois, and while these can be associated with more recent horizontal-wheeled mills in Ireland and elsewhere, where vertical waterwheels are concerned, they are generally associated with Roman and medieval contexts. Further evidence for the medieval date of this mill can be adduced from the wooden-mill components recovered from the site. No less than eight gear-pegs or teeth were found that were similar in size and general morphology to those recovered from English medieval sites at Chingley Forge, Kent, period I (c. 1300–50) and Bordesley Abbey (late twelfth to early fourteenth centuries), along with a small section of the waterwheel's shroud (i.e. a curved wooden plate forming the outer walls of the buckets set on the periphery of the waterwheel).[16] By comparison with similar English mill components, therefore, this must surely be a medieval water-mill. However, while the Chingley and Bordesley Abbey sites were associated with iron-working, the recovery of millstone fragments from the Ballyine site indicate that it was a grain mill. If this is a medieval site, as now seems likely, then it is the earliest-known example of a breast-shot mill in Ireland.

The scarcity of excavated Anglo-Norman water-powered grain mills, given their frequency in existing documentary sources, is somewhat puzzling. In certain cases these sites are likely to have been reused by later industrial mills, but a large number of sites remain to be discovered. Indeed, there are no published examples of Anglo-Norman water-powered millstones nor, for that matter, have any examples of imported millstones from the Anglesey quarries or France been identified thus far. Millstones would have had to be replaced every few years, and so we might expect to find fragments of discarded millstones near mill sites or reused as building stone at other sites.

In the Anglo-Norman period, the expense to the lord of building and maintaining a mill was significant. Frequent repairs necessitated by flooding to mill channels and ponds, including the replacement of worn machinery, would have been a heavy financial burden on the manor. By the fourteenth century, larger, more elaborate water-mills than those investigated at Ballyine and Patrick Street were in operation, such as the King's Mills at Ardee in Co. Louth and at Dublin. These mills were larger and may perhaps be unrepresentative of those elsewhere in the lordship, although in 1305 at Ardmayle, Co. Tipperary, two mills were valued at 24 marks per annum.[17] By the turn of the fourteenth century, both iron and steel were used for mill bearings, and nails were used extensively in mill buildings, as evidenced at Ballyine and in contemporary accounts. At the King's Mills in Dublin in 1314, for example, 53s. 2d. was spent on timber boards and nails for the mill building, while 25s. 6½d. (almost half that amount) was expended on iron and steel for the journals and bearings. By comparison, the mill iron of Leymille and the Maltmille at Ardee, owned by Edward I, was respectively valued at 5s. and 4s. in 1305. In the latter case the lower value would appear to reflect their poor condition. Nonetheless, the millstones of the 'old and broken' Cornmille at Ardee appear to have been originally bound with iron hoops valued at 18s. The use of iron bands as reinforcement for the millstones is a refinement absent in early medieval examples, and was a clear indication that larger millstones were being employed from at least the fourteenth century onwards. Furthermore, it is unlikely that steel – an expensive commodity – was used in pre-Norman Irish water-mills, or indeed in Gaelic areas during the Anglo-Norman period.

The expense involved was necessary to fully exploit the feudal obligation of 'suit to the mill', whereby the lord's tenants were legally bound to bring all of their cereals to the lord's mill to be ground. The miller was empowered to charge a toll (*multura*) for this service (usually ¹⁄₁₆ or ¹⁄₂₀ of the meal or flour ground in the mill), and effectively the private ownership of water-mills or rotary querns was outlawed, the lord's reeve being empowered to seize and destroy them. None of the tenants of Coole and Britway in Co. Cork in 1365 were to have a hand mill (*molam manualem*) without the lord's permission', and they could be fined for having one.[18] As late as 1637 the tenants of Dr John Richardson in the Barony of Tyrhugh, Co. Donegal, were still required to 'grind their corn at the mill built upon the college land [Trinity College, Dublin] by Francis Bressy late deceased and pay the accustomed toll', whilst both the seneschal and the millers were empowered to search the tenant's houses for quernstones.[19] Manorial tenants were also under obligation to assist in repairs to ponds and watercourses, as at Coole and Britway in 1365, where an ordinance states 'they are obliged to clean the millpond (*millepolle*)'.[20]

In the inventory of the King's Mills at Ardee, we find a rare mention of a copper *enee*, a vessel used to measure the toll.[21] The manner in which the grain was poured into the measures was strictly regulated: the grain was mounded over the top of the vessel and then struck off with a strike or strickle. What remained was then pressed into the measure, whereupon the entire process was repeated until the vessel was tightly packed. Deliberate anomalies in this process were a continuous source of grievance for medieval tenants, with millers often being accused of dishonesty. The medieval stereotype of the dishonest miller is best illustrated by Chaucer in *The Canterbury Tales*, and in the *Laws and Usages of the City of Dublin of 1309*. Extremely short shrift was afforded to dishonest millers:

> If a miller take corn to grind, he shall take it by the strike
> measure, and shall take it to the [customer's] house full
> and well pressed two or three times. And if the miller be
> guilty of larceny of corn or flour to the value of fourpence,
> he shall be hanged in the mill on a beam.[22]

In Gaelic areas, however, feudal practices were ignored and it seems likely that both privately owned horizontal- and vertical-wheeled mills, along with rotary querns, continued to be used. This is not, however, an index of technological regression nor of the relative underdeveloped state of the Gaelic agrarian economy. As has been seen, the native Irish had long been familiar with both direct-drive and geared mills, both horse- and water-powered. The Anglo-Normans chose to exploit their estates using the technology of the vertical-wheeled mill, but in other areas of Europe feudal lords used horizontal-wheeled mills. In the Contado of Florence, for example, a region demonstrably more developed in the high middle ages than any region of the Anglo-Norman lordship in Ireland, a considerable number of horizontal-wheeled mills operated under feudal custom.[23] Indeed, apart from iron millstone hoops, there is little difference between the horizontal-wheeled mills of northern Italy in the high medieval period and contemporary examples in Ireland.[24] Needless to say, medieval Florence could hardly be characterized as a technologically backward area.

The Development of the Wind-Powered Grain Mill in Ireland to *c.* 1900

In the early decades of the seventeenth century, the type of windmill that was to become relatively common in Ireland's main grain-producing counties on the eastern seaboard makes an appearance in the Irish Midlands. The tower mill, so called because the mill machinery is contained within a typically cylindrical, masonry tower, is first mentioned in the early 1630s at Warren, Co. Roscommon, and at Knock, Co. Longford. In the tower mill the building is a fixed entity and the moving portion containing the sails and the driveshaft (or windshaft) are carried in a rotating cap section set on top of the tower. A tailpole with a tiller wheel at its lower end was connected to the cap portion, a movement of the pole in any direction enabling the miller to turn the cap and thence the sails into the prevailing wind. At Rindoon, Co. Roscommon, the stump of a seventeenth-century tower mill survives on what may well be a medieval post windmill mound.[25] The automatic fantail developed in England by Edmund Lee in 1745 enabled the cap section to swivel automatically into the wind, but this device was virtually unknown in Ireland.

The design of early Irish tower mills owes much to contemporary British practices, particularly to those characteristic of the western seaboard of Britain. A small number of surviving windmill structures, three in Co. Down and one in Co. Dublin, also have vaulted extensions similar to those found in southern Scottish tower mills. The tower mills built before *c.* 1770 in Ireland tend to be cylindrical, three- or four-storey rubblestone structures, around 10–13 ft in internal diameter and about 20–25 ft high, developing just enough power from their sails to work two pairs of millstones. A good example of this type of mill at Elphin, Co. Roscommon, built by Edward Synge, Bishop of Elphin in about 1750, has recently been restored to working order. Invariably this type of mill survives as a shell, but as in nearly all of the Irish windmills of this period, its gearing would have been of wood, while its movable cap portion would have had a wooden roof covered with thatch. The small tower mill at Tacumshin, Co. Wexford, however, with its tailpole and thatched cap, still retains many of the features of the early eighteenth-century examples, although it was built in 1846.[26]

The period after 1770 and ending around the close of the Napoleonic Wars, during which the cultivation of cereals in Ireland became a very profitable activity, witnessed a spate of windmill construction in Ireland. The windmills associated with this expansion in cereal cultivation were, in the main, larger and more powerful. Nonetheless, while the smaller, cylindrical tower mills continued to be built into the 1800s, these were primarily attuned to local needs, whereas the newer mills produced for much larger markets and thus were designed for increased output. By the early 1800s, tower mills of tapered profile (rather like a truncated cone), around 16–26 ft in diameter and about 33 ft high were becoming much more common. Many had four to five floors, the upper floors housing the milling plant and the rest being used for storage. The increased height of these mills enabled larger sails to be used, and the consequent increase in motive power enabled up to four sets of millstones to be employed. The difference in power ratio made possible by a relatively small increase in height is quite remarkable: a 30-ft-high windmill has twice the power of a 20-ft-high example. As the sails no longer extended to the ground, a wooden staging built at first-floor level was provided to enable the miller to adjust the sails.[27]

The additional height was also necessary for windmills located in urban areas, where tall buildings could adversely affect the flow of the wind. The Thomas Street windmill in Dublin, which now forms part of the Guinness Brewery complex, is one of the tallest tower mills in Europe. Built throughout with locally made brick, it now appears to have been built in the period 1790–1810, its upper section being refurbished in about 1810. Windmill Lane in Dublin takes its name from a five-storey example that formerly stood on Sir John Rogerson's Quay. A number of largely similar mills were built around the same time at Armagh, Balrath, Blennerville, Derry, Dundalk, Lifford and Warrenpoint. A multi-storey example at Blennerville, near Tralee, Co. Kerry, built c. 1800 by Sir John Blennerhassett, was restored in the 1980s. The multi-storey tower mill at Ballycopeland, Co. Down, built c. 1800, has also been restored to working order, but the design of its sails is rather atypical not only of Irish windmills, but of windmills in general.

Some 250 windmills are shown on the first editions of the Ordnance Survey, compiled between the 1830s and 1842. The vast majority are in counties Down (which alone accounted for over a hundred of this total in 1834) and Wexford, which have the largest concentration in these islands. A number of factors were responsible for this eastern distribution. To begin with, both counties were important cereal producers thanks to favourable climatic conditions and proximity to large centres of population. However, as the catchment areas of many of the rivers on the east coast were somewhat restricted, both regions experienced difficulty in expanding their milling capacity based solely on water power. Such expansion was crucial if these regions were to capitalize on the increased demand for cereals in the period 1770–1815, but fortunately wind speeds along the eastern coastal strip of Ireland favoured the construction of windmills. In many cases windmills were used as a supplement to water-mills, particularly those whose watercourses tended to dry up during the summer months.[28]

From the first editions of the Ordnance Survey it is clear that many Irish windmills were already disused by the early 1830s, an important factor being the contraction in demand for milled cereals at the end of the Napoleonic Wars in 1815. But the increasing concentration of mills in Ireland's ports that processed imported grain in newly erected steam-powered mills forced both smaller water- and wind-powered grain mills into decline. Wherever practicable, water power was preferred to wind power. Wind power, unlike water power, could not be stored and was notoriously difficult to control, whereas water could be stored in millponds and regulated by means of sluices or inlet control gates. Furthermore, only by altering the area of the canvas spread on the individual sails could the speed of the windmill be regulated, while in windmills without automatic fantails the cap had to be turned into the wind.

The Development of Large-Scale Mechanized Milling, 1750–1900

In Ireland the large-scale mechanization of grain milling began in the mid-eighteenth century, when a government bounty (offered between 1758 and 1797 on flour brought to Dublin) provided the impetus for widespread structural and technological changes in the Irish grain-milling industry. Unlike many other industries in either Britain or Ireland, virtually all of the processes involved in grain milling had already been mechanized, which encouraged the concentration of production in increasingly larger units. The Irish flour mill was one of the first in Europe to expand vertically, with extra storeys being provided for both more processing plant and additional storage. This development pre-dates Arkwright's multi-storey textile mills of the later eighteenth century. However, there was an earlier but wholly unrelated precedent in the British silk industry, where Thomas Cotchett had built a three-storey silk-throwing mill on the River Derwent in Derby. Cotchett was followed by John and Sir Thomas Lombe in 1721, who built a five-storey silk mill near his own.[29] Nonetheless, Irish merchants were already building what were effectively multi-storey flour factories well before Arkwright's innovations in the English cotton industry of the 1770s. The adoption of steam power in Irish grain mills also greatly reduced the traditional reliance on water power. Large-scale milling could now be undertaken on the quaysides of Ireland's ports, where grain could be unloaded into adjacent granaries, reduced to flour in nearby mills and directly conveyed to and from outgoing ships.

From the second half of the eighteenth century onwards, the means by which cereal grains were cleaned preparatory to milling became increasingly more sophisticated, beginning with the introduction of hand- or mechanically operated winnowing fans. Most of the large, later eighteenth-century flour mills and all of the nineteenth-century examples were also equipped with mechanically driven flour-dressing machinery, which was used to sieve and grade the flour. The mechanical bolter was the first of a series of power-driven devices employed in mills for more efficient flour dressing and it is from its widespread application in early Irish industrial mills that the contemporary eighteenth- and nineteenth-century term 'bolting mill' originates. In a typical

bolting screen, a textile mesh was drawn over a cylindrical wooden framework, which was rotated by an auxiliary drive from the water-wheel. The meal, which was fed in at one end of the drum, was graded by being forced through the mesh from which only flour of the desired grade could emerge. A 'bolting' mill was in existence at Islandbridge on the River Liffey near Dublin in 1738, while according to Charles Smith, Samuel Pike of Cork ran a 'curious' bolting mill near the town around 1750.[30] From the late eighteenth century onwards 'wire machines', which enabled different grades of flour to be separated simultaneously, were also in use in the larger Irish mills.

Millstone set from a nineteenth-century rural mill, near Old Ross, Co. Wexford. This arrangement was largely typical of stone mills up to quite recent times.

The additional grain-cleaning and flour-dressing machinery required that at least a third storey be added to the mill building, largely to accommodate grain storage. Indeed, most of the early bolting mills are likely to have been three storeys high, and to have operated up to three pairs of stones. William Colles' flour and oat mill at Abbeyvale on the River Nore near Kilkenny town, completed in 1762, are described as being 'three stories high' and, if we assume that the early mills at Cork and Dublin were similar in layout, then these were built at least thirty years before Arkwright's integrated cotton mills. Andrew Mervyn's mill at Naul, Co. Meath, had three pairs of French burr stones in 1761 and three flour bolters (all powered by a single waterwheel), along with a weighing room.[31] The drive to three pairs of stones could only have been achieved through either a layshaft or spur gearing, and the introduction of the bolting mill presumably marks the introduction of one or both. Auxillary drives extending through two floors would also have been required for the bolters, grain elevators, a winnowing fan and a sack hoist, altogether more sophisticated gear linkages than would have been in existence elsewhere in Ireland. The importance of these new forms of power transmission to the development of large-scale milling in Ireland has been completely ignored. As we have already seen, flour and meal mills with two or more pairs of millstones, powered by the same waterwheel, were by no means universal when Griffith's Primary Valuation was conducted in the late 1840s, while in a number of midland and western counties these were still in a minority. The machinery of the bolting mill, it is clear, could only have been operated with either a layshaft or spur gearing. As to the introduction of this technology, it seems likely to have been via English millwrights and machine workers brought over to Ireland.[32] In England, spur-wheel gearing in water-mills (which may have been derived from that of windmills) was in existence by the seventeenth century, and was certainly more widespread in English water-mills by the 1730s. Layshaft gearing was also in use in England by the 1720s.[33] It is likely that both means of power transmission were first introduced to Ireland from England with the development of bolting mills.

All of the early mills, although large by contemporary standards, were soon to be overshadowed by developments in Limerick and at Slane, Co. Meath. Between 1762 and 1764 Andrew Welsh and Edward Uzold built what was then the largest industrial structure in Ireland on the bank of the Limerick Canal near the Abbey River lock. The mill, designed by Uzold, cost £6000, and powered six millstones, four bolting machines, and four sets of fulling stocks, all actuated by two waterwheels turned by water from the canal. In addition, the mills straddled an inlet from the adjacent Abbey River, which enabled barges and 'boats of considerable burden' to gain direct access to its granaries. The Lock Mills are depicted on Christopher Colles' map of the city of Limerick of 1769, where they are shown as a U-shaped range of buildings with a rectangular central block. An early twentieth-century photograph of the mills shows the main six-storey mill block, which has a half-hipped roof and a decorative parapet facing the canal bank, and is flanked by what appears to be a grain store.

Two years after the Lock Mills were completed in 1766, the largest water-powered flour mill in Europe was designed and built by the engineer David Jebb near the village of Slane, Co. Meath, using capital mainly supplied by Townley Balfour of Townley Hall, Co. Louth. In 1776, Jebb (the mill manager) showed Arthur Young around the concern, which he described as 'a large handsome edifice such as no mill I have seen in England can be compared with'. The five-storey mill was then the largest industrial building in Ireland, being 138 ft long, 54 ft wide and 42 ft high. It consisted of a gabled block, T-shaped in plan, with a central bay which projected forward with an eaves pediment. In Young's famous description, the grain was lifted to the fifth-storey grain loft, which had a capacity of 5000 barrels, by means of a water-powered bucket elevator. It was then dried in two large kilns which could process eighty barrels in a twenty-four hour period. No less than seven pairs of millstones – the largest number ever operated in an Irish flour mill up to that date – ground some 120 barrels of flour per day.[34] In his capacity as engineer to the Commissioners of Inland Navigation on the Boyne Navigation works, Jebb had overseen the construction of the Boyne Navigation to Slane, which had probably been completed before the mill opened, giving it a waterway to the Irish Sea via the Boyne and thence to Dublin. The mill-race of the Slane mills was also the most impressive in Ireland, consisting of an 800-ft-long walled canal with mooring wharves and a dry dock for boats. In the 1830s the mills had three undershot waterwheels, each 38 ft in diameter. The company that ran the mills also owned large granaries in Drogheda, Dundalk and Balbriggan, along with a fleet of lighters and ships which plied the River Boyne and the Irish Sea. In the early nineteenth century, the Slane Mills, which still stands, was converted to a flax mill and, early in the twentieth century, to a cotton mill.

The 1758 bounty energized the Irish flour-milling industry to the extent that some 166 mills were opened throughout Ireland between 1758 and 1785, even in western counties such as Galway. Large multi-storey mills continued to be built: e.g. Millbrook near Oldcastle, Co. Meath, in 1777, which survives and has a T-shaped ground-plan like the Slane mill; Milford, Co. Carlow, constructed between 1786 and 1790 (originally 125 ft long by 45 ft wide); a seven-storey mill at Ballyduggan, Co. Down, completed in 1789 and recently restored; and the Lee Mills complex at Cork established by Atwell Hayes in 1787. In the 1840s the Milford complex comprised the original six-storey flour mill (since demolished) and a six-storey oatmeal mill (which survives), all powered by a 120 h.p. Fairbairn suspension wheel, which worked twenty-two pairs of millstones. The spread of these mills also ensured increased familiarity with new forms of power transmission, which were often designed by English millwrights. In the final decade of the eighteenth century, two further technological innovations were introduced into Irish milling. The first was the introduction of cast-iron gearing, an early example of which was installed in a mill near Youghal, Co. Cork, in 1792.[35] The second was the steam engine. By 1798 Henry Jackson had established a steam-powered flour mill at Phoenix Street, Dublin, while in 1800 Isaac Morgan of Cork had imported a 12 h.p. Boulton and Watt engine for his flour mill near George's Quay (see colour plate section).[36] The urban flour mill

Henry's Mill, Millbrook, near Oldcastle, Co. Meath, a multi-storey flour mill, completed in 1777.

at once became independent of its traditional source of power, and the existing water-powered mills soon found that they had to install steam engines to compete with the new generation of mills being erected on Ireland's quaysides.

Grain storage in multi-storey mills was clearly a priority from the outset, but expanding demand and capacity necessitated larger kilning facilities and separate warehousing. The construction of corn and flour stores was an important, although often neglected, aspect of the infrastructural development of the Irish flour-milling industry, although the grain stores of Cork city's quayside have recently been studied. From the late eighteenth century onwards multi-storey 'corn stores' or granaries became an increasingly common feature of Ireland's quaysides. The majority of the Cork granaries, for example, were situated either on the city's quaysides or on the side-streets leading to them, and were equipped with large drying kilns and coal storage yards.[37]

An important feature of all grain-storage buildings in Cork was proper ventilation, which took the form of closely-spaced windows on each floor, or louvred vents. The more typical nineteenth-century Cork grain stores had three to four storeys, with central or near-central loading bays on each storey facing the quayside or the street frontage. In most cases the loading doors were situated on the gable end of the building with a projecting overhead sackhoist (complete with a ridge canopy or *lucam*) positioned at the gable's peak. During the second half of the nineteenth century, direct access to the quaysides of Ireland's ports became an important consideration, and increasingly so when the Irish flour-milling industry came to rely on imported grain. One of the most interesting surviving structures of the period is the six-storey grain store at Kilcarbery Mills, Co. Wexford, completed in 1826. This was positioned directly across the wheel pit from the mill's main eighteenth-century block. This curious structure has semi-circular arched windows on all elevations, complete with their original cast-iron frames, a rare survival.

The period 1800–75 is characterized by two major developments, the introduction of steam engines as energy supplements to Irish flour mills and the increase in the number of new steam-powered mills at Irish ports. At mill sites where the steam engine was intended as a back-up for water-powered plant, the engine was either housed in a separate building or linked independently to its own set of millstones. The period 1830–50 witnessed the installation of steam engines at many of the larger Irish mills. By the 1820s Irish machine foundries were already manufacturing steam engines for Irish flour mills. However, when compound engines were introduced, Irish mill owners tended to order new engines from reputable English foundries. Other technological developments included the introduction of new mechanical grain-cleaning plant, principally 'rotary cleaners' and 'cockle cylinders'. Rotary cleaners consisted of a wire mesh drum, equipped with internal rotating brushes, into which grain was fed. The grain in the drum was forced up against its wire mesh by the brushes, which forced out any smaller particles of dirt. Cockle cylinders separated foreign seeds from the grain, while a further device called 'rubble reels' removed dirt and stones.

Nonetheless, in the period 1800–30 water-powered sites remained at a premium, and large-scale water-powered flour mills continued to be built when conditions allowed. Good examples can still be seen at the Santa Cruse Mills, Carigahorrig, Co. Tipperary (1805); the Birr Mills, Co. Offaly (*c.* 1820); and Plassy Mills, Co. Limerick (1824). Laurence Corban's Maryville Mills, Co. Cork, built in 1818 and demolished in 1995, was very typical of the new flour mills of the period, working six pairs of millstones powered by a 20-ft-diameter waterwheel. The Birr Mills comprised an original roughly U-shaped block of buildings, which had internally housed waterwheels, set at one end of the main range of three-storey buildings. Spital Mills near Timoleague, Co. Cork, built *c.* 1829 and demolished in 1992, mirrored the T-shaped ground-plan of the Slane Mill, its five-storey projecting gable in this instance serving as a grain store. Plassy Mills, which drew water from the Shannon by means

Early nineteenth-century multi-storey floor mill at Loughmoe, Co. Tipperary.

The Lee Mills, Cork, built between 1824 and 1832, and converted to a maltings in the 1880s.

of a mill-race almost a mile long, was a six-storey structure set on the bank of the River Shannon, facing the entrance to the Killaloe Canal. It is a unique structure, having a seven-storey tower at one end with a spiral stone staircase running all the way to the top. The tower, which still stands (although most of the rest of the mill survives at ground-floor level only), is built with ornate ogee-headed windows with hood mouldings, along with ornamental gun-loops. When leased in the 1830s by Reuben Harvey (who also had a granary and store a few miles off), carrier pigeons were used to send messages between each site.[38]

The largest water-powered flour mills to be built in this period were the Lee Mills at Cork, which consisted of a series of six- and seven-storey mill buildings, which were entirely rebuilt on the site of Hayes' mills by Beamish and Crawford in the period 1825–31. Henry Inglis, who visited Cork in the early 1830s, was taken aback at the scale of operations involved and what he considered to be the 'perfection of everything connected with them'.[39] Significantly, the original cast-iron waterwheels were supplied by the local

Vulcan Ironworks, but the machinery was supplied and erected by Peele, Williams & Peele of Manchester. By the late 1840s this was one of the largest water-powered flour mills in Ireland, with three 20-ft-diameter undershot waterwheels powering fifteen pairs of stones. However, there was an earlier precedent for the use of English millwork when, in 1820, the Scottish engineer John Rennie (1761–1821) designed the machinery for Thomas Walker's flour mill at Crosses Green, Cork. Indeed this was a common practice in Ireland during the late eighteenth and early decades of the nineteenth century, until such time as English millwrights and machine makers had established foundries at Ireland's principal ports. As Walker explained to Rennie in April 1814:

> ... having seen many mills in this neighbourhood [north Co. Cork] ineffective from any errors in the calculations, we do not like to depend on the engineers here. I will most cheerfully pay the [extra] expense.[40]

From the 1820s onwards the number of steam-powered flour mills in Ireland was beginning to increase, but by and large these tended to be within the environs of ports or near navigable rivers, where coal could be easily obtained. However, while most flour mills continued to rely on water power for the greater part of the year, by the 1830s the larger mills within the vicinity of towns were obliged to install steam-powered plant in order to be able to compete with those established on the quaysides. Indeed, by the 1850s even the larger mills in market towns were obliged to do so. As we have seen, the first moves towards the establishment of steam-powered port mills were made in Dublin and Cork in the period 1798–1800. In 1810 John Norris Russell, a wealthy Limerick city merchant, established what was to become, for many years, the largest port mill in Ireland on Limerick's Dock Road. By the second half of the nineteenth century it was the largest producer of ground maize in the United Kingdom, and in 1837 a nine-storey grain store (which remained the largest in Ireland for many years) was added to it. In Cork city the establishment of a new Corn Exchange on Albert Quay in 1833 hastened the construction of new quayside corn stores and mills. In 1834, William Dunbar obtained the lease to a steam mill on George's Quay, which had ready access to both the river and the Cork Cornmarket, which, by 1844, employed a 35 h.p. engine to work eight pairs of stones in one mill and three pairs in an adjacent one that processed oats. The mill also had a corn store capable of storing 10,000 barrels. John Furlong's Lapp's Quay Flour Mill, Cork, built in 1852, is the best surviving example of a mid-nineteenth-century purpose-built Irish steam mill, which retained its original smokestack until 1998. The five-storey, gabled 'Rock' flour mill, built on the Foyle wharfs in Derry in the early 1850s, is similar to Furlong's in terms of its location and in certain architectural details such as its windows, but it is a much larger structure. However, we should not forget that the overall numbers of steam-powered mills in Ireland were always small compared to the number of mills that used water power only. In 1891, only sixty-eight of the 1482 mills in Ireland were powered by steam only, while a total of seventy-five used a combination of water and steam.[41]

It is evident that from the early medieval period onwards, Ireland's flour-milling technology was relatively sophisticated by European standards. The earliest remains of wooden horizontal-wheeled mills in Europe have come to light in Ireland, which include the earliest known tide mills in the world. Indeed, there are more investigated pre-tenth-century horizontal-wheeled mill sites in the province of Munster alone than in the rest of Europe. This clearly indicates that Ireland was not a technological backwater in the period before the late twelfth-century Anglo-Norman settlement. In all periods of its development, the island was neither isolated from, nor immune to, European influences. Moreover, significant innovation can also be discerned when Ireland's economy became more fully integrated with that of Great Britain during the eighteenth century, when, owing to uniquely favourable conditions, Irish flour mills were among the first multi-storey industrial buildings in the world.

2

Eighteenth-Century Flour Milling in Ireland

L.M. CULLEN

MILLING WAS ONE of the most extensive industrial activities in the seventeenth and early eighteenth centuries. Through the use of water-powered machinery, milling had already evolved substantially from the quern used in domestic production of meal or flour. However, milling was to evolve further and more rapidly in the middle decades of the eighteenth century. This stage in its evolution is significant because it involved a far more elaborate use of water power, and its application to ancillary activities such as raising grain from one level to another; also because such a progression involved the housing of the assembled activities in much more substantial structures than was the case up to then. Milling, in one step, became both a large-scale industrial and commercial enterprise. The use of water power in an extended manner, and the construction of substantial buildings of several storeys, foreshadowed the employment of water power in textile spinning from the 1770s and the appearance of the early spinning mills. Significantly, early spinning mills were not infrequently housed in grain mills.[1]

Mills in the early seventeenth century were as a rule simple enterprises with inadequate millponds:

> Mills be scarce there, and in summer they want water, so
> as they are forced sometimes to go thirty miles off to be

supplied; yet if their millponds were there handled as they be here, and, when that failed, windmills and horsemills were set up in the market towns and other convenient places in some reasonable distance asunder, this might be helped.[2]

The point in this quotation is more that the mills were primitive than that they were few. Mills were a common feature of the manor economy of medieval Ireland; manorial milling rights, either enforced, or as a concept or formality entering into legal documents, are frequently referred to in leases and other legal documents down to the nineteenth century. We know much less of milling in Irish areas outside the Anglo-Norman districts. The water-mill is, however, referred to quite specifically in the legal tracts committed to writing in the seventh and eighth centuries. The Civil Survey in 1654 furnishes for some counties a count of mills (a high proportion of them in ruins at the time of the survey): 91 for Kildare, 118 for Tipperary, 64 for Wexford (excluding the Barony of Forth), 100 for an incomplete survey of Meath.[3]

Little is known of the actual structures of the seventeenth century. Sketches survive from three early Ulster maps of mills at Derry, Coleraine and Omagh.[4] These are all vertical mills; two of the three sketches give the

impression of breast- or over-shot wheels. Mills sited close to towns, especially plantation towns, may have been more elaborate than other mills of that time – the Derry and Coleraine mills appear to have had millponds. But the under-shot wheel was probably common; Dineley's sketch of the village of Staplestown, Co. Carlow, from around 1680 shows quite clearly a mill with an under-shot wheel on the banks of the River Burren.[5]

Seventeenth- and early eighteenth-century mills were very small structures. Dineley's account of his Irish tour

A water-mill in Staplestown, Co. Carlow, sketch by Thomas Dineley, c. 1680. ('Observations on a Voyage through Ireland')

has a sketch of the machinery of a water-mill with the dual purpose of working a millstone, and operating pounders for either finishing cloth or crushing rape seed: the house or structure is barely adequate to house the machinery driven from the shaft.[6] In fact, a single-storey mill would have proved highly inconvenient: it was essential to have one floor or loft above ground-floor level. At this level stood the hopper into which grain was poured from the sacks; on the floor below were the shaft from the wheel and the gearings. For this reason even the early illustrations show two-storey structures.[7] The Halls in their account of Ireland describe such a mill in the 1840s at Lissoy, Co. Westmeath, the 'Auburn' of Goldsmith:

> it is a mere country cottage, used in grinding the corn of
> the neighbouring peasantry, and retains many tokens of
> age. Parts of the machinery are no doubt above a century
> old, and probably are the very same that left their impres-
> sion on the poet's memory.[8]

An accompanying sketch reveals at ground level a structure no larger than a cabin with the shaft from the wheel at a lower level, suggesting that the gearings are housed in a basement or substructure; the wheel was over-shot. Over-shot wheels are also shown on some of the seventeenth-century drawings of Irish mills, and over- or breast-shot mills may have been common enough by the middle of the eighteenth century. By contrast, horizontal mills may have been quite few by that time; Isaac Butler in an account of his travels in 1744 through counties Louth, Meath, Westmeath and Longford makes a point of mentioning a mill at Fore, Co. Westmeath, where the stream ran underneath the mill – a description that seems to suggest a horizontal mill – as something worthy of comment.[9] This fact, together with the relative frequency of over- or breast-shot wheels, would itself suggest some degree of elaboration of mill work to a stage of sophistication greater than that found by the author of *Advertisements for Ireland* in the early seventeenth century.

Whether or not such mills were widespread in the early seventeenth century, it is certain that little mills grinding for a local market were numerous in many parts of the country a century later. The following comment was appended to the abstract setting out details of the bounties paid on the land carriage of flour to Dublin in the year 1 January 1768 to 1 January 1769, as explanation of the large quantity of flour consigned to Dublin from 'sundry mills' in Co. Kilkenny:

> These mills are many in number, and until the high bounty was granted for bringing flour to Dublin, ground chiefly oats, but now for the most part wheat: they send but small quantities in a carriage to Dublin, which are sold in the public market by the carrier or owner.[10]

The great bulk of the milling in such establishments would normally have been done on commission for local farmers and others. In the town of Galway, before the erection of the first flour mill, each baker kept his own chest of grain in the mill:

> Each baker had a large chest in the mill that ground for them with a lock and key, in which he usually kept as much wheat as he judged would be sufficient until the next market day. As he wanted it, it was ground in the mill.[11]

Eighteenth-century multi-storey flour mill at Kilroe, Co. Galway.

Small mills of this kind did the grinding of all types of grain until the middle of the eighteenth century, but by that time larger mills for grinding wheat had begun to appear in England. Imports of flour into Ireland had started to grow, being in the hands of 'at least' twenty mills in England.[12] The rise in flour imports in the 1740s and '50s was much sharper than in wheat imports, suggesting that, apart from the intermittent failures of the harvest in Ireland, English mills in centres such as Chichester were proving more competitive than the diminutive Irish mills of the time. Better quality as well as a more competitive price gave English flour an advantage on the Irish market. The superior quality of the imported variety is borne out in the contemporary comparisons of Irish flour with English, and in the fact that it was English artisans and millwrights who contributed to the improvement of the industry in Ireland at this time. Richard Bonner of Oldtown, near Naas, attributed his self-proclaimed success to 'employing several of the most skilful English artists in constructing the curious machines necessary for such mills'.[13]

The secret of the new mills lay in the addition of processes both preparatory and subsequent to the actual grinding of the wheat. The old mills ground the grain while it was still uncleaned, and the bolting or sifting of the ground meal was left to the bakers themselves. In the new mills the grain was shelled and sifted before grinding. This eliminated the impurities and prevented them from passing into the flour. Once the wheat was ground, it was then bolted mechanically. The latter process had previously been carried out by the bakers, and indeed mechanical bolting seems to have been the most characteristic function of the new 'bolting mills'. The bolters consisted of large sleeves made of woollen cloth or of finely woven wire, to which a shaking motion was imparted by mechanical means. The meal, once ground, was fed into the sleeve and the fine flour passed through the sleeve. As the bolter was fixed at a plane, the balance of the meal passed down the upper surface of the sleeve. It was ground again and passed a second time through the bolters. The 'bolting mills' were therefore quite different structures from the old-fashioned mills, embracing two additional mechanized functions – shelling and sifting, and bolting – in addition to the grinding function to which the older mills had been confined. Flour produced in this sequence of processes was better than that produced in the grist mills, and – through mechanization – also cheaper than that bolted by the bakers by more primitive means.

Catering for a large urban market or, in centres such as Chichester, an export market to Ireland, and thus no longer dependent on earning a commission on the grinding of small quantities as they were brought to the mills, the new generation of miller had also to provide storage for large quantities of grain and flour. The typical structure made necessary by the new milling was one of at least three storeys: the grain was stored on, or at least raised to, the top floor; shelled, ground and bolted on the intermediate floors; and the main shafting and gearings stood at the bottom level. Hoists to raise sacks and elevators to move loose grain or flour, driven from the waterwheel, were an essential feature of the new mills. The operations in a modern mill – that at Slane – were succinctly described in 1776 by Arthur Young.[14]

A large market existed for flour in eighteenth-century Dublin. In this respect the city was unique. The widespread use of flour – as opposed to wheaten meal – was at first urban, and outside the towns uncommon. Even around a centre as large as Cork, the first flour mills worked for the Dublin market; a local flour market only developed later.[15] The bounties granted from 1758 for the transport of grain and flour to the capital[16] were particularly advantageous in the case of flour, the bounty exceeding transport costs. This was certainly an incentive to establish mills, but there were other factors as well. New methods of industrial organization were bound to be imitated in Ireland; an entrepreneurial interest was already evident in investment in up-to-date methods in other branches of industry, and capital was fairly easy to come by in these decades.

The response to the profit on flour held out by the new bounties was slow at first. In 1758/9 and 1761/2, Co. Meath was the only county from which flour was consigned to Dublin. Kilkenny, Meath and Westmeath were alone in 1762/3, and Meath and Kilkenny in 1763/4; flour was consigned from Limerick as well in 1764/5. In the following year (1765/6), flour was consigned from these four counties, and from a further five counties (Carlow, Cork, King's, Queen's and Tipperary). Moreover, the total quantity of flour sent to Dublin rose sharply in that year. This was mainly due to the increase in the quantities consigned from Co. Kilkenny: from 40,517 stone in 1764/5, to 140,700 stone in 1765/6.[17] In the year January 1768 to January 1769, 35,985 cwt came from various unspecified small mills in Co. Kilkenny, and 4102 cwt from the Abbeyvale mills on the account of William Colles.[18] Thus the great bulk of the flour from Kilkenny came at first from the smallest mills. Kilkenny produced both wheat and oats for the Dublin market. But perhaps because the mills in and around Dublin were fully occupied in grinding wheat, Kilkenny had many mills occupied in grinding oats and, as early as the return for 1758/9, the first year of the bounty, it was the only county sending meal in any quantity to Dublin.[19] In the course of the 1760s the attractive bounty on flour encouraged many farmers and carriers to take flour to Dublin as a petty speculation, and the tiny grist mills came to grind for the Dublin market. In 1768/9, according to the return of the bounties made to parliament:

there has been in this year no less than 1,569 premiums
paid to these mills alone, exclusive of what was paid for
the flour brought from Mr Colles's mill of Abbeyvale;
there are but three of them considerable, viz. Archer's
Grove, Warington, and Ennisnag Mills; and of late there
has been large quantities of flour brought from these
mills to Dublin consigned to factors.[20]

The site of the first new-style flour mill in Ireland can only be determined
approximately. A petition from Richard Bonner of Oldtown, in November
1763 seems to imply that he had been milling on modern principles for some
years, and claimed that he had a warehouse in Dublin for the distribution of
his flour.[21] But in fact no flour at all seems to have come to Dublin from Co.
Kildare in 1758/9, or between 1761/2 and 1766/7.[22] Bonner's venture does not
seem to have been as successful as he claimed. He had, moreover, precursors.
A mill with bolting 'mills' for dressing flour was advertised at Islandbridge in
1738,[23] Samuel Pike of Cork was reported in 1750 to have a 'curious' bolting
mill,[24] and Wyse of Waterford had 'flower' mills in 1747.[25] How mechanized
the bolting operation in these mills was is not clear but the evidence, although
equivocal like Bonner's,[26] does suggest experimentation ahead of the large-
scale ventures that had a recognized success in the 1760s. The mills of the 1760s
certainly stood out not only because of mechanical contrivance but because,
catering for the sole large market covering the entire island, they were on a
scale so far unprecedented in the industry. It was probably the inter-related combination of mechanical processes rather than the novelty of the processes
viewed in isolation that made them remarkable. The credit for the first modern
mill may go to Andrew Mervyn of Naul in Co. Meath. At Naul, according to
the report of the parliamentary committee to which his petition was referred
in October 1761:

the mill is built with the best materials, hath one water
wheel and three pair of French stones, two pair of which
go at a time, and the third pair lies by to cool, that there
are three bolting mills, one screw engine, one fan, one
sack tackle, a kiln that dries 45 barrels of corn at every
kilcast and a weighing room, and that in about three or

four weeks the mill may be ready to grind and bolt 24 barrels a day.[27]

The significance of this mill seems to be confirmed by the fact that of the many mills which petitioned parliament for grants, Mervyn's enterprise alone succeeded in getting a grant – £2000 in 1761[28] – and that Co. Meath was the only county from which flour was consigned to Dublin in 1761/2. The next mill to open may have been the mill erected by William Colles at Abbeyvale on the Nore, two miles from Kilkenny town. Colles was an alderman of Kilkenny, proprietor of the Marble sawmills, and had been educated at Shackleton's famous school at Ballitore.[29] The date June 1762 is quoted as the starting date of flour-milling operations in a petition to the Irish parliament in November 1765 for assistance for the expansion of his venture. In the petition he made a point of stating that the mills were three storeys high, a great novelty for an industrial building at this time, describing them as

> mills three stories high, whereby oats are shelled, win-
> nowed from the shellings, ground to meal and sifted, by
> a regular and easy course of progression, and wheat is in
> like manner ground and completely dressed into flour, all
> of which are of a new, firm and convenient structure,
> many parts of which were invented by the petitioner on
> much and long attention after several expensive trials
> with kilns and granaries necessary; and are fully supplied
> with water at all seasons of the year, and so much out
> of the reach of floods that they received but little damage
> from the last extraordinary floods in that part of the
> county.[30]

The next two mills to be built appear to have opened in 1764, one in Limerick,[31] the other in Banoge, Co. Down.[32] A petition to parliament in 1765 from Galbraith Hamilton in Co. Tyrone claimed that he had erected in 1760 a 'wheat' mill 'of the best construction' on the River Mourne, south of Strabane.[33] It is doubtful, however, if this mill was a full flour mill as the peti-tion from Robert Patterson of Banoge presented on the same day, after describing in detail the modern processes in a bolting mill, claimed that no other mill of the like construction hath yet been attempted to be erected in the counties of Down, Antrim, Armagh or Tyrone ... except one in the county of Antrim, which was not begun until he hath made a considerable progress in his said works, and almost completed the same.[34]

The mill to which Patterson referred was that erected by Rowley Heyland on the Crumlin river.[35] Another mill was shortly afterwards worked by the Andrews at Comber, Co. Down.[36]

These early ventures in flour milling in the north were mainly intended to supply a local market. None of the flour from them, with the exception of Rowley Heyland's mill, found its way to Dublin in the 1760s or 1770s. They were relatively small-scale enterprises serving a local market. Yet the establishment of such ventures unrelated to the Dublin market seems to imply some dietary contrast between the north and the rest of the island outside the Dublin region although, given the relatively small scale of the mills, probably a limited one. The largest mills by far were in the south. The mills erected by Andrew Walsh and Edward Uzuld in Limerick – the Lock Mills – were the first really elaborate venture. The granaries and kilns adjoining the mills were 'so constructed over their reservoir as that boats of considerable burden, coming from the sea or by the new navigation, may load and unload out of, and into said granaries'.[37] However this mill, large though it was, was in an intermediate category. The first of the really big mills was that at Slane, which began production in 1766;[38] the property on which the mill was erected had been leased in September 1763. The total cost of the mill, put at upwards of £12,000 in a petition to parliament in 1768,[39] seems to have amounted to £19,187.[40]

Flour milling was still at an early stage of development in the 1760s. The only counties to the fore were Meath and Kilkenny, both of which witnessed a rapid development of bolting mills. In the year ending 31 December 1768, four Meath mills including Slane and Naul were consigning flour to Dublin.[41] From Co. Kilkenny flour was consigned from six named mills, including Abbeyvale, in the year ending 24 June 1770.[42] At the same time the number of counties from which flour came to Dublin rose sharply. In 1763/4 flour had arrived in Dublin from only two counties; by 1769/70 it came from fifteen counties.[43] Tipperary emerged at the beginning of the 1770s as the third most important county in the trade. It also had the mill which, next to that at Slane, was the largest in the country: Stephen Moore's mill at Marlfield, erected in 1769 and consigning flour to Dublin as early as the year ending 24 June 1771.[44] Other counties sending significant quantities to Dublin were Cork, King's, Limerick, Queen's, Westmeath and Wexford. The mill at Belmont, King's County, one of the early, if not the first, large mill in the Midlands, was constructed in 1770.[45] In Cork, according to a petition from the Mayor and Common Council in 1773, several mills had been 'erected in the city … and liberties … and more are intended to be erected for the purpose of making flour and sending the same to Dublin'.[46]

The number of mills sending flour to Dublin in 1770/1 was forty-four (excluding the smaller Kilkenny mills).[47] Considerable growth in milling took place in the subsequent decades: the number of mills in 1790, computed on the basis of those erected since 1758 to supply the Dublin market, was estimated at 248.[48] The data gives an impression of a continued expansion of flour milling from the 1760s. The figure of forty-four mills in 1770/1 compares with a total of 166 mills opened between 1758 and 1785, which suggests a considerable expansion of milling in the 1770s; this is confirmed by the growth in the quantity of flour sent to Dublin: from 87,965 cwt in the year ending 25 March 1771 to 359,044 cwt in the year ending 25 March 1786.[49] Mills that commenced to send flour to Dublin from 1786 are distinguished separately in the account. The parliamentary returns suggest that in counties Cork, Kildare, King's, Longford, Kilkenny, Meath, Queen's and Westmeath, relatively few mills were added between 1786 and 1790. By contrast there was a striking expansion in the number of flour mills in counties Galway, Limerick, Roscommon and Wexford, more than one-half of their mills being opened in these years. In Co. Galway, for instance, twenty-one of the twenty-six flour mills were erected between 1786 and 1790; in Galway town itself eight of its nine mills. Yet only two of the thirty-seven mills in Kilkenny were opened in 1786/90, and one of Queen's County's nineteen mills. Counties like Carlow, Kildare, King's and Tipperary were in an intermediate position: five of Kildare's twenty mills, seven of King's County's twenty-two, and nineteen of Tipperary's forty-seven mills were opened between 1786 and 1790. The overall impression is that mill-building remained an especially active pursuit right up to 1790 in most of the eighteen counties included in the returns.

The erection of new flour mills or the conversion of existing grist mills into flour mills continued after 1790. Some development continued in the counties where milling was already well established. In Ballitore, for instance, the bolting mill was erected by the Shackletons to replace the grist mill in 1792.[50] In Co. Galway, where the significant growth of flour milling began only in 1786–90, 'the great increase of flour mills', according to Dutton, was 'chiefly since 1790'.[51] He was not correct in stating that before 1790 there were only two mills in the town but, writing three decades later, he was not too far wrong in his account. In 1824, Dutton indicated a figure of twenty-three flour mills for the town, and 'upwards of 12 large flour mills' in the county.[52]

Perhaps even more striking than the opening of new mills was the establishment of very large mills in this period. It seems that the wave of mill construction reached its peak during the years of high prosperity associated with the revolutionary and Napoleonic wars. Thereafter, the pace in mill building fell off sharply. The most impressive mill in this period was the great complex of three structures at Milford, Co. Carlow, on the Barrow. The first mill at Milford had opened between 1786 and 1790.[53] According to the Halls, who described the mills in the account of their itinerary through Ireland, 'the mill was originally established in 1790, and was commenced on a large scale'.[54] The castellated structures that they wrote about seem to have been an enlargement of the original mills. The complex was apparently finished by 1813, as a detached house in the valuation dated 1843 indicated that it had been there upwards of thirty years.[55] According to the Halls

> The Milford works have been constructed under the superintendence of Mr William Fairbairn of Manchester: and the chief water-wheel made by him, of iron, cast, hammered, and plate is, we believe, the largest and most powerful in the kingdom: taking water on twenty-two feet – its breadth. It is equal to one hundred and twenty horse power. In the two establishments for producing flour and oatmeal, there are twenty-two pair of millstones in constant work; thirteen of which, with all the attendant machinery, are driven by one wheel.

A sketch of the mills appears in the Halls' work; one of the three main structures still stands, the second – the flour mill – was destroyed by fire *c.* 1970, and the maltings were cleared away recently.[56] In Galway 'two capital mills' were erected, both on Nuns Island. According to Dutton, the mill was erected by a 'Mr Regan' and finished in 1814:

> Mr Regan's, I understand, is composed entirely of metal, contrived and executed by Mr Macky, a very ingenious millwright from Scotland. This mill was begun in 1813; it is erected on five arches, is 80 feet long by 41 broad, has 12 floors, lighted by an hundred glass windows; it was finished and ready for work in one year, and considered to have Cost £10,000.[57]

Clonmel had a complex of mills, the first flour mill in the town being that of the Grubbs.[58] According to Marmion, 'prior to the repeal of the corn law, Clonmel had the most extensive flour mills in Ireland, on the erection of which large capitals were expended'.[59] In 1832, on the same authority, Clonmel exported 230,540 cwt of flour through Waterford.[60]

The bolting mills were large structures. The first were three storeys high: the later and larger mills at least five storeys high. The mill at Slane (138 ft long)[61] was dissimilar to the later buildings, most of which were somewhat shorter and broader; with a breadth of less than 30 ft at both gable ends, it is a singularly elongated, slender and elegant structure. The flour mill at Milford – now destroyed – was 125 ft by 45,[62] proportions which are more characteristic of the bulk of surviving structures. When the first flour mills were erected in the 1760s, large-scale industrial structures were few. They may well be regarded as the precursor of the textile mills, which became common in the 1770s and later. The pattern of the flour mills was that adopted for the cotton mills – several storeys, very commonly five, each storey punctuated by windows at regular intervals. The dimensions of cotton mills conform very closely to those typical of the early flour mills. In November 1783 Joseph Smith was at the stage of roofing over his new cotton mill of five storeys at Balbriggan, about 100 ft in length, and 34 ft in breadth.[63] In the summer of 1787 Deaves erected a five-storey cotton mill at Blarney, which was 110 ft long and 28 ft wide.[64] Water-mills also lent themselves to conversion to textile mills. This happened fairly commonly in England.[65] Among the Foster papers in Belfast, there survives a sketch of a corn mill at Sallybrook, Co. Cork, from about 1805, drawn up when the feasibility of

Late nineteenth-century photograph of the Lock Mills, on the Shannon navigation canal at Limerick, completed in 1764. The cut-stone gateway is the only feature of the mills to survive.

its conversion into a woollen mill was being investigated.[66]

Although the first flour mills were comparatively inexpensive, the new structures represented a substantial capital investment: William Colles' mill at Abbeyvale had cost 'above' £1000;[67] Patterson's mill at Banoge, Co. Down, 'upwards of' £1300,[68] but the Lock Mills at Limerick had cost about £5000,[69] and Heyland estimated that his Co. Antrim mill would cost £3762 to construct.[70] The mill at Belmont, King's County – destroyed by fire three years later – was erected in 1770 at a cost of at least £7000.[71] The mill at Marlfield cost £15,000,[72] and the Slane mill above £19,000 at a final reckoning. These figures represent large amounts for the erection of industrial structures by any eighteenth-century yardstick. Regan's mill, built on Nuns Island in Galway city in 1813, cost £10,000.[73] For purposes of comparison, one may bear in mind the costs of cotton mills in Britain. Chapman has divided them into three categories in terms of costs: type A, not exceeding an insurance valuation of £2000; type B, buildings erected between 1770 and 1790, usually three- to four-storeyed, 70–80 ft long and 25–30 ft wide, valued at £3000–£5000; type C, taller, first erected in the 1790s and (except on a few sites) favoured by generous water-power reserves, steam-powered, costing a minimum of £10,000.[74]

Regan's Mill, Nuns Island, Galway, completed in 1813. The mill later formed part of the Nuns Island Distillery.

There seems to exist a case for arguing that both in functional layout or design, and in scale, the early flour mills in Ireland may be regarded as being among the pioneer buildings of the Industrial Revolution.

The capital requirements of milling were made all the greater by a need for a large working capital. The grist mills, grinding for a local market and on commission, needed little. The flour millers, paying cash for the grain, storing and kiln-drying it, and marketing their flour on their own account on the Dublin market, required a very large amount of working capital.[75] The investment in working capital was as large as the investment in buildings and equipment. Sarah Grubb of Anner Mills, Clonmel, insured the mills, warehouse and kiln for £1700 in 1788, and the goods in trade 'being mostly corn, flour, meal, seed and oil in cask or cistern' for £3500.[76] Both Rowley Heyland at Crumlin and Andrew Walsh and Company at Limerick seem to have represented to parliament that the working capital requirements of their ventures were as large as the investment in fixed assets.[77] William Colles who had spent about £1000 on Abbeyvale and seems to have been envisaging further capital expenditure, maintained that it was 'necessary to have in store grain, meal and flour to the amount of £3000 and upwards'.[78] The promoters of the Slane Mill in 1765 thought the sum of £5000 'absolutely wanting' to lay in sufficient corn.[79] The balance sheet of the Slane Mill totalled £28,944 in

January 1773. The cost of the mill and offices was £19,187.[80] The difference between the figures may be regarded as illustrating in a crude fashion the amount of working capital necessary to enable a mill on this scale to function.

The way in which large amounts of capital were brought together is of interest both in relation to milling itself and the manner of financing industrial and commercial enterprise generally. Much of the capital to establish mills seems to have come from the landed classes themselves. Landlords often had some interest in milling in the form of manorial milling rights. It is possible that this circumstance may have encouraged many landlords to get involved directly in milling rather than to rest content on the income from the leasing of such rights. The Bellews of Mount Bellew, Co. Galway, are an interesting case of entrepreneurial activity:[81] they engaged directly in milling, erected a flour mill and consigned the flour on their own account to Dublin. The details of bounty payments submitted to parliament show that much of the flour consigned to Dublin was on the account of local landlords. In 1770/71, for instance, bounty payments were made to Sir John Parnell in respect of flour from 'Meelick', Queen's County, and to Henry Flood from Paulstown, Co. Kilkenny.[82] The fact that the flour was consigned on their account does not of itself establish that landlords engaged directly in milling – a consignment could represent a speculative purchase of flour from a local miller. But the presumption that in most such cases the mills were run on the landlord's account is strong. There are known instances of this, and in addition the general pattern of the trade was the sale through the hands of Dublin factors of the flour for the account of the mill. The interest of landlords in milling was part of a wider interest within their class in improvement and in the promotion of economic activity. In many cases their direct entrepreneurial interest was limited: they invested in the equipment or buildings but relied on others to provide the working capital and the entrepreneurial ability.[83] This does not seem to have happened in milling to the same extent.

The Slane mill itself represents an interesting example of the financing of a large mill. Viscount Conyngham leased the existing mill at the Bridge of Slane and fourteen acres of adjoining land as well as the weir on the river to the promoters of the new mill.[84] These were another local landlord, Blayney Townley Balfour; William Burton of Dublin, a nephew of Conyngham; and David Jebb, miller. The three partners were to put up £1500 each.[85] Their investment was shortly afterwards supplemented by ploughing into the com-

David Jebb's mills at Slane, Co. Meath, completed in 1766. At the time these were the largest mills of their type in Europe. The structures on the left are later accretions.

pany the proceeds of a lottery ticket amounting to £3750. This was further supplemented by borrowings on bond, mostly from individuals whose names suggest affiliations with the landed classes. The amount due by bond on 1 January 1773, for instance, was £16,706.[86] Not the least remarkable feature of the Slane mill, however, was the extent to which profits were ploughed back into the concern by all three partners. The consequence of this was that by the end of the century the indebtedness had been entirely eliminated.[87] The provision of capital was of course facilitated by the role of the flour factors in Dublin. They advanced money on the proceeds of flour in their hands. In this way they facilitated the task of the mills in buying grain on a cash basis during a very long season. At any given time the Slane mill owed its flour factor a sum rarely below £1000. At the end of September 1771, the amount advanced by the mill's factor, William Colville, reached an exceptional £6077.

The factors' importance in the flour trade was enormous. Without their facilities the millers would have had to curtail their buying. Their importance is also reflected in the prominent place they acquired in Dublin commercial life. Colville, factor for the Slane mill, was one of the largest merchants in Dublin, and eventually became a governor of the Bank of Ireland. The Shaws were another firm in the flour business in a very extensive way. They gradually concentrated on the financial aspects of business as opposed to commodity trade, reducing their flour trade in order to hold the Dublin balances of country banks and merchants, and to open a banking house in 1798 under the style of Thomas Lighton & Co.[88] The Manders, another family to rise to wealth as flour factors, gave Dublin one of its lord mayors in the 1790s.

The financing of the fixed capital of the industry was not of course confined to landed families. Much of it came from merchants. Some Dublin merchants may have invested in mills outside the capital.[89] Merchants who invested in flour mills came from a variety of occupations. Especially intriguing is the case of Henry Jackson who in 1798 had a foundry in Church Street, rolling and slitting mills on the quays, iron mills at Clonskeagh, and a steam engine for grinding corn in Phoenix Street.[90] Coming so soon after the celebrated Albion Mill in England, this suggests the technically advanced and enterprising nature of Irish milling. A distinct group of those engaged in milling in the Dublin area had earlier been specifically flour factors. Given their direct involvement in the trade and ready access to capital, this was a logical development. Arthur Guinness was, for instance, a flour factor as well as a brewer, and had a flour mill at least as early as the 1790s – the Hibernian Mills at Kilmainham.[91] The Manders had a mill at Brackenstown to the north of the city,[92] which was only a part of their investment in milling. In a list of mills in Co. Dublin dated 1802, one of the Manders was identified with two mills in the city and a further mill at Islandbridge.[93]

The Quakers were also involved in the milling industry from an early date, constituting as early as the 1780s an identifiable and influential group in the trade.[94] Their profits from other branches of trade, including textiles, helped to finance their investment in flour milling and indeed the decline in yarn spinning may have facilitated the switch to milling. The main focus of Quaker interest in milling was in the vicinity of Clonmel, formerly a centre of the wool and worsted yarn trades, which emerged as the largest milling centre in Ireland and where the two big interests were the Grubbs and the Malcomsons. Their textile background is reflected in the diversification of the Malcomsons into cotton at the adjacent site of Portlaw where they erected the largest (and most durable) cotton mill in Ireland. In turn, their technological experience in cotton spinning may have influenced their milling. Portlaw, with three engines combining 300 h.p., was the most concentrated instance of the use of steam power in Ireland in 1838; steam engines were installed in grain mills in the Clonmel complex in 1834 and 1837.[95]

The mill at Slane seems outstanding in the development of the industry. It was the first really large mill. When it was erected it was certainly the largest industrial structure in Ireland, and would have been exceeded in scale only by the Royal Hospital, the Dublin Linen Hall, and some of the buildings in the proximity of College Green. Built in cut stone, and characterized by a symmetry and richness of detail unusual for an industrial building, it testifies to the fact that in conception and execution there must have been an awareness of its significance. The first petition to parliament from the promoters of the mill claimed that 'by several persons of skill it is esteemed, both for its size and contrivance, to be equal, if not superior to any structure of this sort in Europe'.[96] Their next petition in 1768 stated that their funds had been expended 'with a view of rendering their works the most compleat of their kind in Europe'.[97] Arthur Young who visited the mill and dined with its manager David Jebb thought it 'a very large and handsome edifice such as no mill I have seen in England can be compared with'.[98] It may well have remained the largest industrial structure in Ireland for several decades. By 1814 it no longer enjoyed that distinction[99] – the huge five-storey malt stores in the Milford complex, for instance, was 222 ft long and 45 ft wide,[100] but at that date it was still exceeded in size by few industrial buildings, and by none perhaps in elegance. Much of the cost of the mill was accounted for by the massive water works, the great weir, and the retaining wall on the river-side of the head race. The floodgates, built to protect the head race and buildings, cost no less than £1800.[101] The head race served as a canal as well. The company owned two to three lighters which carried grain or flour on the Boyne between Slane and Drogheda. The lighters could load and unload in front of the mill, moving upstream through the floodgates, passing above the weir to join the Boyne Navigation Canal upstream and could enter the River Boyne itself again about two miles downstream.

In some ways as interesting as the structure itself is the person who presided over its construction and over its first four decades of operation, David Jebb. A marriage settlement reveals that John Jebb, merchant, was resident in Drogheda in 1751.[102] It seems likely that he was the father of David Jebb – who was to call one of his own sons John. David Jebb is described as a resident in Drogheda in 1763 and 1764.[103] The petition to parliament in November 1765 described 'the petitioner Jebb having served his apprenticeship to Mr Drinkwater, of Chichester, and for some time having had the conduct of his mill, which is the most considerable in England'.[104] Drogheda was one of the main grain markets in Ireland, and in particular helped to supply the north with grain. Chichester was one of the principal ports in England from which grain and flour were exported to Ireland. Flour exports had soared in the year ended 25 March 1746, and remained at a high level subsequently. It is likely that John Jebb, as a merchant in Drogheda, had engaged in the grain and flour trade and, if he had such dealings, he is bound to have had contacts with Chichester. This may be the background to David Jebb's apprenticeship in that port. The petition submitted to parliament in November 1765 was on behalf of Blayney Townley Balfour Esq., Lieutenant William Burton and David Jebb, miller; that in February 1763 was described by the same parties as from David Jebb & Co.[105] From the start it seems that the partnership was under the direction of David Jebb; this is still more amply confirmed by the documents and correspondence from later years. Jebb put up one third of the original stock of the partnership, and ploughed much of his share of the profits back into the firm. In addition, in recognition of his managerial role, he received an allowance of one-eighth of the net profit from the mill. In 1793 Jebb moved with his family to England, intending apparently to run the mill by correspondence with the miller on the spot and with occasional visits to Ireland. His instructions to James Morton were: 'You will move directly on my leaving the mill house into it – I reserve the east parlour and the room above it for myself when I come over.'[106] Jebb did in fact come over from time to time, and in the long intervals between visits, decisions were conveyed by a weekly exchange of correspondence with the mill.[107]

Jebb was one of the sources on which John Foster – the father of the celebrated corn law of 1784 and his neighbour at Collon – relied for advice on the grain and flour trades. Thus the 'great miller of Slane'[108] had a two-fold influence on milling: both through the example of the mill – on an immense scale for the 1760s – and his masterly management of it, and by his access to the powerful and sympathetic figure of Foster.[109] It is ironic that Jebb's departure from Ireland took place only four years before the ending of the bounties on the transport of grain to Dublin. Jebb had felt the bounties gave country millers an excessive advantage at the expense of the millers close to the capital, and he spoke against them at parliamentary committees and no doubt privately to Foster. In reality, the end of the bounties did not affect the structure of the industry greatly. There was little subsequent growth of milling in Dublin.

Other uses which had crowded grain mills off the rivers and streams continued to do so. In 1802 there were only four water-mills in the city, six on the adjacent stretches of the Liffey, and a mere twelve on the tributaries. It is this competition of other users that explains Dublin's leadership in installing steam engines in grain mills – three in 1802.[110] But even this early leadership was a faltering one: Dublin only accounted for four of the sixteen engines in flour mills in 1838.[111]

The growth of the massive port mills, which alone expanded in the second half of the nineteenth century, had to await the inflow of American grain. The industry remained concentrated in the tillage areas with steam sometimes used as an auxiliary in the bigger mills. Big mills continued to be built after 1815, even if fear of American competition may have inhibited some new investment – this was one of the reasons for the Malcomson diversification into cotton. Steam power, usually as an auxiliary, helped to consolidate the industry – millers, even Jebb, had tended to be oversanguine about their water supply, and the Slane mill suffered from summer shortages. One of the most arresting features of the post-1815 period was the dominant position of Clonmel (shipping through Waterford), which completely overshadowed any earlier or contemporary centre and held its place until the collapse of domestic wheat growing in the 1850s.[112] The total quantity of corn, meal and flour shipped from Waterford in 1835 was far larger than from any other port; Limerick was second and, while the quantities include unground as well as ground corn, they probably reflect the first phase in the growth of Limerick's milling in the nineteenth century and the emergence of the Bannatyne and Russell interests in the industry. Unlike Clonmel, Limerick, however, could switch from domestic to foreign grain, and thus preserved in part at least its prominent place in milling: the Russells' mill in Newtownperry at the end of the nineteenth century was the largest single mill in Ireland. The industry remained innovative in terms of technology and business organization in the second half of the nineteenth century, but the price of such a response was a regrouping and concentration in contrast to its diffuse early revolution.

3

A Survey of
Irish Flour Milling
1801–1922*

ANDY BIELENBERG

With the notable exception of the creamery sector, food processing remains a particularly under-researched element within Irish industrial history during the Union. Corn milling falls into this curious gap in the historiography, despite its importance within the Irish economy as one of Ireland's staple industries. With up to 2500 corn mills in operation between 1835 and 1850 it was the most widely dispersed industrial activity on the island, and probably the most important in terms of fixed capital investment.[1] Despite a gradual decline in the number of mills as the industry became more concentrated, down to 1100 by 1916, grain milling still accounted for 10 per cent of recorded gross industrial output in 1907. In the 26 counties, where the greater part of the industry was located, it was relatively more important, accounting for roughly 18 per cent in 1912. By 1907, flour production had become the most important branch, accounting for about 50 per cent of gross output in the milling sector.[2]

The limited historiography on Irish flour milling during the Union has

* I would like to acknowledge the comments of Liam Kennedy and other members of the Historical National Accounts Group for Ireland on an earlier draft, and I would like to thank John McHugh for his significant research contribution, and Peter Solar for his wheat trade figures (forthcoming). The usual disclaimer applies.

focused more on Ulster,[3] where the production of oatmeal was relatively more important than flour milling for most of the nineteenth century. This essay addresses this lacuna by providing a pioneering survey of the industry across the entire island during the period of the Union. A new flour production series between the 1840s and 1920s has been constructed by combining data published in the agricultural statistics (which reveal the extent of native wheat production) with trade data reconstructed by Peter Solar, providing net wheat imports. From this series, it is possible to trace the timing of the shift to foreign supplies and the trend in total production in terms of volume (see Appendix). This series, when combined with a range of qualitative sources, provides a firm basis to re-assess the performance of Irish flour milling over the entire period.

Flour production seems to have expanded in tandem with the general expansion of tillage farming in Ireland between the 1770s and the Great Famine. By 1815, Connell concluded that more land was tilled than ever before, with a good part of the reclaimed land being used to grow corn.[4] Ó Gráda argues that his estimate of agricultural output in 1845, trade statistics and farm accounts, would 'rule out any sharp shift to pasture' prior to the Famine.[5] Since flour was produced almost entirely from native wheat in this period, the expansion of tillage farming in the seventy years or so prior to the Famine contributed to significant investment in Ireland's milling infrastructure. Wakefield noted in 1812 that wheat acreage had been expanding in the previous decades:

> The business of converting wheat into flour is increasing in Ireland, a considerable change with respect to food, having taken place in the habits of the people in many parts of the country, wheaten bread begins now to be much more used then it was formerly.

Wakefield went on to state that the principal land appropriated to tillage ran from Co. Kilkenny through Kildare, parts of Meath and Louth, while areas in Cork, Tipperary, King's and Queen's Counties and Wexford were also identified as significant wheat-growing districts.[6]

In the 1830s it was noted that the advent of steamship navigation on the cross-channel trade led to a rapid increase in the number of grain mills across the country, while others were expanding their capacity, and it is generally assumed that this was a consequence of the growth of the export trade.[7] However, an examination of the export data suggests that this was far less important than rising native wheat consumption. An agricultural report in 1836 noted that native wheat production:

Furlong's Mill at Lapp's Quay, Cork, completed in 1852 and refitted as a roller mill in the 1880s.

> has increased very materially ... there has been more wheat consumed in Ireland the last two years than ever was known ... coarse flour has been so low [in price], that a part of the population which has been in the habit of living upon oatmeal has eaten coarse flour, and there-fore, notwithstanding there has not been a greater export from Ireland, the growth has considerably increased.[8]

The growing application of steam power for grinding grain between the mid-1820s and early 1840s provides additional evidence of investment in flour milling during this period.[9] One witness to the Third Report on Agriculture noted, 'there is a great increase in flour mills and I understand from people that have been connected with them, that it is attended with a great profit'.[10]

The Famine and its aftermath (and the removal of the Corn Laws in 1846) did not precipitate a decline in milling, as the potato failure increased per capita demand for milled cereals. This is evident from the rise in imports of Indian corn in particular from 1846, and also in net imports of wheat over the following decades.[11] By 1852 Carlow town, for example, had four grain mills powered by steam (installed in the previous decade). The borough of Cork city had four steam-powered mills by the beginning of 1852; another had been established by the end of that year when Furlong's Mill on Lapp's Quay was finished,[12] in response to the growth in cereal imports during and after the Famine. Likewise, in the town of Galway there were twenty-five mills prior to 1847 manufacturing flour, oatmeal and malt, and the town's milling capacity expanded during the Famine years.[13]

There is little doubt that bread was an important source of food for much of Ireland's population. Although the consumption of bread (made from wheaten flour) was considered a luxury for the labouring population, by the end of the eighteenth century it was occasionally consumed by labourers and the peasantry in parts of the countryside, and in some towns more consistently;[14] in Dublin (the main market for flour) it was considered in 1803 to be 'the most necessary article of life to the population'.[15] Consumption in urban areas and among the middle classes was widespread, but was more limited among the rural poor before the Famine. Clarkson and Crawford's work on the Poor Inquiry in 1836 reveals that bread was only named as a food consumed by the poor in less than 8 per cent of the parishes in Ireland and it was more commonly consumed in Leinster than the other provinces.[16] Nonetheless, by the late 1830s they suggest that a sizable part of the entire population (i.e. 4–5 million) ate bread at least some of the time.[17] This implies that by the eve of the Famine, the Irish wheat-eating population was somewhat larger than has traditionally been assumed. Dudgeon, for example, suggested that in 1841 the wheat-eating population of England and Wales was less than 90 per cent, in Scotland 40 per cent and in Ireland 25 per cent.[18] It is probable that much of the Irish bread-eating population secured a larger part of their carbohydrates from potatoes than in the rest of the United Kingdom, but even allowing for this, it does not seem unreasonable to assume that well over a third of the Irish population were bread-eaters by the eve of the Famine, and Dudgeon's estimates for Ireland were too conservative.

Solar's estimates of Irish wheat production and net exports in 1840–5 suggest that Irish flour consumption was around 62 lbs per capita just before the Famine. Ó Grádá's estimate of the same period would raise the figure a little.[19] It seems probable that the percentage of bread-eaters had been rising in Ireland between 1800 and 1845, as in the rest of the UK. A growth in native demand for flour seems to be the major explanation for Ireland's extensive flour-milling infrastructure by the 1840s, since flour exports to Britain were minimal in 1800. Though they rose somewhat thereafter, they were significantly less than native flour consumption by the eve of the Famine. How does such a conclusion square with census evidence for this period? Since many millers were engaged in milling grains other than wheat, baking provides a more useful barometer of the geography of commercial baking and bread-eating (though this tells us nothing about the home baking of wheatmeal bread). In 1841 the nine larger towns and cities returned 1652 bakers compared to a total of 6641 bakers for all Ireland. This implies that commercial baking was by no means confined to the larger urban centres, having spread out into the smaller towns. The less comprehensive 1831 census tells a similar story, with 1471 bakers recorded for the thirteen larger towns and cities out of a total of 4565 for Ireland.[20] Commercial oven-baked bread was clearly a well established feature of pre-Famine urban diets. Magee's case study of the major Belfast baker, Hughes, reveals the central importance of bread in the diet of that city and its industrial hinterland.[21] By 1802, the consumption of wheaten bread was noted among the miners of Castlecomer,[22] and by the mid-1830s the consumption of wheaten bread among urban labourers in Waterford had 'increased considerably'. It was also commonly consumed by workers engaged in linen manufacture and the urban population across the north.[23] In rural areas, bread-eaters more commonly consumed home-baked bread.

Surviving business records from flour mills provide additional evidence that the market for flour was not restricted to the larger towns. While many flour millers sold into the buoyant Dublin market, they also sold flour to the local villages and towns in their hinterland.[24] The large mill in Slane sold extensive amounts of flour in counties Louth, Cavan, Meath and the city of Dublin in the 1830s, in addition to handling a large export trade to Britain.[25] The Dundalk flour millers in the 1830s sold to towns in the north, while Belfast at this stage was supplied by flour mills in or near Belfast at Larne, Lisburn, Comber and Bangor.[26] The significance of home-baked bread in the diet of middling and well-to-do farmer households should not be underestimated.

Bread soda, which could be used as a leavening agent for making soda bread with wheatmeal, came into use in the pre-Famine period, while fadge (a mixture of wheatmeal and potatoes), was also consumed. This helped to extend the market for wheatmeal flour and led to an increase in flour consumption in rural households in particular. Though built-in baking ovens were not common outside the town bakeries, inns or the houses of the gentry, iron griddles, pans or bastable ovens were commonly used to bake soda or griddle bread, further increasing the use of home-baked bread in rural and urban contexts.[27]

Solar's estimate of total Irish calorific production in 1840–5 and 1846–50 reveals the greater calorific significance of potatoes over cereals prior to the Famine. However, this trend was reversed during the Famine.[28] Alternatively, Ó Gráda's pre-Famine cereal output estimate (which is less conservative than Solar's) suggests that *c.* 1845, gross value added of wheat and oats combined was £13 million, compared to £8.8 million for potatoes, reflecting the differences between the calorific significance and the market value of cereals and potatoes. Wheat in the latter estimate accounted for almost £4.9 million.[29] Bourke suggests that in normal pre-Famine years nearly 80 per cent of domestic oat production was retained for consumption in Ireland.[30] With the exception of seed oats, almost all of this would have had to be milled for human or animal consumption. The huge significance of oats in the pre-Famine economy provides part of the explanation for the existence of a large and widespread milling infrastructure in Ireland. The expansion of flour milling between 1801–45 contributed to building up the more capital-intensive and technically advanced elements of the sector in response to rising native demand for flour. In terms of size and technical sophistication, many of the larger Irish mills compared favourably with English mills. The largest in the country was Alexander's mill in Milford, Co. Carlow, with twenty-two millstones by the 1840s.[31]

Between the early 1820s and the years of the Great Famine, a number of Irish millers expanded their foothold in the British market. The Corn Laws were protecting them from foreign competition in a growing market. In Waterford, which accounted for half of Irish flour and wheatmeal exports by 1838, flour dramatically eclipsed wheat in significance.[32] The regions that produced a surplus for export were the major wheat-growing districts in Leinster and Munster. Clonmel, situated inland, was the largest flour-milling centre in Ireland, exporting most of its flour through Waterford, where flour exports were high compared to the rest of the country.[33] In 1846, for example, flour

Table 1

The Port of Origin of Flour and Meal Exports from Ireland to GB 1824–38

	Oatmeal (cwt)		Wheatmeal (cwt)	
	1824	1838	1824	1838
Dublin	10,358	142,075	20,694	146,148
Wexford	514	4,308	2,151	5,478
Waterford	8,654	22,577	160,412	663,412
Cork	6,032	9,394	45,859	252,820
Limerick	2,285	51,830	668	30,315
Galway	7,340	—	—	10,220
Westport	3,580	1,860	—	1,458
Sligo	2,307	168,432	—	—
Londonderry	4,221	67,516	220	60
Coleraine	5,187	13,786	—	—
Belfast	20,679	25,772	1,506	5,662
Newry	1,457	77,988	655	18,556
Dundalk	6,682	213,960	3,554	11,220
Drogheda	20,878	319,589	4,062	114,674
Total	100,174	1,119,087	239,781	1,260,253

Source: BPP, 1828, XVIII, *Corn and Meal Exports from Ireland to GB*. BPP 1839, XLVI, *Grain, Malt and Flour Exported to GB from Ireland*.

The Model Mill, Divis Street, Belfast, completed in 1882 and demolished in 1966.

and wheatmeal exports from Ireland amounted to only 724,000 cwt, when Irish flour production was in the region of 5,595,000 cwt. Although flour exports did rise over 1,000,000 cwt in a number of years in the 1830s and '40s, this trade was far less significant than native demand.

By the early 1860s net Irish wheat imports exceeded native wheat production. The increased significance of imported wheat from continental Europe in particular had important implications for the organization and location of the Irish flour-milling industry. These circumstances led to a significant decline of flour milling in many inland locations in Ireland that depended entirely on native wheat. Those centres with a strong flour export trade to Britain in the pre-Famine era also experienced decline, notably Clonmel, where a number of concerns had closed by the end of the 1870s.[34] A witness to the Commission on Irish Industry confirms this picture, declaring in 1885 that the flour-milling business was fairly prosperous in Ireland from about 1850 down to the mid-1870s.[35] The volume of flour produced (see Appendix) increased in these years. Clearly a number of flour mills in locations with access to growing imported supplies of wheat, either in proximity to the major ports, or with connections to them via canal or rail, were able to capitalize on the changing circumstances within the industry at the expense of mills in more isolated locations, who depended on dwindling supplies of native wheat. Those who adapted to the shift in raw material supply retained control of the Irish market for flour by the mid-1870s.

Although some rural mills invested in installing new machinery (such as centrifugal bolting equipment),[36] it was the ports that witnessed greater levels of investment in this period. In the growing industrial city of Belfast there was a steady increase in milling capacity: Davidson's Bridge Mills were opened in 1852; Macaulay & Co. began operating the Steam Flour Mills in Steam Mill Lane in 1858; The Phoenix Flour Mills opened for business in 1861 on Great Georges St; and in 1868 the Brookfield Flour Mills began to operate on Crumlin Rd. Mc Cammon's Mill in King St, which had been initially set up for grinding maize in 1848, was also converted for flour milling during this period.[37] Hughes in Belfast completed 'The Model Mill' in 1877, a large seven-storey structure, which had the latest Simon roller system installed in 1881 (see colour plate section). It was reputed to be one of the largest mills in the UK.[38]

One of the largest mills in Dublin in this period was the Dublin North City Milling Co. Ltd on Glasnevin Rd, adjacent to both the Royal Canal and the Midland and Great Western Railway. Incorporated in 1873, it had thirty-four pairs of stones driven by steam and water power for the manufacture of oatmeal, Indian meal and flour. The company had originally been established by the Murtagh brothers who were corn merchants and millers in Dublin,

Athlone, Longford, Castlerea, Castlebar and Ballina.[39] However, this was eclipsed by developments at Bolands' Ringsend Mill in Dublin, which had sixty-three millstones by the end of the 1870s.[40] These examples give some indication of the growing scale of the larger port-based concerns in this period, and the increasing significance of the large bakeries, which were extending their milling capacity. It was becoming more profitable to mill close to the major centres of population and in the ports, adjacent to where imported wheat was landed.

Cork's traditional position as a strong milling region was sustained through the mid-nineteenth-century transition to imported wheat. The city and county became the principal import, milling and distribution centre in the south of Ireland for both flour and maize meal. It remained the second most important centre after Dublin for importing wheat during most of the second half of the nineteenth century. Hall's of Cork became the largest Irish wheat and maize importers during the same period. The rapid transition in the industry in the latter part of the Famine is evident when Hall reported in July 1849 that 'hard wheat is little known amongst the millers here', but later in October of the same year he commented, 'we find the demand for foreign wheat exceedingly good'.[41] Although local millers at this point were not favourably disposed to hard wheats, Hall's were already building up 'a very good connexion' with the region's flour millers, who were clearly turning to imported wheat supplies to meet the growth in demand.[42] Their letter-books between 1849 and 1851 reveal extensive wheat imports from Poland, France, Egypt, Syria, Leghorn, Marianople and Constantinople. By the 1860s, Hall's had customers all over Cork and the adjoining counties, and from the mid-1870s they were increasingly importing North American wheat, in addition to wheat from Odessa, Danzig, Salonica, the Caspian Sea, France, Spain, Argentina and Australia.[43] A number of mills diversified by milling maize, which was imported more extensively from the Famine years onwards for human consumption and for animal feeds. The provender trade expanded significantly during the second half of the nineteenth century because of the growing importance of livestock in Irish agriculture. While this helped a number of rural mills to diversify, enabling them to survive the contraction in inland flour and oatmeal production, port mills could mill it to even greater advantage.[44] By 1907, Ireland accounted for half the UK output of maize meal,[45] reflecting its greater relative significance in Irish milling, notably in Munster.

Flour milling remained reasonably remunerative down to the mid-1870s, but competition from rising imports of cheap American flour produced in roller mills increasingly reduced profitability, putting many millers out of business. The main advantage of the new system was that it required less motive power to grind a given quantity of corn and it also produced a greater proportion of finer white flour. The diffusion of the new technology was confined predominantly to Hungary and the US by the mid-1870s. Since British and Irish mills were initially slow to adopt rollers,[46] the significant reduction in trans-Atlantic shipping costs meant that American flour could be sold in Ireland at increasingly competitive costs from the mid-1870s. This increased the use of white bread as opposed to wholemeal bread. A witness to the Commission on Irish Industry in 1884 affirmed that 'the great food of the Irish is the white bread'; a number of other witnesses pointed to the major reversals in the Irish flour-milling industry resulting from American flour imports from the roller mills of Chicago and St Paul. The Commission drew much attention to the impact of American competition on Irish flour millers by the mid-1880s.[47] This corroborates reports in *The Miller* in 1883 that there was a lot of American flour in Dublin bread. In the following year the journal noted that 'fourteen years ago the milling trade in this country was in a prosperous condition', being one of the chief industries of Ireland.[48] The flour production series (see Appendix) indicates that this decline was to get much worse in the period leading to the turn of the century.

Imports of North American flour had their most pronounced impact on Irish flour milling in the 1890s, reaching their maximum impact between 1899 and 1903, declining rapidly thereafter. At this point English-milled flour was beginning to make some headway into the Irish market. Taking a more long-term perspective, net imports of flour rose dramatically between 1867 and 1904 from around 300,000 cwt to almost 5,200,000 cwt.[49] Although the amount of flour consumed in Ireland rose considerably, Irish flour production fell from 6,978,000 cwt in 1867 to 4,978,000 cwt in 1904 (see Appendix). This reveals a significant loss of market share for Irish millers to imports, as per capita consumption of flour in Ireland increasingly converged with the rest of the UK.

Table 2

Flour Available per Head in the UK and Ireland (lbs)

	UK	Ireland
1840–5		62
1850–4	259	154
1910–14	257	265

Source: R. Perren, 'Structural Change and Market Growth in the Food Industry: Flour Milling in Britain, Europe, and America, 1850–1914', *Economic History Review*, 2nd ser., xliii, 3 (1990), 425. Net imports from Solar (forthcoming). See Appendix column (5.) for Irish flour production. See endnote 20 for 1840–5.

However, the price decline on the Irish market resulting from foreign competition contributed to a major increase in Irish per capita flour consumption in the last quarter of the nineteenth century. The significance of bread in the diet throughout Ireland increased dramatically in this period. Table 2 reveals a far lower per capita consumption of flour than the rest of the UK in the early 1850s, with Irish consumption rising significantly during the second half of the nineteenth century. By the eve of the First World War, flour consumption in Ireland was slightly higher than in Great Britain. Family budgets for households in the west of Ireland in the 1890s, which were drawn up by the Congested Districts Board, reveal that household expenditure on bread and flour at this stage were highly significant, even among impoverished households. In one district in Donegal, for example, over a fifth of household expenditure went on flour or bakers' bread,[50] and this was fairly typical of the pattern across the western seaboard. The globalization of the wheat and flour market, and the resulting fall in prices, was the most significant factor that increased Irish per capita flour consumption in the second half of the nineteenth century.

Foreign wheat imports into Ireland (the major raw material for the Irish milling industry) provide a useful indication of the timing and intensity of foreign competition in flour on the Irish market. Foreign imports of wheat into Ireland reached a high watermark in 1875, but held up well for the rest of the 1870s. In the 1880s there was a decline in wheat imports as a result of competition from imports of American flour, especially in the second half of the decade. Decline continued in the 1890s to a nadir between 1897 and 1901. Then there was a marked recovery in Irish wheat imports between 1904 and 1912 (see Appendix). It seems probable that English mills at this point were starting to make inroads into the Irish market. While the relative proportions of American and English flour entering the Irish market are impossible to establish, it is very clear from the figures for total flour imports that competition from both contributed to a significant decline in the Irish flour-milling industry between the mid-1870s and the beginning of the twentieth century. By

E. Shackleton and Sons, Carlow Mills. An early twentieth-century view showing barges being unloaded from the adjacent Barrow navigation. (*Milling*, 1924)

1904 imported flour accounted for roughly half of the Irish flour supply, and while the native milling industry recovered some of this lost ground between 1904 and 1917, the volume of flour produced seldom reached the levels achieved in most years between the Famine and the late 1880s. The fall in flour prices in this period reduced profit margins and increased the competitive environment in which Irish flour millers were obliged to operate.

Despite the major reversals experienced by the Irish flour-milling sector as a whole as competition increased, a number adapted to these circumstances by exploiting the major technical innovations and advances within the English milling and machine industries, with some Irish millers contributing to the first phase of innovation. The partial use of rollers for bruising wheat was already being undertaken in Ireland in three mills (at Chapelizod, Lucan and Tanderagee) as early as 1845.[51] Turner of Ipswich installed an early roller system in Russell's of Limerick in 1863–4,[52] and a few years later another was installed by S.S. Allen of Midleton (which was not a success). Although a number of Irish millers had installed Wegmann's patent porcelain roller system by the late 1870s, it was only in 1880 that Messrs Shackleton of Carlow brought a full and complete roller mill into production, using the Simon system (in a converted stone mill), which proved to be a commercial success.[53] Over the following decade a number of Irish mills were either converted or built for roller milling. In Belfast in 1881 D. & W. Carmichael built the Dufferin Mills in Duncrue St and by 1884 the new system had also been installed in mills on Meadow St and the Falls Rd. Others who adopted the system in Ulster included Wilson of the Foyle Mills in Derry, Scott's Omagh Mills in Co. Tyrone, and Walker's Mills in Newry, Co. Armagh. At this stage one of the larger mills in Galway had been converted for roller milling. By 1891, there were two such mills in the port of Cork; Furlong's on Lapp's Quay (with nineteen sets of rollers) and McMullen's on Margaret St (with seventeen sets).[54] Others adapted by relocating: Andrews for example transferred their entire flour-milling operations from Comber, Co. Down, to the port of Belfast in the early 1880s, and by 1900 they were one of the two Belfast survivors. In the next decade, this firm improved its plant and output developing a strong trade in Derry, Donegal and the west of Ireland,[55] presumably at the expense of local milling interests. However, competition in the Belfast market, the fastest growing in Ireland, was intense. From the late 1880s wheat imports into Belfast fell as flour imports rose, which led to a number of reverses in the local flour-milling trade. Even the major industrial bakers, Hughes, who built the Model Flour Mills on Divis St in 1877, closed down their mills in 1900, as it became more economical for them to import flour.[56]

Despite major setbacks, there was an impressive response to greater foreign competition among some Irish flour millers. Carter, another major British milling engineer, later claimed that the first automatic roller system in the world was designed, erected and started by him in Bolands Flour Mill, Dublin, in April 1880.[57] The pace of innovation in Irish flour milling compares favourably with Britain when the smaller population and scale of the Irish industry is taken into account. By 1887, of the 471 complete roller process mills that had been installed in the UK, 73 were located in Ireland.[58] This indicates that a number of Irish flour millers were able to take advantage of the major innovations that were taking place within the English industry in this period. Nonetheless, many of those who failed to adapt went out of business, and flour production by the 1920s became more concentrated in the hands of those who had adopted the new technologies.

The corn supply for the Irish milling industry in this period also became more concentrated in the hands of a small number of larger grain dealers. For example, from 1880 R.H. Hall of Cork opened new offices in Belfast, and subsequently Dublin and Waterford, expanding their trade to all these ports. Despite a depression in the industry, they noted optimistically in March 1886:

> Our millers for many years past suffered very heavily from the competition with American flour, the American mills having exceptional advantages from their new machinery, and their great command of fine wheats. All this has now changed. Out of the twenty-four principal millers in the South of Ireland, sixteen have been remodelled after the American model, and can now defy competition, being fully fitted with the newest machinery. Seven out of the remaining eight nearly always pay cash for what they buy from us. Moreover our millers have now become favourably situated ... to compete with America. The UK has now the produce of all lands and notably the cheap Indian wheats are beating out the American. Milling therefore, which so long has been a staple industry here, gives promise now of recovering its old position ... Many millers have gone down, but those surviving are mostly the largest.[59]

Hall's perspective was that of the major suppliers in an industry which was rapidly becoming more centralized. The extent of their operations in 1893 was dramatically illustrated when they opted to switch their banking operations from the Provincial Bank to the Bank of Ireland to speed up transactions, revealing that their annual turnover was about £2–2.5 million. They indicated that 'in Cork we do about three-fourths of the corn trade, in Waterford the entire, in Dublin and Belfast about half the business done. With the disappearance of several of our competitors during last year, our opportunities for doing business are greatly increased, especially in Dublin.'[60] The company used these extremely difficult years in the Irish corn trade to make cheap acquisitions in Waterford in 1890 and Westport in 1894.[61] It seems probable

The Marina Mills, Cork, completed in 1891, c. 1919.

that the presence of Hall's grain-importing business from the mid-nineteenth century transition to imported grain was a major benefit to the flour millers in the city and county of Cork, as it ensured constant supplies on competitive terms.

A number of mills in Cork city and its hinterland made the transition to roller milling from the 1880s, and as a consequence the city and county still had twenty-seven mills in operation in 1929, which produced over a quarter of the output of the Irish Free State.[62] From the 1880s, much of the industry gravitated towards the port of Cork, where in 1908 there were six large roller mills that used imported grain, including: Messrs John Furlong & Sons Ltd, Marina Mills (a custom-built roller mill established in 1891) and Lapp's Quay; Messrs J.W. McMullen & Sons Ltd, Cork Steam Mills, George's Quay; and Messrs George Shaw & Sons, St John's Mills, John St.[63] Despite the closure of a number of rural mills in the region as a result of this concentration in the port, some survived and even prospered outside the city. Messrs T. Hallinan & Sons Ltd were perhaps the most successful, having taken over the Glandalane Mills in Fermoy in 1861, the Avoncore Mills in Midleton in 1874 and the Quartertown

Mill in Mallow in 1912.[64] Economies could be achieved in medium- to large-sized plants using roller mills, which enabled them to displace smaller mills in their hinterland.[65]

Limerick also became an increasingly important centre for importing and milling foreign wheat in the second half of the nineteenth century, with foreign imports reaching and surpassing those of Cork from the 1890s. Wheat was also forwarded from the port to mills in Clara, Galway, Kilrush and Cahir, amongst other places. With the transition to roller milling from the 1880s, flour milling in the region became more concentrated in two large companies in Limerick city (Bannatyne's and Russell's), which were conveniently located for distributing meal and flour via the Shannon system by canal, in addition to the rail system. However some other mills continued to operate profitably such as Glynn & Sons at Kilrush, Co. Clare, and Maguires Curraghgower Mills at Croom, Co. Limerick.[66] Bannatyne's took over a steam-driven mill in Roches St in Limerick city in 1858, converting to the roller system in 1884, which was extended in 1886.[67] The company was incorporated with a nominal capital of £300,000 in 1894. Goodbody's of Clara became more closely involved in managing the firm, extending their Limerick milling interests when they became associated with Russell & Sons Ltd in 1903. Russell's and Bannatyne's had depots all over Munster and even in parts of Connaught, which facilitated large sales of grain, flour and meal.[68] Although Russell's mills were among the largest in Ireland in terms of capacity, they were ultimately surpassed by Bannatyne's City Roller Mills, which were subsequently considered to be the parent mill in the Rank group and were described as the largest of the Free State flour mills in the 1930s 'during the past generation'.[69] The concentration of ownership evident within the Munster industry continued when the shareholders of John Furlong & Sons (1920) Ltd, one of the largest of the Cork city milling operations, offered to sell all the shares to Bannatyne & Sons Ltd for £121,736. The offer was accepted, anticipating the further concentration of ownership in the Munster industry during the following decades.[70]

In Dublin, the most notable developments were the emergence of the large industrial bakeries – Bolands, and Johnston, Mooney & O'Brien – who milled much of their own imported wheat. Johnston, Mooney & O'Brien had a share capital of £150,000 when incorporated in 1889. Their operations included the Clonliffe Mills, Jones Rd, one of the larger Dublin mills, which had just been fitted with a roller system.[71] Patrick Boland had taken over Pim's Mills in

Ringsend at the Grand Canal Basin in 1873, installing a Carter roller system in the early 1880s. Bolands was incorporated in 1888 with a share capital of £205,000. The amount of wheat ground there can be traced through the company accounts. The quantity remained fairly steady in the 1890s and then rose in the following decade to a peak of 202,779 barrels in 1911, declining slowly over the following decade. By 1921–2, the amount ground was half of that in 1911.[72] This suggests that Bolands flour-milling operation became increasingly less competitive with flour imports from Britain during these years. However, since much of the Irish flour trade was not for commercial bakers' flour, but for the home-baking trade which utilized the coarser flours, Irish mills remained competitive in this important sphere. In 1890, it was estimated that about 80 per cent of the flour sold in Ireland was for the shop trade, while the remaining 20 per cent was for bakeries.[73] Home baking was more significant in Ireland than in Britain, notably in rural areas. This may have been one of the reasons there was less competition with flour imports in the Munster market than in Dublin and Belfast, where bakers' flour for commercial bakeries had a larger market share.

A number of Leinster mills continued to operate at canal and rail heads outside Dublin, or in smaller port towns. The Annagassan Mills, Dunleer, run by Dougherty & Co., was the only survivor in Co. Louth by the 1920s, employing at least twenty persons. The Davis family mill in Enniscorthy was one of the few flour-milling concerns to survive into the twentieth century in Co. Wexford. St John's Mills were acquired by the family in 1858; they were extended and ultimately converted to the roller system in 1885 and produced both household and bakers' flour, in addition to maize livestock feeds.[74] There was a strong milling industry in counties Kildare, Offaly, Carlow, and Kilkenny where a number of medium-sized firms survived as the industry became more concentrated, producing a wide range of products other than flour. The order forms for Perry of Belmount Mills, for example, included superfine flour for bakers' and household grades, in addition to Indian and oaten meal.[75] The Pilsworths took over a range of mills in Kilkenny, and increasingly centred their flour- and maize-milling interests on Grennan Mill in Thomastown (since it had rail access), buying up and closing down other flour mills in the region, or simply using them as sales outlets and stores.[76] Fogarty's of Aughrim were milling native Wicklow wheat, while also taking consignments of foreign wheat off the Dublin, Wicklow and Wexford railway from Dublin, Wicklow or Enniscorthy. They also used the line for delivering flour.[77] But lower through rail rates seem to have favoured the port-based millers or English imported flour. For example Scott's at Omagh claimed, like many other inland mills, that railway rates discriminated against their interests in receiving wheat or delivering flour compared to mills located in Derry or Belfast.[78] It seems clear that the port millers increasingly had greater advantages in terms of transport costs and access to international wheat supplies, while simultaneously commanding larger markets in their immediate hinterland.

To deal with competition from the ports, the Odlum family, who had inland milling interests in Naas, Portarlington, Maryborough and St Mullin's, embarked on a joint venture in 1920, providing them with a foothold in the Dublin trade.[79] The Dublin Port Milling Co. Ltd located at Alexandra Basin, which came into production in 1924, brought together a strategic alliance with experience in grain handling/milling/baking including the Kennedy and Spicer baking interests, Hall's, the grain importers, and Odlums among others. This was indicative of the centralizing tendencies within the industry and the consolidation of resources between companies in cognate fields.[80] The contraction in the number of country mills accelerated from the mid-1870s as prices fell and competition increased. From 1891, it is possible to

The Dublin Port Milling Co. in 1924. (*Milling,* 25 April 1936)

examine the changing geography of the industry. Table 3 records the number of mills grinding wheat in Ireland. This reveals a contraction in the number of mills in most counties, while Dublin grew in importance. The significance of the Cork region also stands out as the county alone accounted for more than twice the amount of flour mills in Connaught and Ulster combined by 1916. In the latter year there were only seven mills in the province of Ulster, reflecting the significant concentration of the industry there.

Table 3

Flour Mills in Ireland 1891–1916

County	1891	1916	County	1891	1916
Carlow	2	2	Antrim	2	2
Dublin	6	10	Armagh	2	—
Kildare	13	3	Cavan	3	—
Kilkenny	13	7	Donegal	1	—
King's	4	3	Down	6	2
Longford	2	1	Fermanagh	1	-
Louth	1	2	Londonderry	1	2
Meath	10	1	Monaghan	—	—
Queen's	7	3	Tyrone	3	1
Westmeath	—	—	Ulster	19	7
Wexford	36	13			
Wicklow	4	2	Galway	20	11
Leinster	95	48	Leitrim	—	—
			Mayo	5	3
Clare	7	2	Roscommon	1	1
Cork	47	33	Sligo	1	1
Kerry	4	4	Connaught	27	16
Limerick	13	8			
Tipperary	13	7	**IRELAND**	**228**	**127**
Munster	87	56			
Waterford	3	2	Source: Agricultural Statistics, Ireland.

With the growing concentration of capital in milling and corn handling, many of the major families invested in each others' enterprises. Family networks were clearly important and their surplus capital could be invested in a related field with which they were familiar.[81] Shareholders in Hall's, for example, included the Hallinan's of Midleton, the Smith's of Cahir, Goodbody's of Clara, and the Pilsworth's of Thomastown, among others.[82] Hall's for their part had £100,000 invested in various larger milling concerns such as Furlong's in Cork city, Donavan's in Kerry (which by 1915 was entirely managed by one of Hall's cousins) and the Dock Milling Company in Dublin, in addition to advancing considerable credit to millers to whom they sold grain. Hall's had a vested interest in keeping Irish mills open, pointing out in 1913 that closure brought increased competition from 'large English millers' and had a bad effect on the trade generally.[83] To restrict competition in a crowded market, millers sometimes co-operated to reduce production. When John Mosse Brown of the Kilmacow mills in south Kilkenny went bankrupt in 1914, the property was auctioned and bought up by a consortium of flour millers in that region including Ardagh's of Pouldrew, Co. Waterford; Going & Smith of Cahir, Co. Tipperary; Mosse of Bennettsbridge; and Pilsworth of Thomastown, Co. Kilkenny, who shut down the flour-milling operation, using the mills solely for commission grinding for local farmers for oats and barley and for selling seed. This effectively reduced local competition and prevented another competitor entering the market.[84] Competition from flour imports, however, was persistently more difficult to counteract.

English flour began to make inroads into the Irish market from the early twentieth century, when the whitening or bleaching of flour was prohibited in the USA. The preference for bleached flour for much of the Irish trade provided British mills with an opportunity in the Irish market, which was augmented by the transition from barm to yeast in Irish baking, which favoured the use of a combination of strong and weak wheats. In these circumstances, large mills at Birkenhead in Liverpool using imported wheats (which they could acquire at lower costs than Irish mills) operated at full capacity with lower labour inputs and the best technologies, thereby enjoying economies of scale. In the decades leading up to the First World War, Liverpool became one of the leading flour-milling centres in the world, its futures market in wheat dominating the UK grain trade. Liverpool-based millers provided increasingly formidable competition for the Irish flour trade, supplying much of the bakers' patent flour by the 1920s, in addition to some household flour for soda bread. Irish mills at this point focused more on slightly cheaper flour for household use. Since the British market was over-milled and over-supplied with flour by the 1920s, and continental exports had been reduced, the Irish Free State market became the most important destination for British flour exports. By 1922, Irish flour mills only supplied roughly half of the Irish demand for flour. Even the larger Irish bakers who engaged in milling found it cheaper to import a large part of their flour needs from Britain. Post-war Irish flour imports were slightly higher than those that prevailed before the war. Although this highly competitive situation was beneficial to Irish consumers in terms of the price of flour and bread (which by 1922 collectively accounted for around 10 per cent of expenditure of the average wage-earning household in the Irish Free State), growing flour imports (largely from Liverpool) contributed to a major downturn in Irish flour milling, which precipitated a number of closures in the 1920s.[85]

Conclusion

This survey provides some tentative pointers towards the development of a more comprehensive appraisal of the history and performance of Irish flour milling during the period of the Union, and some long overdue revisions to the historiography. One of the main conclusions is that both flour milling and bread eating were somewhat more significant before and during the Famine than has generally been assumed.[86] It is virtually impossible to explain the scale of Ireland's pre-Famine flour-milling infrastructure without the existence of an expanding native bread-eating population between 1800 and 1845. Irish flour milling expanded in this period largely as a consequence of a growth in native demand for flour. The statistics for the export trade to Britain in the half-century up to the repeal of the Corn Laws suggest that exports only accounted for a minimal share of Irish flour production. Therefore McCutcheon's argument that following the repeal of the Corn Laws 'the comparative advantage previously enjoyed by Irish flour … on the English market disappeared', may have been quite true. But it was of relatively little significance in terms of total Irish flour output, and it was of even less significance for the Ulster industry in particular (see Table 1), with which he was largely concerned.[87] Although flour exports were important for the port of Waterford and its hinterland and to a far lesser extent for the ports of

Cork, Dublin and Drogheda, the evidence presented here suggests that McCutcheon and other historians have traditionally attached too much significance to exports as the main dynamic in Irish flour milling from the Napoleonic Wars through to the repeal of the Corn Laws in 1846.[88] O'Brien also marks down repeal as the point when 'the prosperous milling industry experienced a reverse'.[89] Perhaps one of the flaws of Mokyr's pessimistic appraisal of the pre-Famine economy was that he followed this traditional line of reasoning that Irish food processing depended largely on exports.[90] In the food, drink and tobacco industries in general, the expansion of native demand between 1800 and 1845 was of central importance in the growth of these industries, and it is evident from this essay that flour milling was no exception.

The repeal of the Corn Laws did not automatically lead to a major downturn in flour production. On the contrary, the severe crisis in the food supply during the Famine raised the demand for flour, driving up flour production in 1847. A bumper harvest and a rise in wheat imports certainly did not lead to any reversals in Irish flour milling. This quantitative evidence is amply corroborated by developments in the baking sector, which also experienced a boom as desperate measures were taken to augment the food supply.[91] The impact of the Famine and its aftermath led to a shift in diet away from potatoes towards milled cereals, which increasingly were imported. By the early 1860s imported wheat exceeded native production, so Irish flour milling witnessed some relocation and reorganization to deal with this major shift in raw material supply, which favoured mills with transport access to the ports. Gribbon notes that due to falling native cereal acreage as well as reduced demand, corn mills closed between 1850 and 1880, while flour mills at the ports and a few inland survivors experienced the effects of American competition.[92] While it seems true that poorly located inland mills declined at the expense of those with access to imported wheat, it is also clear that American flour only began to affect the Irish flour trade from the mid-1870s. Between the mid-1850s and the mid-1870s, the volume of Irish flour production actually increased, despite the marked shift in the wheat supply to continental Europe. While the decline in wheat acreages led to a major contraction of mills dependent on native supplies, the evidence presented here indicates that flour production did not decline overall in the third quarter of the nineteenth century. The industry developed in this period in and around the ports, with per capita consumption of flour rising significantly between the Famine and the 1870s. This evidence completely undermines Fairlie's contention that wheat consumption in Ireland was still probably 'negligible' by the 1870s.[93]

The decisive impact of foreign competition on Irish flour milling was keenly felt in the last quarter of the nineteenth century, when the increasing globalization of the world's wheat supply drove down the price of wheat and flour as UK prices began to converge with those in North America.[94] One of the benefits of this price decline in Ireland was that bread and flour became available to poorer households, reducing dependence on the potato and increasing the variety of the diet. However, while falling prices were good for consumers, they simultaneously dramatically increased competition for Irish flour millers. In 1920, Riordan recalled the crisis of the 1880s resulting from flour imports, and the installation of rollers in a number of Irish mills in response to this influx of cheap flour. Riordan concluded that 'no Irish industry has had to face fiercer competition from outside these shores, and has done it more successfully in the long run than the Irish flour-milling industry'.[95] While this perhaps rings true in the case of the larger players in Irish flour milling, the statistics presented here reveal a somewhat bleaker picture for the Irish flour-milling sector as a whole in the half-century leading up to the 1920s. In the first half of the 1870s it would appear that Irish millers retained full control of the buoyant market for Irish flour. Over the succeeding thirty years they lost half of Ireland's flour supply to competition from imports.

Although a number of Irish flour millers had successfully adapted to new circumstances, and there was some recovery of market share in the first decades of the twentieth century, production did not recover to the levels achieved in the mid-1870s. Output data reveals that in the 6 counties of Northern Ireland, production declined very slightly from 61,420 tons of meal and flour in 1912 to 60,720 tons in 1924.[96] In the 32 counties a similar pattern is discernible: in 1907, 5,182,000 cwt of flour and meal was produced, falling slightly to 5,103,000 cwt in 1926.[97] The production series presented here, however, suggests that the real period of decline and loss of market share took place in the *last quarter* of the nineteenth century. Riordan, therefore, was essentially putting a brave face on the long-term contraction of one of Ireland's staple industries. Nonetheless, flour milling was one of the few Irish industries that was performing reasonably well relative to Scotland, probably because of the stronger history of flour production. The 1907 census (see Table 4) provides a breakdown of UK flour production.

Table 4

UK Flour and Meal Production in 1907

	Cwt	Value
England and Wales	69,847,000	45,325,000
Scotland	4,442,000	2,762,000
Ireland	5,182,000	3,621,000
UK Total	79,471,000	51,708,000

From this point until the 1920s, however, English competition became more intense, displacing American imports. By the 1920s, Liverpool in particular (one of the major milling centres in the world) had carved out a strong niche in the Irish market, replacing the position that American flour had attained by the end of the nineteenth century. Liverpool could operate mills in more optimal conditions than those located in Ireland.

Flour milling is therefore one of the nineteenth-century Irish industries that conforms to some degree to O'Malley's contention that 'the main causes of decline lay in the strong tendencies to industrial centralization, or agglomeration within the United Kingdom'.[98] However, in the case of flour milling this was certainly not just in the United Kingdom; the first and most intensive wave of reversal within Irish flour milling came from trans-Atlantic competition from American flour millers. Furthermore, in terms of timing, the evidence assembled in this essay suggests that the tendencies towards centralization within the UK flour-milling industry (which enabled English mills to acquire a large share of the Irish market by the 1920s) were not a nineteenth-century phenomena, and need to be traced through the first quarter of the twentieth century.

Irish Flour Production 1846–1921 (cwt)*

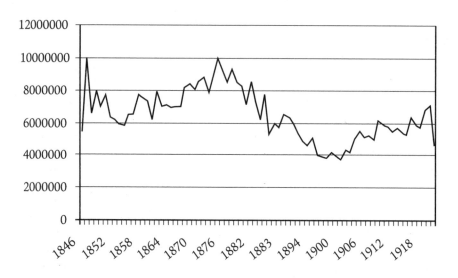

* See column (5.) in Appendix.

Appendix

An Estimation of Irish Flour Production 1846–1921 (cwt)

	(1.) Harvest minus 10% for Seed	(2.) Minus Distilling	(3.) Wheat Supply	(4.) Extraction Rate (%)	(5.) Flour Production
1846	7020000	233000	6805000	80	5444000
1847	11062000	155000	12440000	80	9952000
1848	7144000	219000	8213000	80	6570000
1849	8193000	225000	9991000	80	7993000
1850	5859000	224000	8736000	80	6989000
1851	5645000	217000	9655000	80	7724000
1852	4362000	219000	7953000	80	6362000
1853	4285000	236000	7763000	80	6210000
1854	5544000	223000	7411000	80	5929000
1855	5748000	223000	7246000	80	5797000
1856	6161000	240000	8223000	79	6496000
1857	6286000	266000	8233000	79	6504000
1858	6602000	207000	9764000	79	7714000
1859	5550000	200000	9512000	79	7514000
1860	4806000	129000	9285000	79	7335000
1861	3220000	119000	7903000	78	6164000
1862	2582000	112000	10159000	78	7924000
1863	3167000	121000	8943000	78	6976000
1864	3308000	148000	9069000	78	7074000
1865	3123000	155000	8860000	78	6911000
1866	3043000	148000	9042000	77	6962000
1867	2741000	158000	9062000	77	6978000
1868	3572000	162000	10613000	77	8172000
1869	3007000	178000	10929000	77	8415000
1870	2849000	239000	10408000	77	8014000
1871	2666000	259000	11272000	76	8567000
1872	2303000	299000	11650000	76	8854000
1873	1773000	279000	10313000	76	7838000
1874	2597000	261000	11514000	76	8751000
1875	2086000	296000	13116000	76	9968000
1876	1821000	306000	12178000	75	9134000
1877	1711000	305000	11330000	75	8498000
1878	2077000	327000	12371000	75	9278000
1879	1619000	301000	11369000	75	8527000

	(1.)	(2.)	(3.)	(4.)	(5.)
1880	2005000	262000	11037000	75	8278000
1881	2067000	254000	9551000	74	7068000
1882	1868000	245000	11562000	74	8556000
1883	1167000	260000	9820000	74	7267000
1884	893000	265000	8351000	74	6180000
1885	987000	286000	10495000	74	7766000
1886	906000	286000	7220000	73	5271000
1887	917000	298000	8167000	73	5962000
1888	1230000	306000	7797000	73	5692000
1889	1293000	319000	8927000	73	6517000
1890	1273000	350000	8697000	73	6349000
1891	1261000	388000	8292000	72	5970000
1892	1067000	367000	7340000	72	5285000
1893	803000	358000	6771000	72	4875000
1894	738000	342000	6361000	72	4580000
1895	535000	367000	7042000	72	5070000
1896	576000	385000	5679000	71	4032000
1897	653000	392000	5485000	71	3894000
1898	896000	398000	5410000	71	3841000
1899	834000	390000	5906000	71	4193000
1900	811000	383000	5694000	71	4043000
1901	709000	344000	5354000	70	3748000
1902	772000	335000	6176000	70	4323000
1903	567000	351000	5976000	70	4183000
1904	501000	318000	7112000	70	4978000
1905	689000	341000	7844000	70	5491000
1906	736000	325000	7308000	70	5116000
1907	639000	314000	7448000	70	5214000
1908	672000	329000	7071000	70	4950000
1909	846000	290000	8727000	70	6109000
1910	827000	262000	8495000	70	5947000
1911	798000	263000	8250000	70	5775000
1912	754000	266000	7747000	70	5423000
1913	625000	266000	8151000	70	5706000
1914	682000	276000	7688000	71	5458000
1915	1561000	292000	7373000	72	5309000
1916	1363000	356000	8662000	73	6323000
1917	2205000	334000	7957000	74	5888000
1918	2736000	299000	7614000	75	5711000
1919	1188000	366000	9068000	75	6801000
1920	698000	300000	9433000	75	7075000
1921	743000	300000	6485000	72	4669000

Irish wheat production in 1846 taken from P. Solar, 'The Great Famine was no Ordinary Subsistence Crisis' in M. Crawford (ed.), *Famine: The Irish Experience 900–1900* (Edinburgh, 1989), p. 132. 1847–1921 is drawn from Mitchell (1988), in which 1848 was omitted; this is assumed to be 12.8 per cent lower than 1849, as later estimated for the 26 counties, which accounted for the bulk of Ireland's wheat production. (Agricultural Statistics 1847–1926 [Dublin, 1928], p. 10.) 10 per cent of the native Irish crop is deducted annually to allow for seed, stock feed, waste etc. Net imports of wheat are supplied by P. Solar, (forthcoming), and DATI trade data from 1904–21. The wheat supply is the sum of net imports and native wheat production, with above deductions and also for distilling. Distilling deduction of 300,000 for the 1920s is based on *Application for a Tariff on Flour*, Tariff Commission, R36/3 (Dublin, 1923), pp. 71–2, and A. Bielenberg, 'The Irish Distilling Industry Under the Union' in C. Ó Gráda and D. Dickson (eds), *Refiguring Ireland* (Dublin, 2003), and it has been assumed retrospectively throughout that 1 cwt wheat was used on average for every 37.1 gallons of Irish whiskey distilled. Flour extraction rate of 80 per cent at Famine period taken from Bourke (1976–7), p. 161; 140 lbs of wheat =112 lbs of flour, moving gradually to 70 per cent by the twentieth century. Irish extraction rate was higher than figures given by Perren (p. 425) for UK and the 66 per cent average for UK (*Census of Industrial Production*, 1907). This was assumed to be due to greater demand for coarser grades of flour for soda bread in Ireland. This conforms with the level for the 6 counties given in the 1924 *NI Census of Industrial Production* which is almost 70 per cent. It is assumed that the extraction rate rises in war and post-war years with government control, shortages, etc. *Irish Trade Journal*, May 1926, 153.

4

Irish Quakers in Flour Milling

RICHARD S. HARRISON

THIS ESSAY EXAMINES Quaker involvement in Irish flour milling between the mid-eighteenth century and the 1920s, when their achievements within the Irish industrial sector were significant. Their penchant for industrial innovation has already been noted in the development of the linen industry in Ireland. Throughout most of this period, when Quakers were significantly and visibly engaged in commerce, they deliberately dealt in basic and necessary products such as iron, wool, wood and grain and their manufactured derivatives. They avoided dealing in products that implied luxury and waste and also showed great astuteness in shifting in and out of products when economic circumstances changed.[1] By the 1780s, a number of Quakers engaged in the declining bay-yarn trade, transferred their capital resources into flour milling, including the Pim, Haughton, Grubb and Goodbody families. Irish Quaker flour millers constituted a significant and influential group with a distinctive dress and mode of speech.[2] If their total number was small, they had access on a larger than usual scale to capital and distinctive social networks, which were vital for information flows relating to credit, technology and markets. There were larger Quaker populations in the Midlands and in Wexford, Carlow, Cork and Tipperary, which were mostly tillage areas in the late eighteenth and early nineteenth century. For example, of the thirty-four mills listed for Tipperary in 1790, at least six were Quaker-owned.[3] They were well located to participate in the expansion of flour milling in these regions as wheat acreage and the demand for flour rose.

Flour mills increasingly required larger fixed capital investment and greater working capital, which Quakers were well poised to provide. Firstly, they had the profits from other trades and secondly, in many cases, payments from dowries and legacies could be drawn upon by those entering business for the first time. There were also wider Quaker networks to call on for up-to-date commercial advice, while family and contractual arrangements ensured a degree of safety from ill-considered speculations. Mills show a remarkable tendency to be retained in the same families or to be purchased or inherited from other Quakers. Milling families also tended to inter-marry, which guaranteed access to wider spheres of expertise and capital. It is evident that marriage portions frequently contributed towards a profitable milling business or its improvement.[4] For example, three of the daughters of John Barcroft Haughton, a prosperous Cork iron-merchant,[5] married millers, and each received a marriage settlement. In 1807, Susannah Haughton married Richard Grubb, a miller of Cooleville, Clogheen, where he owned the Tar and the Union Mills.[6] In 1809, Helena Haughton married Archibald Christy Shaw of Lurgan, who was the tenant of her father's flour mill, the Glen Mills at Kilnap.[7] Elizabeth Haughton married her own brother-in-law, Thomas Grubb, in 1819.[8] Haughton, therefore, as a result of each of these marriage settlements passed capital from his hardware business into the flour-milling sector. Samuel Grubb Snr, the father of Thomas and Richard, had married Margaret Shackleton of another important milling family.

The Shackletons were long associated with the village of Ballitore where Abraham Shackleton I (1697–1771) set up the Ballitore School. Shackletons took over the mill on the Griese at Ballitore in 1774.[9] In 1789, Abraham Shackleton II (1752–1818), son of Richard Shackleton (1728–92), had this demolished and built a bolting mill at Griesebank in 1792,[10] letting it initially to Peter Delany, and subsequently to his own sons, George (1785–1871) and Ebenezer (1784–1856), who were partners in the enterprise. By 1805, the mill serviced the local market, with a large proportion sent to and sold via Thomas Gibbins & Son, a Dublin flour factor.[11] An early ledger (1807–10) is a sample of the meticulous accounting procedure expected under the rules of the Religious Society to which they belonged. Increasing business seems to have facilitated further investment in a mill and storage facilities at Athy.[12]

On a much bigger scale were the Quaker mills of Tipperary, and of Clonmel in particular, where the enterprise of David Malcomson was especially significant in the early nineteenth century. Aged twenty in 1784, he had left his native Lurgan to help his widowed cousin Sarah Grubb in the management of Anner Mill, Clonmel.[13] In 1795, Malcomson had married Mary, daughter of Joshua and Sarah Fennell, who were millers in the town of Cahir. His wife brought a dowry of £1500. This marriage allied him with members of the Fennell, Harvey and Jackson families, illustrating the growth of another regional flour-milling nexus.[14] Malcomson chiefly exported flour and grain down the Suir and via Waterford to England. Waterford Quaker merchants such as Max & Blain or Davis & Strangman purchased grain and flour for export.[15] In rapid succession Malcomson had become the owner of a number of Clonmel flour mills, starting in 1808 when his brother bought him the Corporation Mills, Suir Island, for £3000.[16] David Malcomson constantly reinvested profits, expanding his business. His annual inventories reveal a growing export trade in flour.[17] Around 1818, Malcomson set up a partnership with his sons, trading as David Malcomson & Sons. The partnership ran the Corporation Mills and the Little Island Mill in Clonmel acquired a few years earlier.[18]

A period of recession followed the end of the Napoleonic Wars in 1815.[19] This was particularly hard in Munster and resulted in the failure of several banks and businesses including that of John Barcroft Haughton in 1822–3. The Cork Quaker Monthly Meeting would have encouraged Haughton to take responsibility and put all his property on the line in the interest of his creditors. Such a bankruptcy or default could upset the long chains of credit and trust that coalesced around different families of Friends, which is illustrated by a deed agreed as part of the process of sorting out Haughton's affairs.[20] Haughton's assignees included his sons-in-law Thomas Samuel Grubb, Richard Grubb and Joshua Carroll and his nephews John and James Haughton of Carlow. All the parties were involved in the milling, flour and corn commission business and Joshua Carroll was additionally a member of a rich and powerful timber-importing firm.[21]

In the long run, however, the government's 1815 ban on the import of foreign corn following the wars had boosted the milling industry and Irish grain production, also increasing flour exports to Britain. A major beneficiary of this policy was Clonmel.[22] The Limerick Quaker historian Ernest Bennis, speaking chiefly of Tipperary's Quaker millers, noted: 'The bulk of the flour milling was in their hands and walking along the banks of the Tar, Suir and its tributaries I counted eighty-five roofless mills …'[23] The figure that he uses

does not distinguish between the times when the various mills were in operation or became defunct but does give a sense of the scale of industry promoted
by the region's Quaker families. According to *Pigot's Directory* for 1824 there
were twelve mills in Clonmel alone, and different members of the Grubb and
other Quaker families there and in Clogheen and Cahir controlled more than
fourteen mills.[24]

There is little contemporary quantitive evidence for the scale of trade for
any individual Tipperary mill, but it is estimated that David Malcomson's flour
export alone constituted 25 per cent of Waterford's exports between 1816–29,
and in 1827 Richard Lalor Sheil visited his Clonmel mill and wrote, 'here half
the harvest of the adjacent counties as well as of Tipperary is powdered under
the huge millstones'.[25] Something of David Malcomson's moral qualities
emerges in the same account: when Sheil saw a young man shovelling and
covered with flour, he was informed that this was Malcomson's son learning
the business from the bottom up.[26]

At least some consistent evidence about the finances of a flour-milling
partnership emerges in the ledgers of George Shackleton of Ballitore.[27]
Increasing profits are indicated in surpluses that were invested in government
stock. Patterns of expansion can also be identified in the decision of George's
brother Ebenezer to buy out his share in the partnership and to set up his
own mill at Moone in 1826. A figure of £2473 was noted in the Shackleton
ledgers as his share for that year. Ebenezer Shackleton had obtained the
Moone mill and twenty-six acres in 1824 for a rent of £200 p.a. but in 1826,
with an eye to a bargain, paid a sum of Ir£500 and got the rental reduced to
£155 15s. thereafter.[28] George Shackleton's trade had been somewhat more
'domestic' than that of Malcomson and initially less export-oriented. However,
by the 1820s a significant part of his trade was for export, a factor encouraged
on the one hand by the nearness of the Grand Canal. He was not only dealing
with commission merchants James and William Haughton at City Quay, but
also direct with the Quaker Rathbone of Liverpool and other merchants there
and in Glasgow. The element of trust, practical friendship and shared convic-
tions provided a strong bond among these merchants. They also happened to
be among the larger capitalized merchants who had sufficient capital to provide the requisite credit to carry out significant transactions.

The burgeoning flour-export trade offered profit and stability. It encouraged
a bigger capital investment and perhaps even bigger partnerships with 'sleeping

The Kilcarbery Mill of S. & A.G. Davis, Co. Wexford.
(Advertisement from *Milling*, October 1924)

partners'. Signs of growth in flour exports were evident at Wexford, and also at Enniscorthy, where Francis Davis (1777–1863) in 1828 added a double wing six storeys high to his Kilcarbery mill.[29] In Offaly, Quakers such as Robert Goodbody (1781–1860), with his brother Thomas and brother-in-law Anthony Pim, set up the Brusna Mills Co. and Bakery at Clara, with a capital of £4000. Robert Goodbody was 'acting-manager' at a salary of £150 per annum, with the use of the house and lands attached. He had been a land agent to Lord Mornington but, upset by what he felt was unjust treatment of the tenants, left the job, preferring to run a milling business.[30]

The development of commercial and transport infrastructure ancillary to milling was an important feature of the 1830s and '40s, and a significant part in this was played by a number of Quaker families, particularly by the Pims and Perrys, who were simultaneously active in the flour, grain and brewing trades. Branches of the Pim family spearheaded the setting up of the Royal Bank in 1836, which incorporated a core group of milling businesses.[31] One of James Pim's entrepreneurial partners, for example, was his brother-in-law James Perry of Dublin whose brothers and father ran the flour mill at Ballinagore near the extension of the Grand Canal to Kilbeggan, completed in 1830.[32]

Contemporary trade directories reveal strong regional concentrations of

Quaker mills along the rivers Barrow, Brosna and Suir, serving the inland areas of Tipperary, Kildare, Offaly and Laois. Wexford should be noted as facilitating some exports and Dublin and the Midlands were significantly linked by the Grand Canal. Cork constituted an important region of its own, drawing on grain and flour from its hinterland and beyond. The biggest single concentration of flour milling in the 1830s continued to be in Tipperary where Lewis's *Topographical Dictionary* estimated that there were sixty-one major flour mills.[33] Inglis, a visiting traveller, commented that the mills of Clonmel were like the big factories of an English industrial town and attributed their success to the export-based nature of Irish flour milling and that the Irish miller conducted business on his own account.[34] High demand on water resources may have been a factor in members of the Grubb family setting up outside of Clonmel at Clogheen. Samuel Grubb of Clogheen was said to have spent £6000 on his mill at Castlegrace, which employed 30–40 persons.[35] The increasing demands on available water supply were an incentive to millers to make bigger capital investment in the new steam-power technology which also permitted year-round milling independent of water-level and weather conditions. Quaker miller Thomas Samuel Grubbe [sic] at Richmond Mill was one of the first to rely exclusively on steam power in 1828.[36]

Bolands Lock (no. 26), on the Grand Canal, near Tullamore, Co. Offaly.

Cahir was also an important milling centre where the mills were chiefly operated by Quakers.[37] Joshua Fennell had built the Abbey Mills, Cahir, which were taken over by Richard Grubb of Clogheen in the early 1830s.[38] Another was Charles Going (1763–1830), originally from Mountrath, who had been involved in the West Indies trade and in starch manufacture in Cork. When he married Hannah Clendennan in 1798, he had put their fortune into the Suir Mills at Cahir and built a house at Altavilla. His eldest son William Going (1795–1871) subsequently became the reluctant head of the firm.[39]

Quaker flour millers were also of considerable importance in the Midlands. George Walpole (1797–1883), who owned several farms around Roscrea and in the Midlands, operated a milling enclave on the Brosna in Offaly. His mill at Drumakeenan was in 1837 assigned to Richard Dowd Snr, a Maryborough Quaker.[40] Near to Maryborough at Donaghmore was the mill of John Dugdale which could produce 5600 barrels of flour per annum. The mill was not among the biggest in the vicinity; there were six around Maryborough that each had a capacity to produce 12,000 barrels of flour per annum.[41] Also in Laois, a mill at Stradbally was owned by Richard S. Leadbeater, whose mother was a Shackleton.

More significant were the Quaker milling families of Offaly: the Perrys, the Goodbodys and the Robinsons, whose interests were dependent on the Brosna and the Grand Canal. There were four flour mills in Clara, all owned by Quakers and two of them producing 'exclusively for the English market'.[42] The two flour mills of Robert Goodbody at Kilcoursey, with a total of ten stones, seem the most likely candidates for the two noted as exporting to England.[43] Robert Goodbody proved central to the development of the flour-milling industry in Clara. When his brother-in-law and milling partner Anthony Pim died in 1836, Robert Goodbody bought out his interest and set up the partnership of Goodbody & Sons.[44]

Carlow, with its small population of Quaker merchants, shop-keepers and farmers, was a central market and there were four flour mills there in 1837.[45] The flour mills on the Barrow were described in 1841 as 'the greatest establishments of their class in Ireland producing an average of 350,000 cwts of flour and 100,000 cwts of oat meal annually'.[46] One of these mills must have been the Barrow Mills established by John Haughton in 1834.[47] The Barrow, linked with the Grand Canal, was an important artery for the transport of grain and flour to Dublin and Waterford. It was estimated in 1837 that 'in the past 14 years' the trade down-river to Waterford had advanced from 2000 to 15,000 qtrs of flour and corn.[48]

Co. Kildare, which benefited much from the Grand Canal, had a number of Quaker flour millers and Ebenezer Shackleton's business at Moone was also clearly prospering. His mill was stated to be capable of producing 15,000 barrels of flour per annum in 1837.[49] His business owed much to his determination to use the best wheat and ensure the most perfect cleaning his machinery could achieve. A favourite maxim of his was, 'Get rid of a bad grain of wheat even if it takes nineteen good ones along with it.'[50] George Shackleton, Ebenezer's brother, probably sent most of the flour produced at his Ballitore Mill for export or for Dublin consumption via Athy and the branch of the Grand Canal there. By 1839 his ledgers reveal extensive dealings direct to Liverpool to Hunter & Coventry and Rudyard & Leicester, and to May & Co. in Glasgow, among others. Their dealings with James & William Haughton in Dublin continued.[51]

In the 1840s, the increasing domestic demand for bread and the new market for biscuits and fancy confectionery had a bearing on Quaker milling interests, as evidenced by the increasing numbers of bakers listed in contemporary directories. Whilst many merchants such as Harvey's in Youghal or Jacob's in Waterford had experience of producing ships' biscuits, these were hard and designed for long-distance voyages. Specialist biscuit production required finer imported flours and ultimately efficient, clean and specially designed machinery. English Quaker biscuit manufacturers such as Huntley & Palmer had agents in Ireland, and it was not long before Irish Quakers started making biscuits.[52] An early Quaker initiative in 1840 (preceding Jacobs in Waterford) was that of George Baker, later Baker & Simpson of Cork who developed a worldwide export market.[53]

After a downturn of several years, flour milling picked up slightly in 1842–3, just before the Famine. Many Quakers took their part to assist with relief. Members of the Dowd, Perry, Goodbody and Fisher families show up as being involved in local auxiliaries of the Friends' Central Relief Committee.[54] The Great Famine marked a major watershed in agriculture, milling and commercial development. It resulted in the repeal of the Corn Laws in 1846. Immediately, transport statistics for the Grand Canal registered a turnabout in traffic.[55] Where before it had mainly carried wheat and flour down to Dublin, there was now a massive net inflow of grain and Indian corn imported via

Dublin, and the trend was to remain constant in ensuing years. A similar inflow can be detected for Waterford and was reflected in declining native wheat acreage.[56] Midlands-based Quakers had ready-made family links in Dublin to access imported grain for them. The Pims and Haughtons in Dublin were dealers in grain and had the necessary contacts in Liverpool. The Shackletons and Perrys also accessed their grain from these sources in addition to using Liverpool- and Glasgow-based Quakers (sometimes of Irish origin).

Clonmel and the flour mills of Tipperary were perhaps the hardest hit by the repeal of the Corn Laws and the consequent increasing imports of foreign grain. But some flour milling continued both there and at Clogheen or Cahir where the Grubb-owned mills continued to function and with an increased valuation. The Clibborns, who inherited from Sarah Grubb, were also still there with mills at Redmondstown and at Two-Mile-Bridge.[57] But the Malcomsons had disbanded their Pouldrew milling partnership in 1848 and concentrated on cotton manufacture.[58] Other Quakers previously engaged in milling at Clonmel were probably too old to be much concerned with reinvesting or developing new markets and would have been content to retire from business and rely on investments or returns from rentals to keep them going with a lot less risk to their capital.

In some respects, the Midlands were more favourably placed for adaptation than Tipperary. The Shannon and Grand Canal together provided a central artery of traffic that facilitated grain imports via Dublin and Liverpool. This enhanced Limerick as a milling centre. Tullamore was the busiest station on the Grand Canal.[59] A comparison of the Griffith's *Primary Valuation* of *c.* 1852 with the mill-books of *c.* 1838–46 gives some indication of the shifts in pattern in Offaly and Laois where flour mills in the lowest valuations had almost disappeared, while those of a middle or higher valuation increased in number and valuation. [60]

The importance of the canal was evident in the case of John Perry's mill on the Brosna at Ballinagore. They could access grain with little difficulty via the Kilbeggan canal link. Contributing to their post-Famine survival was an expansion of baking in the hinterland of the mill. A bakery ledger from Ballinagore starting in 1843 shows the mill supplying its flour to bakeries over a large area of Leinster.[61] In the Midlands there was a better road system and bigger tradition of bread-eating than in Tipperary, which had been export-oriented. It was said in 1853 that Ballinagore 'would go to ruin' if were not for

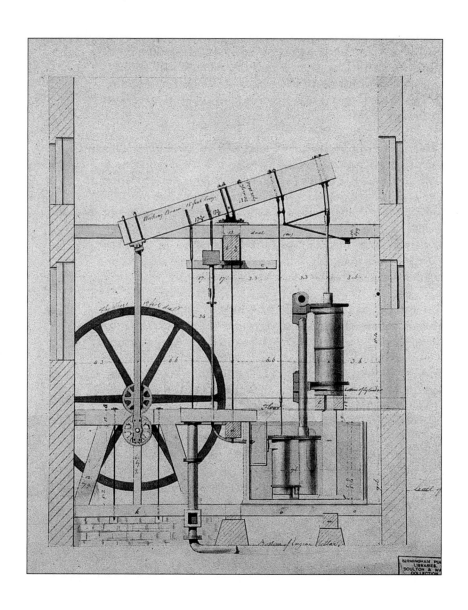

Manufacturer's drawing by Boulton and Watt of beam engine installed in Isaac Morgan's flour mill at Cork, 1800. (Courtesy Birmingham City Libraries. See page 33.)

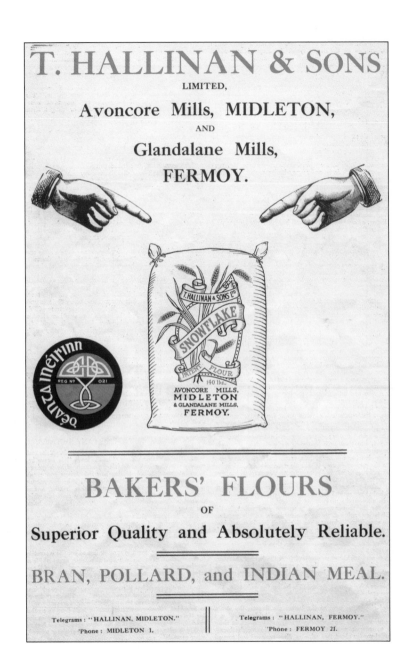

Advertisement for Hallinans of Glendalane, Fermoy, County Cork. (*Milling*, October 1924)

Advertisement for the Clonliffe Mills of Johnston, Mooney & O'Brien.
(*Milling*, October 1924)

Advertisement for Glynn's of Kilrush, Co. Clare. (*Milling*, October 1924)
Advertisement for Going & Smith of Cahir, Co. Tipperary. (*Milling*, October 1924)

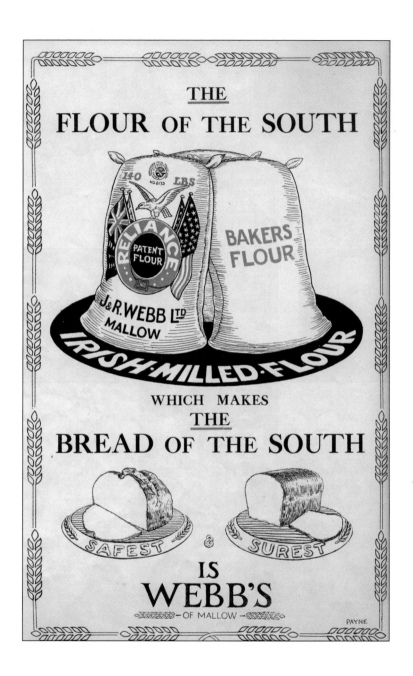

Webb's of Mallow. (*Milling*, October 1924)

Odlums in Naas, County Kildare. (*Milling*, October 1924)

Advertisement for Harp brand, Brown & Crosthwait, Bagenalstown, Co. Carlow.
(*Milling*, October 1924)

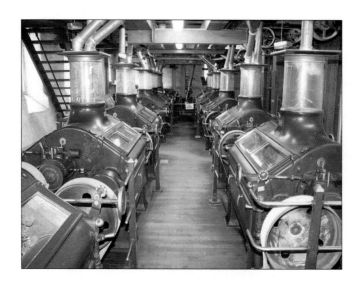

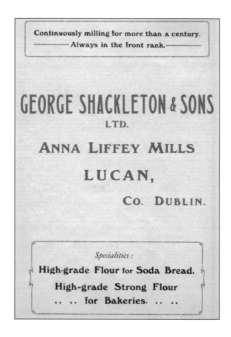

Continuously milling for more than a century.
—— Always in the front rank.——

GEORGE SHACKLETON & SONS
LTD.

ANNA LIFFEY MILLS

LUCAN,

Co. DUBLIN.

Specialities :
High-grade Flour for Soda Bread.
High-grade Strong Flour
.. .. for Bakeries. .. ..

Shackleton's roller-milling plant by Miag of Germany installed in the early 1930s,
at the Anna Liffey Mills, Lucan.
Advertisement for Anna Liffey Mills (Shackleton's), Lucan, Co. Dublin.

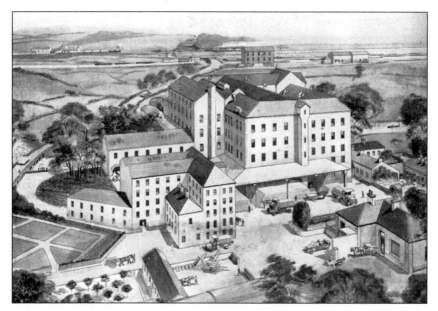

Perry's Belmont Mills, Co. Laois. (*Milling*, October 1924)

the Perry flour mills.[62] A number of Perry's customers were Quakers and they seem to have sold flour retail from their own shop in Ballinagore also. The mill employed seventy men and was capable of grinding 40,000 barrels of wheat in 1838, rising to 50,000 barrels of flour and oatmeal by 1856.[63] This was not the only mill they operated. Under the provisions of the Encumbered Estates Courts, Henry Robert Perry had purchased the Belmont Mill in 1854, which had recently been rebuilt and mechanically upgraded.[64] Robert Perry of Rathdowney and Henry Robert Perry also took over the Clara Mills in 1855.[65] They had taken over the Erry-Maryborough Mill at this point, which was extended by the millwright, Thomas Roberts of Mountmellick, around 1850.[66] The Erry-Maryborough mill had recently been in the possession of John Dugdale & Co. and the Dugdales owned a mill at Donaghmore.[67] The Goodbodys took over the running of the mill in the 1860s, following their 1857 purchase of the Erry Estate under the Encumbered Estates legislation.[68]

In Cahir, Richard Grubb Snr provided for his sons to manage the Abbey Mills. His withdrawal from business was in line with the practice of many older Quakers who sometimes felt a divine 'leading' to do so. His widow showed all the strong character of the Haughtons. She was deaf, but shouted instructions through a megaphone from her bedroom window to her workers.[69]

Though Richard Grubb Snr had chafed at some of the restrictions of contemporary Quaker practice, his son Richard took one dissenting step too far by obtaining a piano and thus, in 1844, his fellow Friends informed him of his de facto disunion from them.[70]

In the post-Famine era grain was imported from the Black Sea, California, Egypt and Australia. Much of the Perrys' imports of foreign grain to Clara and Belmont were accessed from James Pim of 11, Burgh Quay, Dublin and from Haughton & Livingstone in Liverpool, both Pims and Haughtons having Quaker antecedents.[71] Access to imported grain became increasingly essential in the post-Famine era and many young Irish Quakers established new well-capitalized partnerships that were usually family based. Although such arrangements were facilitated by improved banking and legislative provisions that protected investors, family networks were usually critical in terms of capital provision. A prime example of this was the three mills owned by Francis Davis, a Wexford Quaker. In 1856, he vested some of his capital in his sons Francis Davis Jnr, Samuel, Abraham Grubb, Thomas and William Davis to set up a co-partnership to run the Kilcarbery, Urrin and Fairfield Mills, which were used as a collateral to borrow £4000 from the Bank of Ireland.[72]

George Shackleton of Ballitore seized the opportunity to set up improved mills and new milling establishments to be nearer to Dublin's major port facilities, and to access foreign grain and markets. In 1852, he acquired Lyons Mill at the Thirteenth Lock on the Grand Canal. He next took over Grange Mill at the Twelfth Lock and finally, in 1860, entered into possession of the Anna Liffey Mills.[73] His son Joseph Fisher Shackleton (1832–1908) was sent to manage them, and his sister to look after him, a duty she did not greatly relish. In their turn, Joseph Fisher Shackleton and his brother Abraham III (1827–1912) were taken into partnership, and Richard Shackleton Jnr (1841–1916) continued to live at Griesemount, but closed the Ballitore Mill in 1875. It is evident that the family's milling interests were gravitating towards Dublin, attracted no doubt by the expanding demand for flour in the city and its hinterland.

During the 1860s, the membership of the Religious Society of Friends was in constant decline in Munster and Leinster but registered signs of increase in Ulster. Nevertheless there is evidence of an ongoing commercial dynamism by some members. Much of this reflected a creative understanding of contemporary engineering, which was to be a key to survival in flour milling. An amalgamation of Pim and Goodbody interests promoted a steam flour mill at the Grand Canal Dock, but this only survived for four years before it was sold on to Bolands.[74] Technology was also imported.[75] At Belmont, for example, new separating machinery with hoppers had to be ordered from Lüsse, Marky & Bernard of Prague in 1863. The transaction seems to have been made on the recommendation of a fellow merchant in Liverpool.[76]

The marriage in 1867 of Anna Sophia Evans to Robert M. Perry, a son of John Perry of Ballinagore, marked a new phase of enterprise. The marriage brought him into an alliance with other Quaker milling families: the Fayles, the Shaws and the Dowds. When Perry brought home his bride, his native village was decorated with triumphal arches and bonfires blazed while a band of the mill workers welcomed them in with tunes. A local newspaper commented on the good relations between employers and employed. A poem by local bard 'Mike Rickard' shows the importance of the Perry mill to the local economy, to the large hinterland it supplied with flour, and to the efforts of the Perrys to 'drive distress from the needy poor'.

> The human clamour of the skilful farmer
> Does fill the arbour, who comes at will
> With horses harnessed, and drays red varnished
> With loads of corn to Perry's mill
> When weighed and started and neatly clerked up,
> No bills of credit – but the money down;
> There's an inn convenient of entertainment
> With good stout, whiskey, and ale that's brown.[77]

The relative prosperity of the 1860s was not destined to continue and the ensuing decade of the seventies proved a period of great social and economic unrest. Even Ballinagore Mills was affected and during the latter part of 1870 Mr Dowling, the mill manager, was assassinated. The Goodbodys at Clara had received threats and when the Perrys did as well they closed the Ballinagore mills, only opening them again on receipt of a memorial from their employees that described the distress unemployment had caused.[78]

Improvements in communication counterbalanced commercial distress. Railway and shipping systems and the telegraph encouraged further co-operation for business purposes. The use of the telegraph was well established and facilitated the transmission of up-to-date information about the location, arrival, price and movements of grain. It would not have surprised the Perrys to hear that Thomas Stuart, a grain commission agent of Dublin, had 'worked the Nicolaeff all day' to identify supplies for them. Technological advance was mediated by travelling salesmen like J.W. Throop of London who tried to sell them, as he had sold the Goodbodys, patent brush-cleaners for millstones and carefully picked up contacts and recommendations as he moved from country mill to country mill.[79]

Millers were in closer contact than ever before and there is evidence of formal co-operation between the flour millers of these islands. There were between 200 and 250 substantial millers in Ireland alone. Taking a scheme promoted by British flour-millers, Cork millers met in 1875 to discuss mutual fire insurance.[80] Reuben Harvey Jackson, a Quaker corn commission agent, had been one of the speakers at the Cork meeting. He must have recognized the need to make Irish mills more competitive against British milling interests and to have larger units at sea-port locations. In 1877, he invited investment in The Cork Milling Co. using the limited-company legislation of 1862 and 1867. The share capital was for 8000 £5 shares, representing a capital of £40,000.[81] The time chosen by Jackson was inopportune. His endeavour was rapidly outflanked by the new roller-mill technology which could handle the harder imported wheats more effectively, and the Cork Milling Co. soon went into liquidation.[82]

The establishment of the National Association of British and Irish Flour Millers (NABIM) in 1875 was to be a great step forward and encouraged joint-action and the transmission of information. Abraham Shackleton III (1827–1912) took a part in this and his relative Richard (Ebenezer) Shackleton (1836–1900)[83] of Belan and Moone, besides giving leadership to other Irish millers, was to show some of the practical fruits of co-operation in pooling information. In 1871, with his mother Eleanor and brother Patrick, he had taken over Benjamin Haughton's old Barrow Mills at Graigue.[84] The time was ripe to investigate new technology and in 1877, Richard (Ebenezer) Shackleton went with nine other Irish millers, including fellow Quaker Francis Davis Jnr, of Wexford, to Hungary to see the operation of roller mills.[85] Shackleton was the first Irish miller to install a complete roller mill system by Simon in 1879 at his Barrow Mill, which was subsequently introduced at the Athy mills (Moone). His cousins at Anna Liffey Mills installed a roller system in 1883 and another at Lyons Mill in 1887, but this was not continuously

Richard (Ebenezer) Shackleton, who became president of the National Association of British and Irish Millers in 1886. (*The Miller*, July 1886, 82)

used.[86] In 1884, Joseph Fisher Shackleton of Anna Liffey replaced a waterwheel with an Alcott water turbine.[87] The Shackleton family therefore played a particularly innovative role in Irish flour milling in this period.

Taking some advantage of the new technology and incorporating a partial roller system, two of the Grubb mills at Cahir were still in operation.[88] But the Going & Smith partnership, set up in 1864 under the management of Alexander Going (1830–1903), had already taken over the Cahir Mill and the Suir Mill, and now acquired Richard Grubb's Abbey Mill.[89] Going & Smith, like Ebenezer Shackleton, had originally experimented with porcelain rollers but the system was inadequate.[90] They did, however, order Simon plant in 1881 and repeated their order in the next year.[91] In Wexford, Francis Davis who had also investigated the feasibility of using roller mills, opted for the Seck system. The installation of this German system was delayed in 1884 when the ship carrying it was wrecked off the Wexford coast.[92]

The need to set up more efficient partnership arrangements to organize, maintain and expand markets in the face of foreign competition characterized the decade right up to the First World War. The Perry and Goodbody families were crucial to flour milling in Westmeath and King's County. Ballinagore Mill had probably closed by the 1890s and Robert M. Perry shows up as a manager of Webb's Quartertown Mills at Mallow.[93] But Robert Perry & Co. Ltd of Bellmont was set up in 1893, and the company leased back the mills from Thomas Perry with suitable safeguards for his well-being.[94] The Goodbodys made their firm into a Limited Company in 1888.[95] Goodbody capital was used in a number of new incorporations in the milling sector, notably in Limerick, an increasingly important regional centre linked to the Shannon and its associated canal systems, with good port facilities and rail access. Foreign grain imports through Limerick were constantly increasing. James Ellis Goodbody (who had owned the Retford Mills in Nottinghamshire) moved to Limerick in 1891 to manage the family milling interests there.[96] It made sense for the Goodbodys to link up with the Limerick firm of James Fitzgerald Bannatyne and the new incorporation, in 1894, was constituted by a partnership of six Goodbodys and Thomas Archibald Ferguson.[97] A further big move occurred in 1903 when eight members of the Goodbody family and one of the Fergusons took over J.N. Russell's milling enterprise.[98] The Russell Mills at Newtown Perry, Limerick, were noted as having nineteen pairs of rollers for grinding flour and fifteen for grinding maize.[99]

Members of the Shackleton family remained in the forefront of organization for the modernization of Irish milling. In recognition of this role Abraham Shackleton III, a well-known nationalist, was also called the 'Father of the Irish flour-milling industry'. He had long been active in the Dublin Chamber of Commerce and was a 'keen supporter of the Irish industrial movement'.[100] Ebenezer (Richard) Shackleton (1866–1942) was also a significant family member in Irish milling and had been the president of the NABIM in 1886 when it held its annual convention in Dublin. He was educated at Belan and at Trinity College, Dublin, and had a genius for technology. With his friend and fellow NABIM member Brian Nicholson, he had a hand in setting up the 'Rio de Janeiro' mill designed by Henry Simon of Manchester. Reflecting the general growth of Irish economic nationalism in this period, the Irish Flour Millers' Association was set up in 1902. Ebenezer (Richard) Shackleton was a prime mover in its establishment, and was noted to have had 'a scalding tongue and an unpredictable temper'.[101] He was also a member of the Irish Canal Boat Owners' Association. The Anna Liffey Mill was constantly being upgraded as technology improved. During 1900, steel rollers were installed there and new methods for sieving flour were adopted. Bakers' flour for yeast bread was made from more glutinous wheats from the USA, Canada and South America. The 'weaker' flours were made with wheat from Ireland, Australia or the west coast of the USA and packed in ten- or four-stone bags branded as 'First Flour of the Earth' or 'Lily of the Valley'. The flour was delivered to towns and villages in Meath, Kildare, Louth, Westmeath, Dublin and Wicklow.[102] In the early 1900s, the Shackletons owned two bakeries in Meath Street, Dublin, which gave a further profitable outlet for their flour.[103]

Fire was a constant threat to mills and was often caused by sparks that ignited in the atmosphere of dusty grain. A fire destroyed the Shackletons' Lyons Mill in 1903 and it was not reopened. It may have been a factor that prompted a more efficient family partnership set up in 15 February 1904, under the name of George Shackleton & Sons. Abraham, Joseph and Richard Shackleton were listed as the managing directors, with other family members as shareholders. By 1905 the company had assets of £33,076 and employed thirty-eight men.[104] Unrest at home culminated in the Great Lockout of 1913 and the Shackletons were, like the Jacobs, identified with William Martin Murphy and other employers. One of the Shackletons drove a steam wagon to the docks to collect grain and had no Quaker compunctions about bringing a loaded gun with him, which, it was remarked, he 'fortunately did not use'.[105]

The First World War ended American competition and put in place food and supply controls that benefited Irish and British millers. The Ministry of Food required mixtures of grains in bread and the results sometimes proved strange. When soda bread acquired an unintended red appearance, Shackletons' more superstitious customers saw this as a warning that conscription might be imposed on Ireland. Just at the beginning of the war, George Shackleton Jnr (1899–1983), son of William E. Shackleton (1867–1935), was apprenticed to their relative Ebenezer Shackleton. He had been educated at Friends' schools in Newtown, Waterford and Bootham, York. Ebenezer sometimes gave him unusual projects unconnected with milling, but showing a creative engagement with technological problems, as when he asked him to assist in designing an anti-torpedo net to protect vessels from submarine attacks. The war interrupted grain imports and the grain was sometimes not in good condition when it arrived. George Shackleton had one memory of shovelling grain out of a ship and the mites were so thick that the men had to wipe them from their faces as they worked.[106]

With the cessation of hostilities British mills and American exporters began dumping surpluses on the Irish market. But, as with many mills, payments to family members tended to reduce profit. The Goodbody flour-milling business suffered a blow when partner Frederick Goodbody withdrew capital, and then in 1920, competition from imported flour caused a decrease in their profits. There were also too many family members depending on income from the

The Shackletons, George (on left) and Dick (on right), at the Anna Liffey Mills, Lucan, in the 1960s. (Mary Shackleton)

firm. M.J. & L. Goodbody set up a limited company in 1928 and Rank's took over in the following year, but subject to a trust deed of 1902.

In the course of the next decades, many flour mills ceased production. Ebenezer Shackleton was bankrupted and his mills ceased production in 1927, followed by a government-inspired revival as the Barrow Milling Co. in 1933. Other mills with Quaker origins such as Davis of Wexford and Going & Smith of Cahir stayed in business up to the 1960s. But the Anna Liffey Mills, under the management of George Shackleton Jnr and Dick Shackleton (1916–2000), proved the ultimate survivor in this changing world, staying in business until the end of the twentieth century. They attributed survival to finding niche markets when competitors shed business and closed down.

Conclusion

The factors that led to the success and efficiency of Irish Quakers in flour milling apply equally to Irish Quaker merchants and entrepreneurs in other spheres. The encouragement by the Religious Society of Friends of a high standard of probity among its members led to individuals developing a business style that attracted people to deal with them and believe that they received value for money and that their money would be in safe hands. Their Society was not a business or masonic society but encouraged members on the path of Christianity, reminding them of their secular responsibilities, and ensuring that they discharged their proper debts and avoided exploitation and other forms of immorality. Penalties on bad business practice had the positive effect of developing responsible behaviour. Additionally, they would not countenance marriages involving clerical intervention and this practice re-enforced a tendency towards endogamous marriage with consequent protection of family capital and business partnership.

Crucial to successful business was the Quaker network of circulating administrative meetings, which incidentally facilitated a secular purpose at attendant social occasions, in the transfer of information about trade. The experience of members in multi-faceted and mutual review in these administrative meetings was easily transferable to successful 'secular' business. Members were also encouraged to keep accurate records and take stock annually or more frequently. Quaker interest in self-improvement and education resulted, during the nineteenth century, in participation in learned societies and in an interest in practical science and technology, which was an advantage for Irish Quaker flour millers.

Why did so many Quakers become millers during the period in question? Flour milling certainly offered a congenial trade, dealing in a necessary product, which was not tarnished in the way that association with investment in brewing and distilling could be. Flour milling had a certain meditative quality conducive to Quaker ways of worship and to the avoidance of more worldly company, which struck a balance between co-operation and competition. However, by the late nineteenth century allegiance to the Quaker tradition had been much eroded. Some Quaker millers were attracted to the newly disestablished church with its concomitant and activist evangelicalism that offered them an identification with their Protestant peer group. Some were attracted to careers as civil engineers, architects, solicitors, doctors and stockbrokers. Some Quaker flour millers survived until well into the twentieth century; they were also reasonably represented among the shareholders and on the boards of directors of some of the major Irish flour-milling companies in this period. To a large extent this was a residual presence in an industry in which they had played a far more significant role in the nineteenth century.

5

The Introduction and Establishment of Roller Milling in Ireland, 1875–1925

GLYN JONES

PRECURSORS

BY THE MID-1880s it was recognized that gradual reduction roller milling was replacing traditional flour-milling practice in the UK, and this movement was clearly represented in Ireland. In place of millstones to grind the grain, and crude sieving and separating equipment to remove much of the bran from the endosperm within the husk, more gradual processing methods were used. Rolls (or rollers) opened the grain; rotating sieves separated the granulated constituents, began the process of bran removal, and sorted components into fractions graded by particle size. Air currents were used in purifiers to extract small bran particles and further rolls were employed to reduce the endosperm to flour fineness.

A central feature of this major phase of innovation over the previous decade was the technical journal *The Miller*, founded in London by William Dunham in 1875. Until Dunham launched this journal, there was no means of spreading technical ideas on roller milling. *The Miller* grew rapidly in size, coverage, and circulation throughout the United Kingdom, and members of the new profession of milling engineering used the journal to promote their latest machinery. Dunham had experience of global travel and of mill-furnishing contexts throughout Britain. He enthused, commented, advised and prompted, supplying up-to-date news on expanding businesses, and providing an ongoing chronicle of technical change, notably the development of machinery design within the industry. Aged only sixty-five when he died in 1894,[1] he recorded and evaluated the introduction and establishment of roller-milling processes as they were improved and scaled up, replacing cruder traditional machinery. Dunham's encouragement of new methods and stimulus from Austria-Hungary led towards the 1878 inauguration of the National Association of British and Irish Millers (NABIM). By August 1881, membership of NABIM was well over 200. The Irish membership was twenty-three at this point, rising to sixty by 1886,[2] but diminishing thereafter. The establishment of NABIM provided both formal and informal opportunities to increase shared knowledge.

In 1891 G.J.S. Broomhall founded the journal *Milling*, published in Liverpool, which from the turn of the century increasingly became the more prominent source of information. Whereas Dunham had to rely on woodcuts to depict machinery, mills and personalities, Broomhall could make use of photographic illustrations, and published many descriptions of mills and their equipment, frequently including reports of visits to Ireland. *The Miller* and *Milling* are therefore important sources for the history of the Irish flour-milling industry between the 1870s and the 1920s, apparently overlooked by historians of Irish economic history. Drawing extensively from these journals, this essay examines developments in the Irish industry during this important period of transition.

The American Problem

From the mid-1870s, as the USA became by far the most important supplier of wheat to the UK, millers needed to consider alternatives to standard mill-stone practice, which was not suitable for harder wheats. A new term became central to the discussion: strength, conferred by a protein substance known as gluten, which was acknowledged as necessary for the production of well-risen loaves. Cereal chemistry was at a stage of surmise. Trial and error in laboratory and bakehouse led to useful practical knowledge, but scientific understanding evolved only slowly over many decades. A public preference also emerged for whiter bread. UK wheat (notably from Ireland) was soft and had high moisture content. There was an insufficient supply of native wheat, especially in poor harvest years, and it lacked strength.

Wheat supplies from overseas were essential, but millstone milling methods abraded the bran, especially of hard strong wheats, producing flours of an inferior quality. Solutions for these problems became important as market criteria changed. By 1880 *The Miller* was forcefully proclaiming the merits of 'Pure flour': 'Neither Edinburgh, Glasgow, Dublin or Belfast would be satisfied with the bread that is consumed in the metropolis.' Critics referred to the inferiority of bread in the capital as 'London greys'. Elsewhere, though not yet in predominantly rural areas, the popularity of livelier, whiter bread was widespread by the early 1880s. In 1881 the milling engineer Harrison Carter, with sound experience as a practical miller in Ireland, wrote for *The Miller* on 'Milling in Ireland and England', stating, 'There is a large and increasing demand for strong flour' in Ireland.[3]

Unfortunately for the UK millers, supplies of American flour increased rapidly – with surges in 1879 and 1883[4] aided by poor UK harvests – when it was becoming clear that the policy of American millers was to press flour on the UK market rather than wheat. The intention was often stated explicitly, and pressure was maintained by cost-cutting and later by dumping. Highly refined Hungarian flours had provided the initial surprise for traditional millers, but as prices were very high and quantities would be limited, its impact was negligible. But the arrival of ever-increasing quantities of good quality American flour at competitive prices quickly affected confidence. Vague awareness of the existence of roller mills in Hungary and America progressed towards active interest in trying new methods, even if only tentatively until the early 1880s.

Early Experiments
Dunham and *The Miller* supplied news of roller milling in Hungary and UK millers went to investigate, notably in 1877 when a party of about forty visited Budapest to study gradual reduction roller milling. J.R. Furlong of Fermoy, R. Shackleton from Dublin, and F.W. Davis from Enniscorthy were named among the eight Irish members of the party.[5] Hungarian innovation was concentrated at Budapest, where many of the mills adopted new methods gradually through the 1870s, though even then methods were still labour-intensive. Some of the visitors helped to form NABIM, though the prime influence was a new mood of purposeful enquiry encouraged by Dunham. However, to search for the names of early innovators in Ireland, it is necessary to examine information provided by the milling engineers and inventors of machinery.

Members of the British and Irish millers who visited Vienna and Budapest in 1877, organized by J. Harrison Carter. The Irish members of the party included G.F. Penrose, J.R. Furlong, J.W. McMullen, F.W. Davis, F. Davis, R. Shackleton, J. Hodder and D. Carmichael. (Glyn Jones, *The Millers* [Lancaster, 2001], p. 36)

Practical progress within the mills can be traced to the extent that representatives of the milling journals made visits.

The names and achievements of the earliest experimenters and users of new ideas are part of any account of technical change, but amongst millers they were not the long-term technical leaders; this is true of Ireland and England. There were early piecemeal trials of unfamiliar machines, which certainly did not constitute milling systems, in which an increasingly sophisticated series of operations formed an integrated, highly mechanized processing plant. British and American milling engineers quickly improved, extended, and scaled up the operations, with plants at Minneapolis in particular being notable for their rapid enlargement. In Ireland, there was marked technical advance in the early 1880s but, not surprisingly, usually for smaller scales of production than in Britain. A fairly early customer for Henry Simon's rapidly developing design work was Bernard Hughes' mill at Belfast with plant of much more than average capacity.[6]

The earliest partial experiments, other than those with pairs of simple crushing rolls applied extensively in other industries to grind or pulverize a diversity of materials, were with machines designed by Gustav Buchholz, a German engineer working in England, and Friedrich Wegmann of Switzerland. Various versions of Buchholz's methods were tried in England and Ireland, including simple pairs of small rolls, hulling machines to remove husk by abrasion, and complicated composite machines containing a series of pairs of small rolls. The label 'Buchholz's system' was used indiscriminately. In 1872 S.S. Allen stated that he was introducing Buchholz methods at Midleton, Co. Cork;[7] he was optimistic, but numerous later reports at technical meetings and in journals concluded that Buchholz's various schemes were unsuccessful. E.R. & F. Turner of Ipswich, who manufactured Buchholz's machines and became Harrison Carter's machine makers, stated that 'as long ago as 1863 or '64 we fitted up Messrs Russell & Sons at Limerick' with Buchholz equipment.[8]

Buchholz's composite machines were sometimes called semolina mills, semolina being the bulk of the endosperm. In traditional milling, middlings (hard particles) were usually discarded. Friedrich Wegmann devised a method of grinding the middlings, which produced good quality flour. His early roller mill for this useful adjunct to the process consisted of two pairs of small porcelain rolls, and its popularity was intensively advertised. It was a short-term answer to an old problem, and a stimulus towards more general experimentation with the purifying operation. By 1882, Wegmann's first few customers in Ireland had increased to twenty-eight.[9] Many subsequently well-known millers' names appear in his advertisement lists, though few had acquired more than one machine. In mainland Europe, Wegmann rolls became a continuing fashion; in the UK the porcelain roller mill was at a trial stage of innovation, not suitable for the initial gradual reduction stages of breaking the grain. Buchholz had not solved the intricacies of the break stages and had not attended to the reduction roll stages of main flour production. Neither he nor Wegmann advanced the subject of the purifying operation.[10]

From 1878 to 1881, Henry Simon and Harrison Carter developed plant design ideas from rudimentary principles towards systematic solutions of UK milling problems, which were more complex than those encountered in Hungary and America because of the more diverse mixture of wheat types that had to be handled. From 1880-1 they were preparing for intensive involvement in the modernization of the milling industry; their breakthrough included experience and developmental progress in Ireland. Both adopted chilled iron rolls: fluted for the break stages, and smooth for the reduction stages. Each improved the design and action of centrifugal sieve-sifters for scalping (separation of break stage products), particle size grading, and flour dressing. They used continental-type gravity purifiers, but soon started development work on superior sieve purifiers. Carter formed a close relationship with the engineer principals of E.R. & F. Turner at Ipswich.[11] Simon had his roller mills manufactured by Bühlers in Switzerland,[12] while concentrating on the basis of evolving plant designs and consultancy in a rapidly expanding business. Carter was originally a practical miller, apprenticed in Sussex, and experienced in flour-mill management at Davis Brothers, Enniscorthy,[13] and at the famous Coxes Lock Mill in Surrey. Born in Silesia, Heinrich (Henry) Simon (1835–99) studied at the Zurich Polytechnic, practised as a mechanical and construction engineer and became a British subject in 1862. He continued collaboration with colleagues in Switzerland and Germany, to the advantage of his work in the UK and elsewhere.[14]

Simon's first roller plant in Ireland was ordered by Ebenezer Shackleton in 1879 for his mill at Carlow. It was presumably a small plant, though not as

Shackleton's mill, Co. Carlow, in 1879. This was one of the first mills in either Britain or Ireland to be fitted out with Simon's roller-milling system. (Henry Simon, *Occasional Letter*, June 1928)

small as many country mills: probably of about 3 sacks of flour per hour output capacity (one sack = 280 lbs or 2.5 cwt). Shackleton ordered a second plant for his mill at Athy,[15] possibly soon afterwards. While supervising the Carlow installation, Simon met William Stringer, the young Irish mill manager there, and at the celebrated milling exhibition at Islington in 1881 Simon confirmed his initial favourable impression of Stringer's talents. Stringer joined Simon's staff and became the firm's milling expert, a title recognized amongst milling engineers as appropriate to an ability to advise millers and collaborate with engineering design staff.

Late in 1879 Carter referred to the 'large mill I have lately started for Messrs White Brothers, Muckamore', Antrim, where he introduced roller mills and centrifugals of his own design.[16] There may have been continued use of millstones; if so, it was a 'combination plant', not a complete roller plant as Simon called his installation at Carlow. In 1880 Carter installed a complete roller plant, to replace forty-one pairs of millstones at Ringsend Road Mill in Dublin owned by the prominent bakery firm of Patrick Boland; the order was given by James Mooney who was to become very well known as an advanced innovator in Ireland and also as a leading member of NABIM. Carter regarded

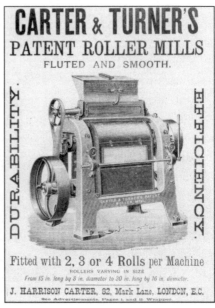

Left: John Mooney (1841–1923). (*The Miller*, April 1923) **Right:** Carter's roller mill. (*The Miller*, March 1883)

the project as the 'first roller mill in the world which finished off all the products in one continuous operation'. Mooney retained twenty-two pairs of stones out of his previous total of sixty-three, to be used separately. Carter included Austrian Escher Wyss break rolls and a few Wegmann machines, but by 1883 E.R. & F. Turner of Ipswich were manufacturing the whole range of machines required in applications of the Carter system. In 1883 Mooney acquired the Clonliffe Mills in Dublin and discarded the fifteen pairs of stones and commissioned Carter to install a roller plant of 10-sacks-per-hour capacity.[17]

Reluctance and Despondency

In March 1882, Harrison Carter read a paper to the Regular Millers of Ireland Trade Society in Dublin on the 'Relative Merits of Millstones and Rollers'. It was an advocacy for gradual reduction roller milling by an experienced speaker who remained good-humoured when confronted by antagonistic responses:[18] Mr Lawrence Murphy, president of the Society, read a statement from America that 'the roller system is but a bubble'. In May, Murphy gave his view that 'the roller, as a rival to the millstone, carries within it the marks and tokens of its own condemnation'. In November there was misinformation about iron rolls and reference to the risks of 'new-fangled systems'. John Mooney wrote to the Society to counter 'the condemnation' of rolls.[19] In May 1882 Mooney had spoken strongly in favour of new methods and machinery during the AGM of NABIM at Leeds. He commented on the American competition in the flour market, and urged 'his Irish friends' to use the best available machinery, not wait for 'the millennium'.[20]

The Society's meetings were reported in *The Miller* and in 1884 Dunham was made an honorary freeman of the Guild. The effects of publicity were more far-reaching than the members could have expected. After Carter's visit to Dublin, he was invited to address the Amalgamated Society of London Operative Millers, and in July 1882 he encountered similar opposition to his ideas, though with longer discussion and eventual constructive results. A 'rollers versus stones' controversy stretched from 1879 to about 1885, a rearguard action by traditionalists, largely in increasingly marginalized country mills.[21] By 1884, the Irish Society was considering admission of operatives working in roller mills, and heard a member say that rollers were 'being adopted everywhere'.

In England, outspoken operatives complained at meetings about wages, while more eloquent colleagues wrote to *The Miller* to oppose modern machinery. In

Ireland, operatives' activity included visits to bakery firms to lobby against use of foreign flour. In 1884 the Dublin Society was formulating protective trade policies, which they hoped employers would espouse. In Dublin, Murphy urged 'the Irish people to use only Irish-made flour and boycott foreign importation'. He alleged that similar action had been taken in Cork, where the people of all creeds and classes had combined for the purpose of preventing the sale of 'American flour'.[22]

The Dublin Society was invited to send delegates to the first annual convention of NABIM at Stockton-on-Tees in 1884, but did not accept. After the convention, Dunham concluded that the NABIM members, necessarily master millers, had recognized that 'a revolution had taken place' in milling methods. By the autumn, the views of the London operatives were much altered, partly by public resolution of the 'rollers versus stones' controversy, and tangibly through Carter's efforts, particularly his invitation to both operatives and master millers to visit one of his main installations; he was highly instrumental in convincing operatives that roller milling was the acceptable way forward. Operative millers could assist future trade and their own employment prospects by acquiring proficiency in new highly mechanized processes, radically different from traditional milling in method, scale, and potential for continuing technical development.

A more dramatic version of events was recorded in 1885 by the Select Committee of the House of Commons on Irish Industries. While reporting the Irish milling situation, the main aspects were stated to be:

1. large import of American flour, to the injury of Irish flour millers
2. question of the adoption of improved machinery by Irish millers; 'great decadence' meanwhile
3. suggestions for an import duty on foreign flour[23]

In the report there was much pessimism and some optimism, the former being emphasized in statements of numbers of mills closed, the latter being diluted by absence of technical witnesses. The traditional industry was most affected, but those millers needed to read the statement in the report that 'the great food of the Irish is the white bread'. An important point about the evidence to this committee is that larger and innovative millers did not appear, so it did not provide a balanced assessment. But it did indicate the extent to which American flour had penetrated the Irish market.

The Spread of New Ideas

Simon and Carter and the Survival of Flour Milling in Ireland

There was a surge of innovation in UK milling from 1883 to 1885, and enough evidence of Simon's activity has survived to show the spread of these changes amongst Irish millers. Information about Carter's contribution is sketchy, but during 1884–5 he was supplying plant to W.P. & R. Odlum at Portarlington, R. & W. Pilsworth at Thomastown, and R.W. Newton at Londonderry. In 1886 he was reported to be equipping a 'large new mill' for Messrs Russell at Limerick.[24] Simon customers for complete plants from 1879 to 1885 are shown in Table 1. In addition, Simon was always willing to supply individual machines and to remodel existing installations. Many names appear in the table of millers who were to continue successfully, though with varying long-term experience. In 1884 Simon was advertising that he had 'built the largest complete roller plants in the UK', including two plants of 5000 sacks per week for Mr B. Hughes of Belfast;[25] working absolutely continuously, that was equivalent to an individual plant capacity of 30 sacks per hour, ten times the size of Simon's very early plants. Bernard Hughes (1809–78) had been a prominent Belfast baker and flour merchant.[26] He was succeeded by his son Edward (1835–93) who enlarged the business.[27]

Myths of Hungarian and American Leadership in Innovation

The earliest notable experiments in the UK with roller mills and purifiers were in the 1870s. When improved and integrated, these piecemeal attempts to explore a series of processing operations led to the development of comprehensive milling systems. By the early 1880s, several milling engineers had devised designs for gradual reduction roller-milling plant suitable for both hard and soft wheats. They had eliminated most of the laborious aspects of milling, and were learning from trials and alterations in the mills. With an increasing field of activity there was bound to be variation of design and effectiveness. Simon, Carter and Robinsons were the best-known consultants and suppliers; many other small firms joined the field.

Table 1

Customers for Simon Complete Roller Plants[28]

MILLING FIRM	LOCATION	DATES OF ORDERS FOR PLANT						
		1879	1880	1881	1882	1883	1884	1885
Alexander, J. & Co.	Belfast		*					
Andrews, I. & Sons	Belfast					*	*	
Bannatyne & Sons	Limerick					*	*	*
Bennett, J.	Clonakilty					*		
Brown, J.	Waterford						*	
Budds, C.	Graigue					*		
Furlong & Sons	Cork							*
Gilliland & Sons	Londonderry				*	*		*
Going & Smith	Cahir			*		*		
Halligan, J.	Dublin			*				
Hallinan, T. & Sons	Midleton, Cork					*	*	
Hannon, H.	Carlow					*		
Haughton, T.C.	Athy				*			
Hughes, Bernard	Belfast			*		*	*	
Lyons, H.	Croom						*	
McRobert, J.	Listooder							*
Odlum & Pemberton	Naas							*
Perry, R. & Co.	Banagher						*	
Reeves, J.R. & T.B.	Newbridge						*	
Roche, D.	Croom						*	
Scott, W. & C.	Omagh						*	
Shackleton, E. & Sons	Athy			*	*			
Shackleton, E. & Sons	Carlow	*			*			
Spicer, J.	Navan							*
White, T.H. & Co.	Belfast							*
Wilson, A. & Co.	Londonderry						*	

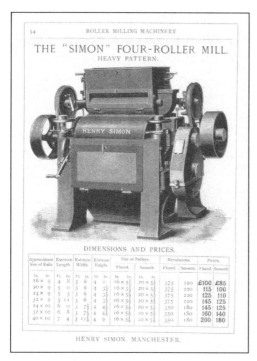

Simon's four-roller mill of 1885 onwards. (*Simon's catalogue*, 1892)

For a few years many machines were imported from America and Austria-Hungary, but that supply dwindled. G.T. Smith's purifiers from America were an advance on continental gravity types, but a variety of American roller mills had little long-term impact, even the Gray roller mill, prominent in America. The closest machinery connection with Hungary was through J.A.A. Buchholz, son of Gustav, who for a short time used Ganz roller mills from Budapest.[29] Simon used European machine-makers, but his plant designs and many principles of machine design were fundamentally for UK situations. A few UK mills adopted the word Hungarian, for instance the Bernard Hughes site at Belfast was often called the Model Hungarian Flour Mills, which was eye-catching but inappropriate. Henry Simon vigorously denied that his system was a direct descendant of Hungarian practice, which was vastly different from the methodology needed in the milling situations in Britain and Ireland.[30]

Dublin Convention of 1886

In 1886 NABIM held their convention in Dublin; R.E. Shackleton of Athy and Carlow became president. Papers were given by Carter's manager, Gilbert Little, by S. Sealy Allen on water power, and by T.W. Hibbard, principal of J. Reynolds & Co.'s Albert Mills at Gloucester. Hibbard's subject was 'Gradual Reduction by Roller Milling, Applied to Soft Wheats', which was of special interest to country millers, particularly in western Ireland and eastern England.[31] Hibbard stated that 'foreign and generally hard, dry, brittle wheats [were] mainly used', but apart from UK wheats, which were always soft, imported varieties also included soft wheats. Some opponents of roller milling had argued that rolls were unsuitable for milling soft varieties, so Hibbard's paper was a potentially helpful corrective. As Hibbard was one of the leaders in the provision of the City & Guilds scheme of study and examination for millers, he had a position of constructive influence. Bakers considered colour, strength, flavour, and profitability of the bread they could make. Native wheats might confer flavour. Some market sectors required cheapness. Increasingly, attention was focused on whiteness and strength. NABIM members were invited to inspect mills in Dublin and district, presumably an especially interesting opportunity for the large number of Irish millers named on the visitors' list. The Patrick Boland Bakery and Johnston & Co.'s new machine bakery were also available for visits.

Table 2

Mills Visited in the Dublin Area during the 1886 NABIM Convention[32]

OWNERSHIP	LOCATION	SYSTEM INSTALLED		
		NAME	Capacity Sacks/Hr	DATE
Patrick Boland	Ringsend Road	Carter		1880
Boland		Millstones used separately		
Walter Brown & Co.	Hanover Street	Robinsons	6	Recent
William Brown & Son	Dock, Barrow Street	Robinsons	8	Recent
J. Comerford	Rathdrum, Co. Wicklow	Carter	5	1886
Maconchy & Co.	Templeogue	Throop	6	1884
McMullen, Shaw & Co.	Custom House	Simon	6	1886
John Mooney	Clonliffe	Carter	10	1883
S.R. Roe	Leixlip	Millstones		
G. Shackleton & Sons	Anna Liffey, Lucan	Fiechter		

At that stage, Carter (1886) had prominence around Dublin, and was completing 'the largest [plant] yet erected on the Carter system in Ireland' for Messrs Russell at Limerick, but at the end of the 1880s he withdrew from milling engineering; his business was taken over by E.R. & F. Turner. Thomas Robinson & Son of Rochdale then attained second place to Henry Simon.

During the next two years there was anxious discussion in the UK milling industry about depression in trade. As President of NABIM during 1886–7, Ebenezer Shackleton of Moone Mills, Athy,[33] considered that the depression in agriculture was 'caused mainly through foreign competition'. Within NABIM there were conflicting attitudes; a committee was appointed to investigate, which reported to the London Convention in 1887. Shackleton was mindful of free-trade principles, but stated, 'Some people say that we should call a spade a spade, and propose protection and impose a duty on foreign flour.' The committee's conclusion was that the depression was 'not from want of skill and enterprise, or lack of suitable machinery, but from the action of external causes, which they hope may not be permanent'. The report contained the first and only extensive statement of the supposed numbers of complete roller-process mills. NABIM had counted 461 in the UK, of which seventy-two were complete roller-process mills in Ireland, listed by counties as follows:

Table 3

Numbers of Irish Roller Process Mills as Reported in 1887[34]

Antrim	5	Dublin	12	Limerick	5	Tyrone	1
Armagh	1	Galway	1	Londonderry	2	Waterford	2
Carlow	3	Kildare	4	Meath	1	West Meath	1
Cork	14	Kilkenny	4	Queen's	4	Wexford	3
Down	3	King's	1	Tipperary	2	Wicklow	3

There were thirty-six in Leinster, twenty-three in Munster, twelve in Ulster, and one in Connaught, but numbers of mills do not indicate strength of contribution, nor the technical state of particular mills. Capacities of mills are more difficult to find. In 1885, the *Irish Times* commented on 'tremendous American competition', but referred to 'ten or twelve mills in the neighbourhood of the City of Cork' that had been remodelled. It remained difficult for millers to assess the state of their industry. In a lengthy survey provided for *The Miller*, the conclusion was that it was not possible to form a comprehensive archive on the Irish flour-milling industry. Apart from Hughes' mill at Belfast, most Irish mills were much smaller than the well-known mills in Britain, where capacity was to increase considerably at the main ports. However, the large numbers of small country mills in Ireland and England did not indicate undue backwardness. Technical change from the later 1880s laid a foundation from which the roller-process mills would become capable of producing most of the flour required, without needing a large contribution from small traditional sites.

Commercial Uncertainty and Perseverance

Between 1888 and 1892 there was a second surge of mill modernization in the UK, bigger than the wave of 1883–5.[35] Successful innovators expanded. Late innovators turned to roller milling, provided they had adequate finance and potential market prospects. In Ireland there was lively activity. Newly registered, Bolands Ltd in 1888 owned three bakeries in Dublin and the Ringsend Road Flour Mills, where E.R. & F. Turner installed a roller plant to replace the twenty-two remaining pairs of millstones; reported capacity was 10 sacks per hour.[36] During 1889–90 Robinsons supplied a 10-sacks-per-hour plant to J.W. McMullen & Sons Ltd at Cork Steam Mills, George's Quay, and also plant to J. Good of Ballincurra, Co. Cork, R. Ardagh near Waterford, and W. & S. Mercier at Belfast.[37] During the same period Simon received an order from Going & Smith at Cahir to enlarge their mill and increase output, also from Howard Brothers of Crookstown, Co. Cork. Furlong & Sons at Cork ordered a new 10-sacks-per-hour plant, which Simon was keen to illustrate in his 1892

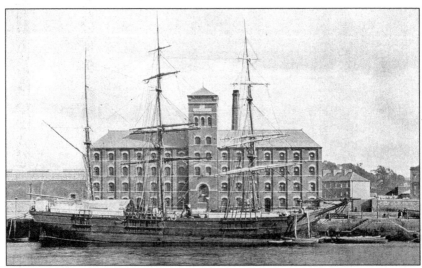

J. Furlong & Sons' mill at Cork. (*Simon Catalogue*, 1892)

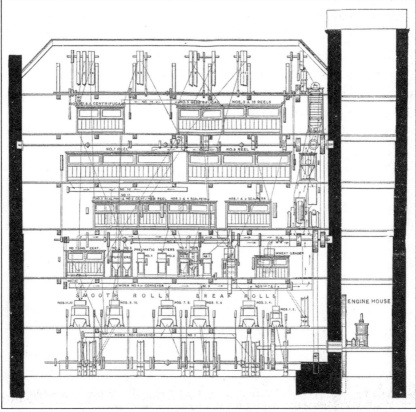

Detailed drawing of Bolands' mill. (*The Miller*, June 1888) Longitudinal section of Bolands' Ringsend Road Mills at Dublin. (*The Miller*, June 1888)

catalogue,[38] the second of three impressive volumes between 1886 and 1898. Another plant was for J. & C. Gardner at Belfast. Hallinan & Sons of Fermoy ordered a remodelling, to increase output. In 1892 there was another remodelling for Going & Smith at Cahir: new purifiers and roller mills. Simon had so much work in the UK and overseas that his previous practice of publishing lists of names of customers became less appropriate. He continued to publish a map of customer locations each January; successive editions showed his involvement in Ireland.[39]

In 1893 Simon received an order from Hughes at Belfast for reconstruction of the roller plant, including new purifiers, and provision of wheat washing,

Henry Simon's installations in Great Britain and Ireland up to 1889. (*The Miller*, January 1890)

drying and conditioning plant.[40] In 1895 there was an order from J. Hannan & Sons of the Prumplestown Mill, Carlow, for reconstruction of their newly acquired Ardreigh Mill, Athy. J. Halligan of the City of Dublin Flour Mills, Usher's Island, was noted as a customer for at least the third time, requiring additional heavy four-roller mills. In 1897 George Shackleton & Sons of Anna Liffey Mills, Lucan, wrote to Simon, expressing pleasure and satisfaction after the installation of a 6-sacks-per-hour plant.[41] Also in 1897 there was a 10-sacks-per-hour capacity plant for Johnston, Mooney & O'Brien Ltd at Dublin; in 1890 the three constituent bakery businesses had amalgamated, in combination with the Jones' Road mill which Mooney had acquired in 1883.[42]

In 1894 the NABIM convention was at Belfast, with John Mooney as president; he emphasized that Irish bread eaters demanded 'nothing but the whitest flour … irrespective of its flavour, sweetness or nutriment'.[43] American flours had an added advantage of bleaching while in transit and in warehouses. There was an enormous rise in UK flour imports in 1892, the pressure continuing to 1903.[44] It is still puzzling how survivors amongst UK millers retained confidence through the very difficult trading conditions of the 1890s, created by external forces and sharpened by competition within the milling industry. In 1894 Simon noticed that the journal *North Western Miller* of Minneapolis had surveyed American flour exporters, who were reporting that Irish and English flours were improving.[45] He published his observation in his newsletter to customers and many others. The well-known cereal chemist William Jago offered similar encouragement. In 1894 Simon also wrote proudly about Hughes' mill at Belfast as 'a good example of a first class mill'.[46] Unfortunately production stopped there in 1900. It was reported that the bakery could buy foreign flour cheaper than it could be manufactured in Belfast.

Modernization: The Next Stages

Survivors and a New Era

When Sidney Leetham of York presided at the NABIM convention in 1900, he described the industry as dominated by the mills located at the principal wheat ports. He observed that existing firms were 'survivors of the fierce competition of the last 15 years'.[47] Commercial overlapping had been a growing feature since 1893, as local and district trading areas expanded towards regional and national boundaries. By about 1904 the pressure of American flour imports eased; major combines in the United States had over-stretched their own resources, and had been countered by UK port mill development. Despite Leetham's idealistic search for mutual understanding and William Vernon's diplomatic support, the business priorities of individual millers could not be regulated by collective discussion and national agreement. Local millers' associations had varying perspectives and problems in defending their territories. Milling firms with entrepreneurial drive and strong trading positions set future patterns.

Few Irish millers remained members of NABIM, ten appearing in the official list of 1899–1901, twelve in 1906–7, and ten in 1913–14. Names appearing in all three were Bolands; Brown & Crosthwait; Walter Brown of Dublin; S. & A.G. Davis of Enniscorthy; Johnston, Mooney & O'Brien; R. Morton & Co. of Ballymena; Robert Pilsworth of Kilkenny; and George Shackleton. Isaac Andrews & Sons were named in the second and third lists. A South of Ireland Millers' Association was formed at Cork in 1886,[48] and a stronger basis for policy-making followed in 1902 with the formation of the Irish Millers' Association.[49] Meetings were held at the prestigious Shelbourne Hotel in Dublin, with regular attendance by increasingly well-known firms. The membership represented the hopes of the Irish industry. In addition to their official records, their names appeared in trade directories, notably the voluminous *Kelly's Directories*. *Thom's Directory* of 1908 listed forty-nine members, twenty-five of whom had large celebratory advertisements in a special 'Irish milling and bakery' issue of the journal *Milling* in 1924.[50]

Milling industry prospects depended on the will to make use of technical change and firms' resources. There were three aspects of milling system development: improvement, enlargement and extension, and UK millers needed to be innovative within their own businesses on a continuing basis. There were many improvements of machinery. Roller mill designs evolved, the lastingly modern configuration of roll pairs arranged at an angle to the horizontal being important from about 1904,[51] after which previous arrangements were recognized as antiquated. In place of previous sieving and sorting machinery, many new means were devised to separate components as the wheat was broken, to classify material by particle size, and to extract the required end-product. These culminated about 1910 in progress with plansifters, gyrating plane sieves, in contrast with previous rotated centrifugal separators. Overall plant enlargement was increasingly evident, particularly at port sites. System extension included provision of wheat-preparation plants for washing and drying the raw material, and putting the wheat into good milling condition. For larger sites there were bigger and more efficient wheat storage installations and more efficient mechanical handling facilities, ideally alongside deep water quays.

Between 1904 and 1906 the biggest firms in Britain adopted many or most of the technical advances, setting standards that much smaller firms could not fully emulate; for these others competition depended on regional tastes, niche positions, or unusual skills. William Vernon was the first with a new class of large well-sited port mills, concentrating his firm's capacity at Birkenhead instead of Liverpool in 1899 – Henry Simon's last major project.[52] Simon registered his firm as Henry Simon Ltd in 1897, a private company which maintained the leading position amongst milling engineers. Simon's had very large projects for Joseph Rank at Hull, then during 1904–6 at London and Cardiff, and in 1913 at Birkenhead.[53] Spillers acquired a Birkenhead site in 1914 but completion was delayed, the Robinsons plant only being started in 1926. In May 1914 *Milling* reckoned 'the capacity of mills actually in Liverpool and Birkenhead' was 'nearly 800 sacks per hour'. Obviously a concentration of milling capacity and shipping facilities there could markedly affect supplies of flour in Ireland.

Action in the Irish Mills

In 1903 *Milling* reported 'A Visit to the Emerald Isle', mainly to Belfast survivors: Isaac Andrews & Sons at the Belfast Mills, W.S. Mercier's Dufferin Mills, and James Neill & Co. Ltd's King Street Roller Mills. Andrews' capacity was stated to be 20 sacks per hour, the others 10 and 8 sacks.[54] Despite Ulster's difficulties, Andrews had advanced to twice the output of many Irish mills. *Milling* had suggested in 1901 that there were 'between two and three hundred' mills in the UK with over 10-sacks-per-hour capacity. By 1901 the North Shore Co. at Liverpool, where two members of the Andrews family had gained experience, had an output of 100 sacks per hour. By 1904 there was a revival of activity in Bernard Hughes' premises, Hughes, Dickson & Co. taking a lease and acquiring a new Simon plant.[55]

The word 'revival' was often used, for instance in 1910, 'the first cause of the revival was the invention of bleaching by Mr Sydney Andrews'. In the 1880s the Andrews family, descendants of several generations of millers, had moved their business from Comber to the Belfast Mills, previously owned by John

Alexander. In 1901 Sydney Andrews devised his method of using nitrogen peroxide to bleach flour, and obtained patent protection. The Flour Oxidizing Co. Ltd was formed by Isaac Andrews & Sons and Ross T. Smyth & Co. of Liverpool, who defeated opponents after lengthy litigation.[56] Whiteness was no longer equated with American flour, and bleaching was soon applied by many UK millers, despite criticism led by the Birkenhead miller William Buchanan. William Vernon preferred flour with a golden bloom. In 1911 there were official reports to the local government board on bleaching, flour improvers, and the nutritive value of breads. There was anxiety in the Irish Flour Millers' Association; but bleaching had become familiar, and continued.

By 1905 general trading confidence was more assured. *Milling* reported on 'The Revival of Flour Milling in Ireland', and visited the North City Mills at Dublin,[57] where Robinsons' double diagonal roller mills had been installed to provide a capacity of 'eight to ten sacks per hour'. In a 1907 appraisal of 'the present position of Irish milling', it was stated that 'the output of Irish mills has been steadily increasing for some years and since 1903 their capacity has been increased by something like 100 sacks per hour'. Also it was said that the 'four principal milling centres are Belfast, Limerick, Dublin and Cork ... the largest output probably being that of Messrs James Bannatyne & Sons, of Limerick'; that might have surprised other districts.[58] There were four problems for discussion, but no clear solutions:

1. the need to concentrate production at the ports
2. disadvantages of Ireland being undermilled
3. lack of good milling-quality Irish wheat
4. increasing competition from English millers

In August 1910 *Milling* reported: 'Quite a goodly number of mills in the Emerald Isle have been remodelled during the past twelve months and several plants have been enlarged.' There was a warning to examine efficiency rather than to increase capacity. The Dublin North City Milling Co. decided to enlarge their 10-sacks-per-hour plant at Phibsborough Mills by 50 per cent, a complete remodelling to include a new scalping method.[59] That autumn the Irish Flour Millers' Association estimated the total capacity of the members' mills as 412 sacks per hour, but their potential market was regarded as eroded by imports.

The mills of John Furlong & Sons at Cork were visited at Lapp's Quay, and Victoria Quay where the Simon plant was described as 'a most up-to-date kind'. Cork Steam Mills at George's Quay, owned by J.W. McMullen & Sons had been 'entirely reconstructed', including 'latest diagonal pattern' roller mills, but capacity was not much increased. St John's Mill at Cork, owned by G. Shaw & Son, was rebuilt after a fire in 1910. It was decidedly up-to-date as a so-called 'plansifter mill' with double diagonal roller mills, supplied by Turners, and electrically driven. Within the county, T. Hallinan & Sons had been at Glandalane Mills near Fermoy since 1861 and at Avoncore Mills, Midleton, since 1874. The family had worked other mills in the county and had, amongst ancestors, 'a long line of millers' in Kent. Their current mills had Simon plants with recent improvements in wheat preparation stages and scalping methods. Elsewhere, there was the Going & Smith Ltd mill at Cahir in Tipperary, a business stretching back to the Suir Mills of 1795. In the early 1900s, they had bakeries at Cahir, Cashel and Clonmel. Their scalping methods included rotary sieves, reels and centrifugals. Power was obtained mainly from turbines for an 8-sacks-per-hour plant, which was remodelled from a Simon system to Samuelsons of Banbury equipment in 1912.[60]

William Odlum succeeded an uncle in business at Maryborough in 1865 and the family built a mill at Portarlington in 1880. W.P. & R. Odlum extended the firm to St Mullins near Kilkenny and Naas, Co. Kildare. The last two mills were water-powered, each 4 sacks per hour; the others had each reached 9 sacks per hour. After a fire, the rebuilt Maryborough mills were started in 1911 on the Simon system, with double sieve purifiers and the inclusion of plansifters.[61] At M.J. & L. Goodbody's mill at Clara, the Fiechter roller milling machinery of 1886 was replaced in 1899, and in 1911 there was a report of new milling plant, supplied by Samuelsons of Banbury, to provide an output of 7 sacks per hour. It was stated that Goodbody's had a 'controlling interest in James Bannatyne & Son's large flour mills at Limerick, operated under the titles of Messrs James Bannatyne & Son Ltd, and Messrs J.N. Russell & Son Ltd'.[62]

In mid-1912 Simon's reported work for eight Irish mills: reconstructions of roller plant for Russell at Limerick; Neill at Belfast; the North City Mill at Dublin; J. & R. Webb at Mallow; and reconstructions of wheat-cleaning plant for the first four firms, for the Dock Milling Co. and Johnston, Mooney & O'Brien at Dublin; and Gilliland at Londonderry. There were three plansifter installations and, additionally, three orders for ancillary equipment.[63]

Wartime Difficulties

The general situation of wartime control of the UK flour-milling industry, and the delayed return of ownership and management to the mill owners and millers after the war, is a subject mainly concerned with stringency and bureaucracy, not technical development.[64] Disparity between the Irish milling industry and the rest of the UK had been increasing since the 1870s or '80s, different positions resulting from the effects of a variety of technical and other factors. Commercial practices, transport facilities, social backgrounds, and geographical layout shaped different environments, which in many respects were not to the advantage of Irish millers. In Britain there was much more scope for the exercise of entrepreneurial vigour and scale economies, clearly exemplified by Joseph Rank (1854–1943) whose Alexandra Mill at Hull was started in 1885 with a capacity of 6 sacks per hour; his capacity of 20 sacks per hour at the Clarence Mill at Hull, in 1891, was trebled by 1894.[65]

Wartime obscured many gradually emerging issues: the need for rationalization, the imperative of not standing still technically, socio-political change in the UK and particularly in Ireland. The first issue was discussed in England before the war, but during 1914–18, and for some time afterwards, the division of port mills and large urban mills from small predominantly rural mills was temporarily of secondary importance. Wartime restrictions on trading distances curbed the trade of leading firms. Rivalry was resumed later when there were efforts to recover lost territory. From 1914 there were attempts in Ireland to encourage renovation of small and remote country mills. In 1916 instruction was being offered by the Irish Department of Agriculture at Albert College, Glasnevin.[66] By 1917, as there were attempts to make districts 'self-supplying', it was reported that more than 200 small mills had been restarted, partly supported by loans. It was said, 'Many of the little mills are of the "rattletrap variety"; few of them survived after the end of the war.'[67]

In 1917 supply conditions became hazardous throughout the UK. There were reports of shortage of flour in several parts of Ireland, and concurrent stories that in some counties flour was used in pig and poultry feeds. Official extraction rates were imposed at the mills, a major setback, but not an isolated effect of dissatisfaction with product quality; under official control there was a loss of opportunity to exercise wheat buying and blending experience. Millers' skills and determination were blunted and milling criteria obscured. Priority demand for whiteness led to increasing mixing in of maize flour.

For many years Irish millers and activist operatives had deplored a lack of national support for Irish-made flour. Pricing was sensitive, and in 1914 the chairman of Bolands was already alleging that English millers were 'dumping' flour in Ireland.[68] It was simultaneously reported that 'practically every Cork bakery firm used some Irish flour', by which was meant 'Irish milled', not necessarily from Irish wheat, and that was hardly a confirmation of adequate national milling capacity and quality. After the war and the drawn-out control period there were unresolved difficulties. Would Irish wheat supply and its milling quality improve? Could the Irish country mills prosper? Would the port mills and others be in contention?

In 1924 G.G. Kirby stated, 'the impoverished state of the milling trade is not, as we should like to allege, "a war problem" ... The circumstances arising out of the European and the Irish war certainly made trade embarrassments more acute for Irish millers, but the problem was before them in 1904 to 1914.'[69] That seems to have been a crucial period when further innovation was necessary, when American domination of the flour import market had eased, and English flour millers were not yet so clearly regarded as a foreign force and English competition was far less marked than it was to become in the 1920s.

BEYOND 1920

The end of 1920 was marked by optimism, for instance: 'The position of the industry [in Ireland] was never more hopeful.' Nevertheless it was also reported that Dublin and the North 'depend a good deal on supplies from outside the country'. The UK milling industry remained under government control until 1921, by which time overseas flour supplies were increasing alarmingly, and remodelling was essential.[70] A return to production of higher-grade flours in 1921, led by Rank, was a counter to imports, but matching flour supply to demand was an elusive ideal: undermilling in London and Ireland encouraged imports; surplus capacity led to sharply competitive price-cutting. There was continual anguish and quest for a more balanced trade throughout the 1920s; the whole of the British milling industry was seriously affected.

The first formal industrial relations practices were instituted in 1919, with A.E. Humphries leading in Britain, in conjunction with the Union leader Ernest Bevin.[71] In Ireland there was less harmony, with strikes, occupations of premises, and even the kidnapping of a well-known miller. While some of these interruptions were brief, disruption continued into 1923: in March *Milling* reported that 'After six weeks of idleness, varied with the joys of picketing, operatives in the flour mills in the Free State area commenced to return to work on Monday last … without imported flour, the population would have gone breadless', a condition which could have caused panic in wartime.

Tariff protection was advocated, but a new mood was required amongst millers and their potential customers. British millers slowly realized the importance of advertising, but were not quick to learn how to do it, and how to pay for it. Irish millers and bakers needed concerted campaigns in support of Irish-made flour. The suggestion by the chairman of Bolands that 'the Irish public should look at the whole situation' was sound, but overshadowed by his contention that trading activity by British millers represented 'a deliberate and sustained attempt to suppress the Irish industry'.[72]

In Britain, NABIM continually discussed trading anxieties and the effects of imports, forcefully increased after 1918: Scotland was said to be 'overwhelmed' with American flour. Leading Irish millers could focus attention on particular difficulties at official enquiries. In 1922 transport costs were examined by the Irish Railway Commission, where W.E. Shackleton stated that the forty-three members of the Irish Flour Millers' Association comprised 'with a few exceptions, the entire flour and milling trade in Ireland'.[73] From evidence to the Fiscal Commission in 1923, it was reckoned that Irish flour mills were supplying about half of the requirements, and perhaps they could have supplied 80 per cent if not hindered by imports.[74] Unfortunately, enquiries could result in bureaucratic misdirection, rather than assistance.

In 1924 there was substantial activity. The journal *Milling* published a special issue to commemorate the opening of the Dublin Port Milling Co.'s new mill, convincingly described as 'a very definite step forward in flour milling practices in Ireland'. Built alongside the Merchants' Warehousing Co.'s granary, it had a capacity of 25 sacks per hour, with intention of doubling later. Granary and mill were both equipped by Henry Simon Ltd. The mill was on the Alphega-Plansifter system, and included use of the largest size Simon roller mills, and purifiers of latest design.[75] G.G. Kirby, who was research chemist to Vernons at Birkenhead and then to Spillers, was appointed as assistant manager and research chemist. Apart from a lengthy description of the new mill, there were two other valuable features: background papers, including two by Kirby, and extensive representation in advertisements of leading milling firms, two-thirds

Odlums advertisement. (*Milling*, October 1924)

of Association members joining in; Odlums should have been given first prize for impact, with Robert Perry & Co. second.[76]

Attempting to put full capacity into use, British millers used an advertising theme: 'Eat more bread', which was also a response to dietary changes and public interest in new breakfast and other packet foods. Johnston, Mooney & O'Brien at Dublin launched their own campaign with the slogan 'Eat the best'. During 1924, Simon's reconstructed their Clonliffe Mill to incorporate Alphega-Plansifter methods, with up to 14-sacks-per-hour output. In 1925 the journal *Milling* described the remodelled mill and the Ballsbridge bakery.[77] The combination of milling and baking facilitated comprehensive advertising to promote a variety of bread and associated foods, deriving added experience from their own catering business.

So Dublin had good models of port mill design, and of combined milling and baking enterprise, but when summarizing Irish milling difficulties of 1924, *The Miller* suggested that 'the prevailing feeling was one of waiting' rather than action. Unhelpfully, there were 'customs duties imposed south of the Boyne upon imports of goods such as machinery and other milling essentials, which (otherwise) might have helped to an improvement'.[78] Also, it was reported that in Ireland, 'The growers made all sorts of excuses for not growing wheat.' In Britain there had been energetic attempts since 1902 to improve the milling quality of UK wheat, led by A.E. Humphries on behalf of NABIM, but wheat hybridization and the study of protein action during bread making became an ever-extending investigation. In several ways, therefore, Irish millers were frustrated. To resolve the block to progress in British milling, it was suggested that a new concept was needed; in Ireland it might have been called 'repositioning', a framework and strategy to encourage enterprise.

A survey of each decade still prompts the questions: 'What happened next?' and 'Were opportunities missed?' After the troublesome 1920s, new mills were built in Britain, surprisingly soon in the 1930s. Rank's built a large mill at Belfast, an impressive project on a quayside site.[79] In the Irish Free State there was definite expectation of revival, concurrent with complications of government regulation. The Dublin Port Mill was increased to 50-sacks-per-hour capacity. Bolands remodelled to 30 sacks per hour. Simon's were particularly active in Ireland, which was indicative of the general upgrading of plant during the 1930s; they claimed that 'over 75 per cent of flour manufactured in the Free State is produced on Simon plants'.[80] Irish flour milling had changed dramatically since the widespread introduction of roller technologies in the 1880s. These new developments had made many of the old inland flour mills redundant, which was later to be conjured up by the mellow imagery of Elizabeth Bowen, who referred to 'those great abandoned mills which, all over Ireland, gauntly stare down the river valleys'.[81] While the new Irish state assumed more responsibility for the general positioning of the Irish flour-milling industry from 1932 onwards, progress beyond temporary equilibrium still depended to some degree on enterprise in individual firms. Some were in a better position to exploit the new circumstances more effectively, and amongst them, a number of the Irish flour millers who had adopted roller-milling technologies in the last decades of the nineteenth century were very prominent.

6

The Political Economy of the Irish Flour-Milling Industry

1922–1945

AKIHIRO TAKEI

Introduction

THIS ESSAY EXAMINES the impact of government policy on the flour-milling industry of the Irish Free State between 1922 and 1945. In the immediate aftermath of the First World War, the prospects of the Irish flour-milling industry were far from promising, as domestic and foreign markets were saturated, so the most serious matter for millers was how to cope with overcapacity. This essay will focus on the extent of state intervention in the flour-milling sector, comparing and contrasting the non-interventionist stance taken towards the industry by the Cumann na nGaedheal government as the era of free trade drew to a close, with the Fianna Fáil government, who favoured greater state intervention and import substitution in the industrial sector at large. In particular, this essay will identify the business strategies adopted by Irish flour millers in response to these changing economic and political circumstances.

The Crisis in the Flour-Milling Industry

By the early twentieth century, overcapacity was becoming a serious problem in the British flour-milling industry, and imports of flour into the UK exacerbated the situation, which made the Irish market highly competitive. However,

JAMES COMERFORD & SONS

XXX HOUSEHOLDS FLOUR excels in
QUALITY, COLOUR AND FLAVOUR.

XXX BAKERS FLOUR excels in
QUALITY AND STRENGTH.

□ ▪ □

GRANULATED AND
OTHER
INDIAN MEALS.

□ ▪ □

Rathdrum Mills
Co. Wicklow.

James Comerford & Sons' mills at Rathdrum, Co. Wicklow. (*Milling*, October 1924)

the outbreak of the First World War provided an opportunity to strengthen the business position of Irish flour millers. The government controlled the purchase of wheat, its manufacture and the sale of flour.[1] Riordan noted at the end of this period of restriction and control that it 'resulted in Irish flour mills … being kept going to the maximum of their capacity, producing flour for which there was an immediate outlet'.[2] Effectively, the Irish industry enjoyed temporary protection in this period, but after the end of the war, overproduction resumed in Ireland and Britain. The supply of wheat and flour was growing year by year but by the early 1920s Irish and British flour millers were compelled to run their mills on short time. An influx of cheaper flour, largely from Britain, weakened the position of the Irish industry.[3]

National independence coincided with a period of economic stagnation and many Irish flour millers with memories of prosperity during the war years hoped that the Irish government would provide them with full protection from British competition and the dumping of surplus British stock on the Irish market. *Milling*, the British trade journal, frequently reported on the issue in 1922 and 1923.[4] One of its comments in 1923 highlighted the difficulties of the smaller Irish millers:

On the West Coast of Ireland, we are told, the flour trade was so bad in certain districts, as the result of improved flour being used in such large quantities, that the milling operatives, who are also members of their Trade Unions, actually subscribed money themselves to get posters print-ed appealing to the Irish people to purchase nothing but home-milled flour, so that the local mills could be kept running.[5]

The Irish Flour Millers' Association sent a report to the government calling for protection in 1926, explaining the critical situation in the national industry. The total home requirement of the state was roughly 3,000,000 sacks, and the potential output of the Irish Free State mills was 2,961,000 sacks of flour per annum. However in 1925 they delivered only 1,624,272 sacks. The balance came from flour millers located outside the state: this included 868,170 sacks from Britain, 170,061 sacks from Northern Ireland, and 297,221 sacks from abroad. The Association indicated that the output of the flour mills in the Irish Free State were running at 75 per cent of their capacity in 1925, declining to 61 per cent by January 1926.[6] The report noted the serious downturn in the industry:

At the time of writing ALL the Mills in Cork and Limerick areas are either shut down or have their men under notice for stoppage next week. This is to enable them to clear off stocks of flour accumulated owing to scarcity of orders. For the same reason most of the Dublin Mills are either shut down or on short time; the reports are similar from the various Ireland Mills.[7]

The number of flour mills in the 26 counties was estimated to be forty-four in 1918, falling to only thirty-one in 1929, and by 1932, the final year of the Cumann na nGaedheal government, it had fallen further to only twenty-eight.[8]

Difference of Interests

The Irish Flour Millers' Association repeatedly lobbied for the imposition of a tariff on imported flour to protect their interests, but their efforts were initially unsuccessful. The Association first suggested protection as a solution to their problems to the Fiscal Inquiry Committee in 1923. The Committee did not support a protective policy: firstly, on the grounds that the industry was not 'in the infantile stage'; secondly, that protective policies were frequently misused; thirdly, that it would raise the cost of living; and lastly, that it would be disadvantageous for bakers and biscuit manufacturers.[9] As the Fiscal Inquiry Committee had no power to determine policy, their rejection was not decisive. The Association sent a report to the Department of Agriculture in mid-February 1926, which outlined how the circumstances of the domestic flour-milling industry could be improved by the imposition of a duty on imports.[10] The Department considered a tariff, but did not implement it.[11]

The Association did not abandon the prospects of protection, applying for a tariff of 3s. per sack to the Tariff Commission in 1927, but again their efforts were in vain. Patrick McGilligan, the Minister for Industry and Commerce, stated in the Dáil that his government would not impose a tariff on imported flour before the Commission submitted their report to Ernest Blythe, Minister for Finance:

> We have operated successfully so far as certain tariffs are concerned, and we intend to operate on those lines in future with regard to other industries. We are not going to face up to putting a tax on flour, still less to a prohibition on wheat, until we find out that there is going to be manu-facturing or milling done in this country. We will find out what the cost will be and what the offset is going to be. We would hesitate to impose a tariff on flour until we find that the firm of Jacob and Co. have had their fears resolved and that we are not going to lose the present employment and industry which they gave.[12]

Although the Commission recognized that Irish flour millers were suffering from British competition, they took the view that this would help put weaker and outmoded mills out of business, while simultaneously encouraging the concentration of the industry in the larger and more modern concerns.[13]

The Irish Flour Millers' Association proved to be a weak lobby. Many prominent Irish flour millers were from Protestant families, who seemed to have limited political influence with the government of the day. Furthermore, the Cumann na nGaedheal government supported the interests of Jacob's, the biggest biscuit manufacturer in Ireland, who provided extensive employment in the city of Dublin; Jacob's were referred to by the Tariff Commission as having provided 'one of the most formidable objections to the granting of the tariff'.[14] If protection proceeded, it was probable that the cost of flour (native and imported) would rise, which would run counter to the biscuit manufacturers' business interests. Since Jacob's used weak British flour (which was suitable for biscuit making), the Association sought to reach an agreement with them, and Blythe reportedly intended to intervene between the parties. He understood that there was no difficulty in treating Jacob's as an exception, which could be permitted to import foreign flour free of duty, even if their product was sold at home.[15] However, the Commission ultimately determined that the economic merits of a tariff were little or nothing compared to Jacob's business activity. The biscuit manufacturer let it be known that if a tariff was implemented they might relocate more of their operations to Aintree near Liverpool (where they had a plant since 1912). They employed around 3000 workers in Dublin, while it was estimated that only 153 additional persons were expected to be employed in mills in the event of a flour tariff being implemented.[16]

There were other reasons why the lobbying activities of the Association were ineffective. Irish wheat growers had limited political influence compared to the powerful non-tillage farm lobby. Wheat acreages had continually shrunk since the mid-nineteenth century, with the exception of a brief spell during the First World War, and millers depended on importation for most of their wheat supply. Secondly, the flour millers were not all firmly in the pro-tariff camp. The Dublin Port Milling Co. Ltd and Bolands Ltd, the major firms with highly capitalized facilities in the port of Dublin, were less active in seeking protection within the Association, since they were more capable of competing with imported flour. Rank's and Spillers, who were both based in Britain, opposed the tariff on behalf of the South of Ireland Flour Importers' Association to the Tariff Commission.[17] Shackleton's, who were located near Lucan on the Liffey upstream from Dublin, supported the implementation of a tariff, as did Senator J.P. Goodbody (of James Bannatyne & Sons Ltd and J.N. Russell & Sons Ltd, Limerick, and M.J. & L. Goodbody Ltd, Clara). The others who joined them came from the two most severely depressed milling regions: E. Shackleton of Carlow (E. Shackleton & Son), who went out of business by 1930, and C.C. Mercier of Cork (John Furlong & Sons [1920] Ltd). Rank's, having opposed the tariff, took over a number of the above mills in Cork and Limerick in 1930 which enabled them to operate in the Irish Free State behind the tariff barrier in what had been one of their major markets.[18]

The central principle of Cumann na nGaedheal's economic policy was to support Ireland's traditional emphasis on exporting agricultural products, since the agricultural sector contributed 32 per cent of GDP and 54 per cent of total employment in the economy in 1926.[19] Patrick Hogan, the Minister for Agriculture, placed particular emphasis on the maximization of farmers' income through the production of livestock and livestock products for export to Britain.[20] The Department of Agriculture had given some consideration to tariff protection as a means of encouraging wheat growing. Professor Whelehan's suggestions in this regard were published in the Tariff Commission's report as an addendum. He also intended to promote domestic cultivation through the encouragement of domestic flour milling 'by means of a bounty on wheat milled into flour'.[21] However, Whelehan's plan did not materialize and the representations of the Grain Growers' Association were ignored.[22] In the case of the industrial sector, the recently established and far less influential Department of Industry and Commerce was largely preoccupied with the Shannon Scheme in this period. Especially after McGilligan became minister, it was more supportive of the larger export-orientated companies in the industrial sector such as Guinness, Jacob's and Ford who supported the policy of free trade, as opposed to the numerous smaller employers who largely produced for the home market and sought protection from British competition.[23] The flour millers within the state did not, therefore, get a good hearing from the government in the 1920s, and their position deteriorated over the course of the decade.

Cumann na nGaedheal and the End of Free Trade

The balance in attitudes to the merits of protectionism or free trade were ultimately transformed by the onset of the Great Depression, which had important implications for Irish economic policy. First of all, the government was challenged by Fianna Fáil, which made strong efforts to have the position of flour milling reconsidered by Dáil Éireann after the Tariff Commission's rejection.[24] Moreover the investment strategy of Joseph Rank's Ltd over Cork and Limerick, two of the major sites of flour milling in the new state, sparked off a strong degree of economic nationalism, which led to proposals within the Dáil in 1930 to implement greater national controls over the sector, such as quotas, restrictions against foreign capital investment, and the encouragement of native wheat production.[25] The government did not follow up on this with legislation. Instead, McGilligan met the representatives of the Irish Flour Millers' Association, offering state intervention and credit for the industry, but it was obviously not attractive for Irish millers:[26] he noted that 'the answer I got was flat and decisive, that they preferred an amalgamation with the English Mutual Millers' Association'.[27]

The formation of a cartel was a common way to reduce excessive competition in a particular sector. Members of a cartel usually agreed on a production quota, fixing prices, thereby restraining the impact of market forces. In Britain, flour-milling firms had adopted cartel-style quotas on production. Rank's and Spillers, whose milling capacity was nearly half of the total capacity of the British industry, took the initiatives to form the Millers' Mutual Association in 1929, under which their industry was rationalized.[28] Irish flour millers had already been negotiating a rationalization of the flour trade in the Irish Free State with the British flour millers in 1929. When J.V. Rank visited Ireland in the following year (when he purchased mills in Cork and Limerick), he was interviewed by the *Irish Times* and cited as one of those responsible for the rationalization scheme in Britain. He explained its effect and importance in the case of Britain and also insisted on the necessity for rationalization in Ireland: 'When the Government were asked to put on a tariff they refused, and the millers found that they had to do something to help themselves.'[29]

The Irish flour millers set up the Flour Millers' Economic Association on 1 May 1931.[30] This cartel fixed each miller's share of flour production, thus securing existing Irish and British millers' interests in the Irish market. This agreement seems to have been advantageous for Irish millers; official statistics indicate that the net output of the Irish flour-milling industry (including non-wheat products) increased from £523,549 to £787,038 between 1929 and 1931.[31] The profits per sack of the Dublin Port Milling Co. leaped from only 4*d.* to 2*s.* 7*d.* between 1931 and 1932.[32] With the drop in wheat prices and the restriction of competition, the profitability of flour milling in the Irish Free State began to improve dramatically.

In the 1920s, the Cumann na nGaedheal government took the view that the policy of free trade gave stronger Irish flour millers an opportunity for further development at the expense of the more inefficient millers. However, as the era of free trade drew to a close at the end of the decade with the onset of the Great Depression, this policy came under severe pressure. Their tacit approval of the establishment of a cartel effectively indicated that the government at this point approved of protection for the Irish flour-milling industry. Under the cartel agreement, no mills had to be closed, but as with most cartels it increased costs for consumers. Although the government did not place a tariff on imported flour, it was prepared to tolerate a cartel initiated by a British firm. But it was reluctant to alter the established pattern of Irish agricultural production away from cattle farming to tillage, and from export-orientation to self-sufficiency, which Fianna Fáil were advocating as an alternative economic doctrine. Hogan's rigid refusal to introduce state intervention in native wheat cultivation,[33] and McGilligan's tolerance of the formation of a flour cartel joined by British interests, resulted in the following comment in the *Irish Times* in 1931, which expressed the fear that there would be a rise in flour prices but accepted that 'without restriction it seems that Irish mills will be allowed to rationalize themselves out of existence'.[34] Up to this point, the Irish and British flour millers had taken the initiative, while the government had as far as possible pursued a policy of non-intervention in the industry.

The Self-Sufficient Policy of Fianna Fáil and its Impact

As protectionism became more commonplace globally, the economic policy of the new Fianna Fáil government sought to encourage native manufacturing industry more effectively through import substitution. They advocated industrial and agricultural self-sufficiency, through the creation of employment in tillage in place of cattle farming, and the full use of indigenous resources, with greater state intervention in the economy, notably in the industrial sector. They proposed to develop industries by tariffs and quotas and by encouraging foreign investment (with legislative controls over foreign ownership), and through strengthening the Irish capital market. The Control of Manufactures Acts of 1932 and 1934 sought to control foreign management and investment in the Irish Free State. The Trade Loans (Guarantee) Acts of 1924–39 aimed to assist small businesses, while it was envisaged that the statutory creation of the Industrial Credit Company in 1933 would provide industrial capital. A number of industries benefited by these means and the industrial sector experienced expansion during the 1930s.

The flour-milling industry was directly affected by the new trajectory in economic policy that Fianna Fáil undertook: food self-sufficiency and the creation of employment through the expansion of tillage farming had important implications for milling. Fianna Fáil envisaged that they could achieve this by the encouragement of wheat growing, and that mills would produce more flour as a consequence of this expansion of native production.[35] Seán Lemass, the new Minister for Industry and Commerce, initiated this policy of expanding the flour-milling sector as part of the new government's wider programme of industrial expansion. The Irish Flour Millers' Association played no role in this, and since the cartel agreement made prior to the election of the new government was beneficial enough to Irish millers, their attitude to the full scope of Fianna Fáil's new programme for industrial development was negative. When Lemass called a meeting with their representatives they expressed publicly that 'millers are perfectly satisfied with their status quo, and that any interference would not react to their benefit'.[36] This is hardly surprising since Lemass wished to break the cartel that had been initiated by Rank's, and reduce their influence in the Irish market.[37] In contrast to the previous government, he gave far less consideration to the interests of Jacob's, the strongest anti-tariff lobbyist to the Irish Flour Millers' Association, who sold much of their output on the British market. Jacob's had already decided to transfer a considerable proportion of their manufacturing capacity to Aintree in April 1932 before the Fianna Fáil government had begun to proceed with their new economic policy. But Jacob's still employed 2500 in Dublin in the mid-1930s, and the total quantity of biscuits exported from Ireland only declined from 84,407 cwt in 1931 to 72,851 cwt in 1933.[38]

The government launched its protection policy for Irish flour with the imposition of a tariff on imported flour. The Finance (Customs Duties) (No. 3) Act, which came into effect from 1 September 1932, placed 5s. on each sack of flour imported.[39] Importers of British flour into the Irish Free State market consequently had their business seriously reduced without compensation.[40] Furthermore, the Agricultural Produce (Cereals) Act of 1933 placed rigid regulations on all parties concerned in the milling business in the state (including corn dealers), encouraging farmers to cultivate more wheat. Under these regulations, flour millers could not operate their mills without a licence. The Minister for Industry and Commerce exercised very considerable powers to grant, refuse or revoke licences.[41] Therefore, according to the Cereals Act,

Seán Lemass performing the opening ceremony at the National Flour Mills, Cork, in 1934. (Odlum Group)

newcomers to the flour-milling industry were to be selected by the Minister.[42]

The Cereals Act prescribed wheat and output quotas for each miller. After consultation with the Minister for Agriculture, the Minister for Industry and Commerce was to fix at the beginning of the cereal year the percentage of the total production of the wheat harvest to be milled by all flour mills. The output quota was allotted to each miller and a miller who produced in excess of this was to be fined 3s. per 400 lbs of wheat (normally the equivalent of 280 lbs of flour).[43] The figure was produced after careful examination as to what was 'a fair margin of protection for the small inland mill against the highly capitalised port mill'.[44] For example, the milling costs per sack of flour (including profit) milled by the Dublin Port Milling Co., a 'highly capitalised port mill', in 1932 was 35s. 1d. (with a profit per sack of 2s. 10d.).[45] The figure of 3s. seemed to be well calculated to cap the business activity of efficient flour mills; the figure was balanced so that an efficient flour mill could sell flour more competitively than in an area where an inefficient mill was also operating.[46] The Cereals Act did not assure an outlet for the quota and it did not prohibit overproduction, provided the miller paid the fine. Therefore limited competition was allowed, and it was envisaged that this would help to rationalize the industry. Industrial relations also effectively came under the control of the government. The Joint Industrial Council (which consisted of officials of the Department of Industry and Commerce, the employers and the unions) was formed in order to settle any matters relating to working conditions.[47]

The impact of protection was significant for the industry. When the Cereals bill was examined in the Dáil in 1932 the journal *Milling* criticized Fianna Fáil's industrial policy on the grounds that the Irish flour millers were 'placed under a form of control that resembles that imposed on the millers of this country during the war'.[48] Four years later, the same British trade journal seems to have envied the new policy that had been implemented in the Irish Free State:

> the main difference is in the attitude of respective govern-
> ments to the millers in the two countries ... we may say
> confidently that flour milling in the Irish Free State is in
> a flourishing condition, and that the Government, the
> millers and their employees are successfully working
> together to carry on and build up a sound, well-equipped
> and harmoniously working industry.[49]

The number of flour mills increased from twenty-eight to thirty-seven between 1932 and 1936. The production of wheat flour increased from 3,930,852 cwts to 6,804,113 cwts in the same period (see Appendix 3). The gross output of all products (including non-wheat products) also increased from £3,669,782 to £6,746,765. With the rise of native flour production, imports of flour fell rapidly from 3,377,092 cwts in 1931 to only 586,040 cwts in 1934 (see Appendix 2). It was said that the imposition of a tariff on import-ed flour would increase the number of employees only by 153, but the number of employees (engaged at mid-October and excluding piece-workers) increased from 1979 to 2739 between 1931 and 1936.[50]

Oligopoly

Between 31 May and 30 July 1933, nineteen flour millers were penalized for over-production, amounting to 15,343 sacks of wheat milled. In the following quota year between 1 August 1933 and 31 July 1934, a further fourteen flour millers were penalized for 93,085 sacks.[51] As the total wheat requirement for producing flour in the Irish Free State was about 4,300,000 sacks (approximately 3,000,000 sacks of flour) the amount over quota in the year 1933–4 was nearly 2.2 per cent of national requirements. Over-production by this amount could have reduced the weaker millers' share severely. *Milling* reported a mill in Co. Clare that had to go so far as to close their mill temporarily in March 1934 'owing to heavy stocks of flour on hand and poor demand'.[52] Internal competition under the fine system came into play immediately after the enactment of the Cereals Act, and the Flour Millers' Economic Association ceased to function in 1932.[53] This system seemed to be successful in rationalizing the industry in an orderly manner.

From 1932 to 1934 the area under wheat expanded from 21,388 acres to 93,817 acres, and wheat production within the state increased from 445,000 cwts to 2,038,000 cwts.[54] The success of the wheat-growing policy instituted under the Agricultural Produce (Cereals) Act of 1933 caused several problems: most notably the lack of facilities for drying and storing the increasing native wheat supplies with high moisture content, which was only one of the reasons there was a preference amongst millers for foreign wheat. Another problem was the growing cost of the wheat bounty.[55] Initiated by the Department of Agriculture, the Cereals Act of 1935 was enacted to resolve these problems, arranging the minimum storage accommodation or drying plant to be provided at specified mills at the expense of the millers. The payment of a bounty on wheat was repealed and the Minister for Agriculture could fix minimum prices for native wheat to be paid each month by millers and wheat dealers, and flour millers were forced to use a fixed amount of native wheat.[56] The percentage of native wheat to the total amount of wheat milled jumped from 5.05 per cent to 15.64 per cent between 1934 and 1935.[57] The net effect of all this was that millers' costs rose.

The Irish flour-milling industry at this stage was being reorganized by two major groups. One was Rank's, who started to acquire a controlling interest in the Goodbody Mills and their associated company Furlong's in 1930. Their strategic reason to target mills in Limerick and Cork was very obvious; about half of Irish flour output was produced in Munster, substantially in these two cities.[58] Rank's also acquired a controlling interest in the mills in Cork held by the Hallinan family. They incorporated the Cork Milling Co. Ltd, a holding company, in 1932, under which the mills in Cork were owned as subsidiaries, and also Rank's (Ireland) Ltd in 1934, which owned the Goodbody's mills.

The members of the old milling families continued to be engaged as members of the boards of directors, which was usually the case in British mergers.[59] Spillers lost their large business in the Irish Free State,[60] while Hovis, another British flour miller, sought to enter the Irish market but this was not permitted by Lemass, effectively restricting competition in the Irish market.[61]

The other group was the Dublin Port Milling Co. Ltd, the largest and most modernized mill in the state, which had been operating during the 1920s. Its various founders were already engaged in different aspects of the grain and milling business. The cornerstone of this native alliance were the Odlums, who had substantial milling interests in Kildare, Laois and Kilkenny, and the Halls, who were Ireland's premier grain importers, and as such had an excellent knowledge of the raw materials market.[62] The industrial location of this new group was more advantageous in the long term than Cork and Limerick, as the market for flour in Dublin and its hinterland was expanding to a greater degree. Between 1931 and 1936, the percentage of gross national output produced in Munster declined from 50.0 per cent to 44.2 per cent, while in Leinster it increased from 42.1 per cent per cent to 49.5 per cent. The total value of gross output in Munster increased from £1,750,072 to £2,980,909 in the same years, while in Leinster it increased from £1,473,547 to £3,342,435. The increase in the number of mills was by two in Munster and five in Leinster.[63] Rank's (Ireland) had the second and third largest mills in the state but their facilities were becoming comparatively less competitive.

W.P. & R. Odlums Mill at Portarlington. Original 1880 mill in foreground with additions from the 1920s–'30s. (Loftus Odlum, Tilson Collection)

By 1937, it is estimated that both of these groups accounted for roughly 70 per cent of total flour production in the state.[64] Since the market was at this point closed to foreign flour imports, these two major players effectively controlled the Irish flour market. In other words, an oligopoly now existed. The market was saturated by the mid-1930s: flour production did not increase significantly thereafter until the latter years of the war.[65] By the end of 1934 when the Department of Agriculture proposed the Cereals bill (later enacted as the Cereals Act of 1935), which planned to burden flour millers with the higher costs for using native wheat, the flour millers responded by forming cartels in different regions; the Cork Flour Millers' Association, later the Cork and District Flour Millers, the Waterford and District Flour Millers and the Dublin City Flour Millers aimed to control the conditions on the sale and price of flour.[66] All the preparations for an increase in flour prices were now in place.

Failure of Rationalization

The Fianna Fáil government introduced a system of price supervision within the Prices Commission, which monitored the price of flour. A formula for fixing flour prices was prepared by the Commission for application during the quarter ending 31 March 1934, and the Irish Flour Millers' Association informed Lemass that they were complying with it.[67] However, the price of flour jumped sharply after mid-1935, reflecting a rise in the average price of native wheat and other milling costs; approximate average prices of flour increased from 10s. 4d. per cwt in 1934 to 12s. 7d. in 1935. Native wheat prices for millers increased from 7s. 8d. per cwt to 10s., while imported wheat used by millers increased from 6s. 3d. to 7s. 3d.[68] Price increases were repeatedly questioned in the Dáil after 1935.[69] The higher price of flour was the result of a contradiction in Fianna Fáil's industrial policy as Lemass stated:

> If we were to allow competition to have full play, we would keep in existence only the large port mills and necessitate the closing down of the inland mills and that might be a bad policy. To what extent the price of flour charged by the port mills could be reduced, without wiping out whatever legitimate profit these mills may be getting, I cannot say, but there is a problem there which can be

solved only by such an extensive rationalisation of production and cereal control and ownership of the machinery
of production that the problem cannot be easily removed,
and a solution applied without very considerable reactions
in other directions.[70]

Milford, Co. Donegal. The mill was completed in 1936.

The Cereals Act of 1933 was put in place to rationalize the milling industry, but when the Cereals Act of 1935 was enacted, this programme was substantially suspended. The government seemed to overlook cartels as long as they
used native wheat. The Irish Flour Millers' Association also established
another cartel in 1936, the Flour Millers' Quota Association, which aimed to
facilitate the Cereals Act of 1935. The purpose of the Quota Association was
to control the sale of flour for protecting inland mills.[71] Moreover, Lemass
granted licences for millers to operate their inefficient mills (some of which
had failed prior to 1932).[72] He had stated in the Dáil in 1932 that policy was
geared 'to encourage wheat growing', but he also stressed the 'need to decen-
tralise industries'.[73] He and his department clearly recognized that it would
be extremely difficult to simultaneously reduce the price of flour and preserve
inefficient mills. The interests of industrial and agricultural producers were
deemed to be of greater significance than those of consumers.

The issue of flour prices continued to be a matter of concern. Several plans were discussed between the Departments of Industry and Commerce, and Agriculture: first of all, an excess profits duty was considered. The efficient mills enjoyed excess profits due to the cartelized market. The duty, it was argued, could be effective in bringing down flour prices. However, this was not deemed to be workable without the kind of tight control exercised over the industry during the years of the First World War. Secondly, a subsidy for inefficient mills was considered. However, this option would simply have transferred the burden of increased flour prices from consumers to taxpayers. Thirdly, the gradual reduction of tariff rates was considered as this would stimulate competition with foreign millers, but the Irish market would be partly lost to them. The final option was the amalgamation of all mills into one company, which could have been easily pursued, given that the industry had already been reorganized into two groupings.[74] Various other schemes to close inefficient mills were considered. The Department of Industry and Commerce even considered the possibility of the nationalization of the entire industry, but the government decided to back away from this option on 25 April 1938.[75] Ultimately, the creation of new jobs and the preservation of existing jobs in tillage and milling took priority over the rationalization programme and the problem of the rising cost of flour.

The War Economy

Although the Irish Free State pursued a policy of neutrality in the Second World War, it was not immune from the economic impact of the conflict. The Irish government established the Department of Supplies, to which Lemass was moved from the Department of Industry and Commerce for the duration of the emergency. Supplies played a central role in sourcing and distributing agricultural and industrial products in co-operation with the Departments of Industry and Commerce, and Agriculture. The Irish government, before the setting up of the Department of Supplies, had already discussed a national scheme of wheat supply with the Irish Flour Millers' Association in September 1938. At the request of the Department of Industry and Commerce, the Association decided to set up the Wheat Reserve Committee, which would purchase, store and control a reserve of wheat collectively, and after the beginning of the Emergency, Lemass (now Minister for Supplies), wished to form a standard company in each industry. Grain Importers (Éire) Ltd was established by the end of 1939 for flour millers to purchase imported wheat collectively. Irish Shipping Ltd was established in 1941 to deal with the difficulties of securing cargo space for Irish supplies during the war. One of its most important functions during the remaining years of the war was the importation of wheat to supplement native wheat production.[76] As the war intensified, it became increasingly difficult to import wheat, and the cultivation of native wheat became an urgent priority. The Department of Agriculture introduced Compulsory Tillage Orders in 1941, which expanded native cultivation. Wheat acreage increased impressively from 305,243 acres in 1940, to 463,206 acres in 1941, rising to 662,498 acres in 1945.[77] Meanwhile the guaranteed price was set and the prices for wheat per barrel of 20 stones were repeatedly revised from 27s. in 1938/9 to 55s. plus credit voucher value at 2s. 6d. in 1944/5.[78]

One of the major tasks of government during war was to prevent major price increases where possible. The Departments of Industry and Commerce, and Supplies were responsible for enforcing the Emergency Powers (Control of Prices) (No. 1) Order, which fixed the price of most consumer goods, including flour, on 7 September 1939.[79] The control of prices was reasonably effective, but as the importation of wheat became more difficult and the guaranteed

Mills on the Grand Canal Docks, Dublin: an aerial view from the late 1940s. Dock Milling Company in foreground with Bolands Mill behind. (Neil Higgins)

prices were successively increasing in order to extend wheat acreage, prices continuously increased. Supplies of flour were increased by degrading the quality of flour: the percentage of flour extraction from wheat, which was normally 70 per cent, was increased to 100 per cent in 1942, and barley was mixed with better percentage extraction wheaten flour in 1944.[80] A subsidy was also adopted to restrain price increases. The expenditures for the subsidy expanded from £742,400 in 1941/2, to £2,565,178 in 1944/5.[81] Since Lemass was anxious that flour millers should share the cost of the increase of wheat prices, the Department of Supplies introduced a proposal to limit the return on capital to all flour millers in 1941 to not more than 6 per cent. To facilitate this, the Irish Flour Millers' Association formed the Millers' Control Committee in the following year under the direction of the Department of Supplies.[82]

Labour policy during the war years was handled by the Department of Industry and Commerce. The Trade Union Act of 1941 limited the activity of all trade unions and prohibited employers from negotiating wages or working conditions without holding a negotiation licence. As the Act centralized the trade union movement and placed it under national control, it was imperative for the Irish Flour Millers' Association to register themselves as a trade body, to be called the Irish Flour Millers' Union. They were given a licence by the Department of Industry and Commerce on 28 September 1942. Negotiations between labour and management on industrial relations matters continued in the Joint Industrial Council.[83] The Wage Standstill Order (Emergency Powers Order No. 83) prohibited any wage increases and restricted union activity in 1941.[84] Government control was so rigid that flour millers and the unions were unable to improve working conditions, but successive bonus orders by the government at least increased wage levels for mill workers; the average increase of wages for grain milling increased 32.2 per cent between 1938 and 1945, whereas the average for Irish in industry was 29.6 per cent.[85] Even so, this did not make up for price increases, and in fact, real wage levels declined to such an extent that they only recovered to pre-war levels in 1949.[86]

In short, the impact of the war on flour milling in terms of price was far less dramatic than for other basic foodstuffs. The aggregate cost of living index increased by 70.6 per cent and the average food price index by 64.9 per cent between 1938 and 1944. Prices of sugar, potatoes and eggs rose by over 80 per cent in this period. Those of bread, household flour and fresh milk increased by 25.6 per cent, 46.2 per cent and 39.5 per cent respectively, and beef, bacon and butter (Irish creamery) 60.5 per cent, 76.9 per cent and 63.5 per cent each.[87] As the increase in flour price was relatively modest and the government avoided operating a consumer-rationing scheme on flour (although the quality of flour and bread deteriorated), a reasonably stable supply of flour could be chalked up as one of the successes of Fianna Fáil wartime governments. It was due to the wheat reserve schemes from 1938 that a large extension of native wheat production got underway. However, rationing of flour and bread had to be introduced in the immediate aftermath of the Second World War, which indicates that problems relating to the wheat supply became relatively worse in the Irish Free State at that point than during the Emergency itself.[88]

Conclusion

In conclusion, neither the laissez-faire strategy adopted by Cumann na nGaedheal nor greater state intervention by Fianna Fáil helped to increase the process of rationalization within the Irish flour-milling industry during the period in question. The millers had already reached a cartel agreement one year before Cumann na nGaedheal left office. Even in the more interventionist regime established by Fianna Fáil, the government conceded enough to provide a framework for millers to develop oligopolistic business practices. The number of employees and mills (including inefficient mills) and the price of native wheat and flour all dramatically increased and cartel bodies revived. Flour production in the Irish Free State during the 1930s, and subsequently during the Second World War, rose to much higher levels than in the 1920s when the industry had been relatively depressed. While the consumers had to spend more than before, employment in milling was assured and the rationalization programme suspended. The Fianna Fáil government formed a national economic regime in which Irish flour millers had less freedom of choice than previously, but also less business risk and less competition.

Appendix 1

Wheat Acreage and Production Growth in Ireland, 1922–45

	Acres	cwt(000)
1922	38,221	715
1923	36,443	638
1924	32,612	554
1925	22,252	402
1926	29,386	619
1927	34,466	761
1928	31,350	635
1929	28,583	634
1930	26,740	585
1931	20,848	418
1932	21,388	445
1933	50,491	1,063
1934	93,817	2,038
1935	163,473	3,582
1936	254,521	4,200
1937	220,263	3,744
1938	230,426	3,963
1939	255,280	5,106
1940	305,243	6,257
1941	463,206	8,708
1942	574,739	10,230
1943	509,245	8,708
1944	642,487	10,922
1945	662,498	11,461

Note: Wheat acreage in 1851 was 428,705 acres.

Sources: *Statistical Abstract* (1931), p. 26; (1939), pp. 44–5; (1941), p. 40; (1946), p. 40.

Appendix 2

Imports of Wheat and Flour, 1924–45 (cwt)

	Wheat	Flour
1924	6,087,976	3,760,439
1925	5,278,813	3,161,507
1926	5,414,783	3,196,263
1927	6,373,136	3,380,984
1928	4,899,600	3,174,719
1929	5,865,578	3,112,567
1930	5,316,189	3,331,924
1931	5,636,926	3,377,092
1932	5,917,849	2,964,923
1933	8,208,894	1,387,503
1934	9,437,475	586,040
1935	7,558,412	227,951
1936	8,024,622	139,408
1937	6,487,911	117,345
1938	7,597,152	101,235
1939	7,257,581	96,322
1940	6,637,177	79,611
1941	1,000,014	30,769
1942	3,897,906	10,353
1943	1,942,202	577
1944	4,462,682	688
1945	4,567,718	220

Sources: *Trade and Shipping Statistics* (1924), p. 10; (1926), p. 18; (1928), p. 18; (1931), pp. 27–8; (1933), pp. 27–8; (1936), p. 31; (1939), pp. 30–1; (1939–42), pp. 30–1; (1943–4), p. 29; (1945–7), pp. 28–9.

Appendix 3

Flour Production (cwt) and the Number of Flour Mills, Grain Mills and Employees 1926–45

	Flour Production	Flour Mills	Other Mills	Employees	
				Flour Mills	Grain Mills
1926	3,783,902	34	71	2,087	3,048
1929	4,016,295	31	74	2,023	3,127
1931	3,847,591	29	75	1,979	3,215
1932	3,930,852	28	80	n.a.	3,321
1933	5,765,275	30	70	n.a.	3,406
1934	6,410,884	32	86	n.a.	3,791
1935	6,852,277	36	89	2,677	4,000
1936	6,804,113	37	100	2,739	4,188
1937	6,700,334	38	102	2,709	4,201
1938	6,517,072	n.a.	n.a.	n.a.	4,346
1939	6,918,063	n.a.	n.a.	n.a.	n.a.
1940	6,940,773	n.a.	n.a.	n.a.	n.a.
1941	6,573,966	n.a.	n.a.	n.a.	n.a.
1942	6,347,334	n.a.	n.a.	n.a.	n.a.
1943	7,364,360	n.a.	n.a.	n.a.	n.a.
1944	7,721,219	n.a.	n.a.	n.a.	3,568
1945	7,921,705	n.a.	n.a.	n.a.	n.a.

Notes: 1. Flour means wheat flour. 2. Number of employees is number of persons engaged at mid-October (excluding piece-workers). 3. The number of employees in grain mills excluding flour mills did not dramatically increase except for in Co. Cork. Sources: *Census of Industrial Production* (1926–9), pp. 38, 43, 46; (1931), pp. 36, 42; (1932–5), pp. 16, 26, 31; (1936), pp. 46, 51–3; (1937), p. 46, 51–2; (1938–44), pp. 84, 86; (1945–7), p. 63.

7

Irish Flour Milling
Since the Second World War

NORMAN CAMPION

IN THE DECADES after the Second World War, the flour-milling industry in the 26 counties remained diverse and geographically dispersed; even remote areas were still in many instances supplied from local flour and feed mills. The industry at this stage remained more production- than market-orientated and this continued into the 1950s. Since flour tended to be distributed on a regional basis, there were often duplications of brand names, e.g. Glynn's of Kilrush, Davis's of Enniscorthy and Goodbody's of Clara used White Rose.[1] Ten-stone (63.6-kg) cotton bags of flour were collected from the local grocer and conveyed home on the horse and cart to stand near the hearth, becoming the source of daily bread for the family. The tradition of home baking was still strong in the 1940s, and household flour (bought in shops) for home baking still accounted for almost 43 per cent of the total market for flour in the state by the end of the decade. A government inquiry provided a breakdown of the market in the 26 counties in 1947–8, as shown in Table 1.

The cotton bags were very much a reusable packaging material and few were dumped. Many 8- or 10-stone cotton flour bags became sheets with brand names such as 'Purity', 'Hearts Delight' or 'Magnificent' stamped on them. Smaller bags became dishcloths, pillow cases, straining bags for crab apple jelly, or even shirts. Bakers, in contrast, largely used refundable jute bags:

Table 1

A Breakdown of Flour Consumption in the 26 Counties, 1947–8.

	Sacks	% share
1. Flour used by confectioners, biscuit manufacturers and industrial users	150,000	5.1
2. Flour used in commercial baking of bread	1,533,000	52.2
3. Flour used in home consumption	1,254,000	42.7
Total	2,937,000	100.0

Source: *Flour and Bread Inquiry: Interim and Final Report* (Dublin, 1950), p. 51.

Rank's, for example, had an entire office in Limerick dealing with returnable sacks, which was not unusual among Irish millers.

The industry faced many problems after the difficulties of the war years. Although there was a world wheat shortage, flour consumption immediately after the war was 20 per cent higher than pre-war levels, owing to the scarcity of other foods and the fact that it was subsidized. Flour and bread subsidies continued until May 1957. The flour extraction rate was controlled again after the war and various measures were taken to ration flour and bread between 1947 and 1952. During this period, Canadian flour was imported to supplement some of the shortfall in native production. This was blended in at 10 per cent. The Millers' Control Committee (established during the war) continued to control millers' profit margins until 1953.[2] Despite a brief recovery during the food shortages in the wake of the war, Irish flour consumption began to decline from over 300 lbs per head in 1945, to 220 by 1958. This contraction of demand reflected a wider European pattern in the decades after the war, with rising living standards facilitating a more diversified diet, in which bread was displaced by more exciting foods. Medical advice in this era turned against starchy foods, while some slimming diets excluded bread entirely. In the post-war era, automation and mechanization lightened the work of labourers, who worked fewer hours a day, fewer days a year and with less intensity, thereby reducing the demand for high energy foodstuffs like bread. Table 2 provides a comparison of consumption patterns in Ireland with other European countries.

Table 2

A Comparison of per capita Consumption of Flour in a Number of European Countries in 1959

Country	Flour consumption (lbs)
Ireland (ROI)	210
United Kingdom	168
Denmark	89
Belgium	180
France	213
F.R. Germany	110
Switzerland	165
Norway	126
Sweden	112
USA	115
Canada	140
Australia	185
New Zealand	159

Source: Department of Agriculture and Fisheries, *Report of the Survey Team Established by the Minister for Agriculture on the Flour-Milling Industry* (Dublin, 1965), p. 108.

Table 2 reveals that Irish bread consumption was at the higher end of the European scale, only exceeded by France. Per capita consumption in the 26 counties had risen dramatically to 308 lbs just after the war, declining thereafter. The consequence of this (combined with a slight fall in the population) is that the amount of flour produced in the state declined from 411,000 metric tonnes in 1945, to 270,000 in 1965.[3] As a result, overcapacity in the industry became even more acute, and the following mills were gradually taken out of production in these years: T. Hallinan & Sons, Fermoy, Co. Cork (1953); J. & R. Webb, Mallow, Co. Cork (1957); James Comerford & Sons, Rathdrum, Co. Wicklow (1957); T. Hallinan & Sons, Midleton, Co. Cork (1960); George Shaw

Johnston, Mooney and O'Brien's Clonliffe mills in 1948. (Hugh John de Lacy)

& Sons, Cork (1960); and Johnston, Mooney & O'Brien, Dublin (1961). This initial voluntary rationalization programme was initiated by the Irish Flour Millers' Association and ran from 1953 until 1961, and a further scheme introduced in 1962 resulted in additional closures.[4] These mills were compensated, which was funded by a levy on the production of the remaining mills. The following mills therefore also ceased production as a result of the various rationalization schemes that had been implemented by 1965: Thomas Palmer & Co., Galway; McDonagh Milling & Trading, Galway; Ballina Flour Mills, Mayo; Byrne Mahony & Co., Dublin; Bennett & Co. Ltd, Shannonvale Mills, Clonakilty, Cork; Walter Brown & Co., Dublin; M. Glynn & Sons, Kilrush, Clare; Going & Smith Ltd, Cahir, Tipperary; Brown & Crosthwait, Bagenalstown, Co. Carlow; R. Pilsworth Ltd, Thomastown, Kilkenny; W. H. Mosse Ltd, Bennettsbridge, Kilkenny; Owen Fogarty Ltd, Aughrim, Wicklow.[5]

After all of these closures the surviving Independents were: Milford, Donegal; Barrow Mills, Carlow; The Dock Milling Co., Dublin; Bolands, Dublin; G. Shackleton & Sons, Lucan; and S. & A.G. Davis, Enniscorthy, Wexford. The number of mills in operation was reduced to seventeen by the end of 1965,

Above: Odlums' bulk flour tanker in Dublin during the 1970s. (Odlum Group)
Left: The Dock Mill, Dublin in 1949.

with the Odlum Group operating seven of these, while Rank's had four. After all these closures, the Independents' licences were adjusted downwards with sales allocated as follows: the Independents 27.45 per cent, from 34 per cent previously; Rank's increased to 32.67 per cent, from 30 per cent; and the Odlum Group increased to 39.88 per cent, from 36 per cent. Despite rationalization, overcapacity continued to be a problem as the consumption of flour continued to decline at over 2 per cent per annum. This situation only reversed in the 1980s when more wheat-based products were being consumed.

In an attempt to counteract falling demand, marketing and general advertising using TV became more common from the 1960s, with product identity becoming an increasingly important factor to ensure brand loyalty and establish good brand images. Odlums commissioned Arks Advertising, who came up with a new image for their cream and self-raising flours. This involved the introduction of the now famous Owl symbol (part of the Odlum family crest). Rank's for their part promoted Rank's Friendship Flour and McDougall's Self Raising Flour. A group of the independent flour millers got together and brought out a common brand named 'Success', with more limited results in the market place. In addition, there were all kinds of in-store promotional activities, demonstrations of baking at the ICA (Irish Countrywomen's Association) and other similar groups, while special-offer items like kitchen scales were not uncommon. Rank's, Odlums, Bolands and Andrews had specialist demonstration teams.

This shift towards greater marketing was accompanied by an equally dramatic shift away from the way flour had been stored, presented and sold in shops. Large 8- and 10-stone bags had traditionally been brought into stores and dumped in a bin (which frequently contained ancient residues at the bottom). From this it was scooped into 7- or 14-lb. bags. The new supermarkets adopted a somewhat more efficient and hygienic approach, selling off the shelf prepacked flour in various sizes with strong brand images. The supermarkets brought similar changes to the presentation and marketing of bread, which they wanted wrapped, sliced and unsliced, with bakers developing and marketing their brands more forcefully.

Despite these major changes in marketing and packaging, and a considerable reduction in the number of mills, there were other problems to contend with. When the Republic of Ireland entered the EEC in 1973, the Irish flour market was still fully protected. Rank's and Odlums almost reached an agreement to merge their milling interests, but the Minister for Agriculture, having first considered this desirable, reversed his position because the government had concerns about a monopoly in the flour market. In 1974, the social impact of high inflation following the 1973 international oil crisis saw the re-introduction of a subsidy on flour and bread and this continued until 1982. It was only at this stage that Irish flour milling was finally exposed to the full forces of international competition. Rationalization continued and, in 1978, a host of mills were closed by the Odlum Group at Waterford, Portlaoise, Ballysadare and Naas, and these were replaced by newly built mills at Portarlington in 1978 and in Cork in 1981–2. These were significant developments as they were the first new mills to be built in the Republic since 1935.

Despite the absence of any new flour mill construction in this period, the late 1950s and early '60s witnessed great technological change in baking, and

Quality control meeting at Portarlington Mills in the 1960s. From left to right: Sam Lewis, chemist; Loftus Odlum, general manager, Odlums, Portarlington; Cecil Tilson, technical manager. (Tilson Collection)

this had important implications for flour milling as many bakers were also millers. Automation reduced manning levels, notably the demand for skilled labour. The steady decline of the traditional Irish batch loaf in favour of the sliced pan was a further factor in the development of those types of processes, with greater uniformity in quality. All of this facilitated the use of larger plants and the growth of larger bakery units in Britain and Ireland.[6]

Against this background the links between milling and baking increased. Odlums, for example, purchased Johnston, Mooney & O'Brien; Rank's owned Rourke's Bakery in Dublin, the Marina Bakery in Cork and Kelly's of Kilcock. Milford Donegal was a flour-milling and bakery group. The Dock Milling Company held minority shareholdings in Joseph Downes & Sons of Dublin and Peter Lyons of Drogheda. Bolands erected a modern bakery with high-speed mixing and travelling ovens. These firms invested most heavily in the new baking technology, and between them they had a significant influence on the entire sector. The development of supermarkets and multiple groups also initially helped these larger firms. The multiple retailers wished to restrict the firms they dealt with to the ones whose products sold best. In the early 1970s the miller bakers' position looked promising. The voluntary limitation of production agreement and the agreed quotas it embodied ensured that there was no price competition in the milling industry. They took the profit in the mill and set the price of flour at a level to discourage new entrants to the bakery trade. The Department of Industry and Commerce set the maximum retail price for bread. The bakeries of Johnston, Mooney & O'Brien, Bolands, Mothers Pride in Dublin and Cork, Downe's Butterkrust, and Peter Lyons of Drogheda and Millford in Donegal, together with independents such as Thompson's of Cork, Keating's of Kanturk, Lydon's of Galway and a few others adapted best to the advent of supermarkets. When in 1971 the venerable Dublin firm of Peter Kennedy decided to close, the remaining Dublin bakeries were strong enough to agree a compensation package.

In 1966, Bolands bakery installed a new line of plant. The bakers' union refused to operate the new plant unless they received a new productivity bonus. Still reeling from the effects of the 1965 strike, Bolands conceded the demand. Over the next few years, all the traditional Dublin bakeries conceded to this bonus. The unions also set their face against any dilution of the Night Work in Bakeries Act (1936). Thus, while the position of the traditional bakers looked promising, there were ominous signs of the problems ahead, including the five-day delivery week, the prohibition of night work, over-manning and intense demarcation. The high level of investment traditionally required to enter the trade was being undermined by developments in the United Kingdom, where the consolidation of bakeries into larger units with larger plants and the rapid improvement in technology meant that many relatively new automated plants were coming on the market at moderate prices.

A new kind of bakery therefore emerged in the Republic. They purchased the plants almost new from the United Kingdom at a fraction of the cost of new ones. They recruited new staff who, while properly paid, did not have the disadvantages of the union houses, demarcation, productivity bonuses, the ban on night work or a five-day delivery week, etc. Rather than provide their own fleets with employee drivers with the high capital and running costs this involved, all their sales were carried out through self-employed distributors. They had no aversion to Monday deliveries, in fact Monday deliveries with night baking were the two platforms that enabled them to enter and ultimately increase their share of the market. Joseph Brennan Bakeries, M&B in

Dublin, The Higgins family of Pat The Baker in Granard, the O'Connors of Western Pride in Ballinrobe, Kiely's of Tipperary, William's of Taghmon, and Fitzgerald's of Cork, all began to develop and grow.

By the early 1980s a major battle for survival was going on and the traditional bakeries with their high cost base and total labour inflexibility were under real pressure, as one of Ireland's most regulated industries became liberalized. This resulted in the closures of Mothers Pride in Dublin in 1984, the Marina Bakery in Cork, Bolands Bakery and Mill in 1984, Thompson's of Cork in 1984, and Joseph Downes & Sons in 1987. When finally Johnston, Mooney & O'Brien closed its bakery at Ballsbridge in 1989 (having been in business since 1835) the last vestiges of the old order went with it.

Another feature of the industry in this period was the tenacious survival of a number of independent mills in private ownership. Two of them built new mills in the mid-1930s revival – Murphy Brothers of Ballina and Milford Mills, Co. Donegal. Farther south, the two 4-sack capacity mills of Thomas Palmer & Co. and MacDonagh's were in a unique position at Nuns Island, Galway; the two mills butted onto each other, straddling a branch of the Corrib River, deriving their power through turbines. M. Glynn & Sons, Kilrush, Co. Clare, distributed their flour on their own ships along the Shannon estuary, up as far as Limerick where they had a depot. They also developed the car ferries across the Shannon, which gave them easy lorry access to the Kerry market.

Bolands Mills in Dublin and their neighbours, Dock Milling,[7] were located on the Grand Canal Basin, providing access to small coasters and barge transport for incoming grain supplies. Johnston, Mooney & O'Brien located at Jones Road (near Croke Park) was also an Independent, but was closed after being damaged by a dust explosion in 1961.[8] Their Ballsbridge bakery was amongst Dublin's biggest. Byrne Mahony was located at Usher's Quay, near the Guinness brewery. Walter Brown & Co., who were located at Hanover Street, Dublin, were part of the loosely knit Brown Family group of mills.[9] In a rural context, the Pilsworths' at Thomastown and the Mosses' at Bennettsbridge played a significant role in the affairs of the Irish Flour Millers' Association, as did many of the other independent millers (see list of presidents of the Association in appendix). After Mosse's mill closed in 1965 they set up a joint enterprise with S. & A.G. Davis, Enniscorthy – Davis/Mosse. That alliance continued until the acquisition by Bolands. The Barrow Milling Co., Carlow, was one of these mills, which was restarted in 1936, with Lemass performing the reopening ceremony.[10] George Shackleton & Sons, Lucan, on the River Liffey, had been operated by the same family since 1866.[11] There were two mills in Co. Wicklow: Fogarty's of Aughrim was almost self-sufficient with power from turbines giving almost 120 h.p., which was enough to also generate their electricity for lighting. They had their own rail sidings. Comerford's closed in 1957 and Fogarty's in 1962.[12] Milford (Donegal) Bakery & Flour Mills was established in 1936 by the Sheils family. It was newly built. Manus Sheils subsequently became Technical Director of Robinsons (Milling Engineers) before coming back to Milford as managing director in 1956.[13] He was president of the IFMA in 1968 and in 1980. It was taken over by a subsidiary of Halal Meats in 1989 but closed a year later.[14]

Bolands were the largest of the Independents.[15] After the war the Grand Canal Street Bakery was rebuilt, but this was just before great changes were coming about in the trade and it was out of date by the time it had been completed in 1952. Bolands Mills on Barrow Street had increased its capacity in the 1950s. Their household flour was a big seller in country areas. With the post-war decline in bread demand, Bolands decided to augment the sales of confectionery and bread by a return to biscuit production, but on a much more ambitious scale. In 1957, a new biscuit factory was opened at Deansgrange in south Dublin. The Anglo Irish Free Trade Agreement of 1965 forced Bolands and Jacob's to look at their respective positions. They decided to pool their resources and in 1966 all production was centred at the new biscuit factory in Tallaght. In 1976 a reverse take-over of Bolands by The Barrow Milling Company saw both operations continue until the Barrow Milling Company went into liquidation in 1984. Philip Lynch and the Irish Agricultural Wholesale Society Ltd (IAWS) acquired Bolands Mills from the receiver in 1984, increasing its capacity so that it not only supplied the general market, but also the developing group of Irish Pride bakeries. This situation continued until 2001, when investment considerations and a close look at the Irish flour market indicated that it would be wiser to concentrate on the IAWS (Irish Pride bakeries). Bolands Mills therefore finally ceased production in 2001.

The Odlum Group of mills displayed a greater degree of flexibility in their strategy than other Irish flour millers, which goes some way to explaining the longevity of the Odlum name.[16] It is worth tracing the fate of the various mills in this group that were shut down as part of this strategy of survival, which enabled them to be among the few millers who constructed new mills in this period so that they were able to concentrate production in state-of-the-art facilities. W. P. & R. Odlum Ltd was located at St Mullins on the banks of the Barrow and was home to Ross Odlum and later his son Douglas. This was finally closed in 1964. W. P. & R. Odlum (originally Odlum & Odlum Ltd, and before that Pembertons) was located at the Leinster Mills on the banks of the canal branch to Naas. It was also the home of Mr Claude Odlum, and rumour has it that the mills did not run at night so as not to disturb his sleep! It closed in 1978.[17] Maryborough Mills, Portlaoise, was the head office for W. P. & R. Odlum Ltd. It was where John Scott presided, having previously been the last general manager of the Grand Canal Company before Peter Odlum brought him into the company in 1951 for his general managerial skills. This 14-sack mill was also closed in 1978 and subsequently demolished. W. P. & R. Odlum, Portarlington, is the only surviving country mill in Ireland.[18] New mills of 60-sack capacity were built in 1978. Loftus Odlum was general manager until his retirement in 1994 and Nigel Odlum remains the operations manager in 2003.

Odlums' connection with R. & H. Hall brought them into direct involvement in the following mills in which Halls had a shareholding: George Shaw & Sons, St John's Mills, Cork, which was closed in 1960 and its license transferred to The National Flour Mills, Cork; Johnston, Mooney & O'Brien, Jones Road, Dublin, which was one of the early mills to be converted to pneumatic conveying in Ireland. Its connection with the Ballsbridge Bakery, which required 83,000 sacks per annum, made them an attractive target for investment by Odlums. Sadly, in 1961 a dust explosion in the screen-room threatened the stability of the buildings and the mills never worked again, the licence being transferred to the Dublin Port Mills. Even by 1962 W. P. & R. Odlum Holdings had only a 30 per cent share in the Dublin Port Milling Co., but Odlums had provided the management since its formation in 1924. It eventually became the flagship for the Odlum Group. Peter Odlum was appointed general manager in 1948. Gradually the original 25-sack plant installed in 1924 had been increased; by the mid-1930s it was up to 50-sack. Currently (2003), it is a 70-sack plant with all the most up-to-date computer controls. It runs seven days a week with short shutdown periods for maintenance purposes, like all the Odlum mills.

As Odlums were short of wheatmeal quota, they bought Howard Rowe's of Wexford in May 1956. Howard Rowe & Son Ltd (established in 1850) were

The *Moshula* at Victoria Quays, Cork, in 1961. This was one of the last sail ships to deliver grain to Cork. (Odlum Group)

located at Paul Quay and had a large wheatmeal quota of 10,000 barrels per annum. They continued to operate it for a period but eventually transferred production to Dublin Port Mills in 1972.[19]

The National Flour Mills, Cork, was purpose-built during the 1930s revival. It had all the advantages of a port location with accompanying grain silos – it was the first mill built by Buhler in Ireland. Miag of Germany replaced

The National Flour Mills, Cork, in 1963. (Odlum Group)

it with new plant in 1967. Miag was a serious competitor with Henry Simon Ltd in the field of engineering and machine making for flour mills. Eventually Simon built a new mill in 1981–2 of 60-sack capacity (250 tons of wheat in twenty-four hours). Another associated company with this group was W. & G.T. Pollexfen, Ballysadare, Co. Sligo, which had connections with the Yeats family (through family and direct shareholdings) going back to 1901. It was probably the 'greenest' of all the Odlum Mills, deriving some 700 h.p. from the Ballysadare River both by direct drive from the turbines and electrical generation and distribution (some was sold to the ESB). The employees indulged in a certain amount of 'salmon fishing' with an efficient early warning system saying 'manager on his rounds'. The 15-sack mill closed in 1974, while the Westport branch had been sold to a local co-op in the previous year. The Waterford Flour Mills, which were purpose-built in 1936, adjoined Hall's silos on Waterford quayside. This was one of the great training centres for many millers, not only for Odlums and their associates. The mill closed in 1979.[20]

In 1953, Peter Odlum took over his father's position and successfully guided the company to its position of strength until his death in March 1983. Odlums found that in order to remain competitive, it was necessary to rationalize production. As there was a connection with R. & H. Hall who had milling interests in Cork and Sligo, the first step was to bring these interests together by the formation of a new company called Associated Mills in 1963. This arrangement continued for a while until it became apparent that some of the smaller mills would have to be closed, as they were uneconomic to run. The first to close was St Mullins in 1964, followed by Pollexfen's in Sligo in 1974. To strengthen the company's position, the mill in Dublin was remodelled in 1970, a new mill was built in Portarlington in 1978, and the mills in Portlaoise, Waterford and Naas were closed. Finally, to complete the rationalization programme, a new mill was built in Cork in 1981–2.[21]

Rank's Ireland Ltd[22]

To appreciate the problems of Irish flour milling in the 1970s and early '80s it is worth looking in some detail at the saga of the decline and fall of Rank's Ireland Ltd, one of the two leading groups.[23] Rank's problems were shared in varying degrees by the rest of the industry. To deal with overcapacity between the 1950s and early '70s, Rank's reduced their production facilities to three mills, one in Limerick, one in Cork and one in Dublin.

With dropping flour consumption and over-capacity in the industry, they decided to further concentrate their production facilities. An announcement was made in October 1975 that they would close the Limerick mill, as the plant was too big, too old and too much of a burden on the company. The plants in Dublin and Cork were to be remodelled and production concentrated there. Almost immediately tremendous pressure was applied from a range of individuals and groups, including politicians, unions, clergy, etc., asking the company to change its decision. The plan to close Limerick was shelved, although some minor rationalization was achieved through staff reduction.

In 1978, Rank's Ireland again reviewed their objectives and priorities in a report that highlighted falling profits and obsolete milling plant; the company to a large degree was simply living on its name and was being overtaken by its major competitors. Rank's still had three mills, each requiring modernization, but these were more than demand warranted. However the attempts to rationalize were not a success. A new feed mill was completed in Cork in January 1980, and almost immediately there were difficulties. The market turned down sharply and the mill soon started to incur heavy losses, so it was closed and sold to Southern Milling. The loss to the company would amount to £1.8 million in a full year. The position of Rank's in 1982 was that they were sustaining losses in feed milling and bakeries,[24] in addition to the cost of extrication from loss-making activities. All this necessitated heavy borrowing from the banks, with the high interest charges of the period further crippling the company, curtailing

Top: Lord Rank inspecting voluntary fire brigade at Rank's, Limerick, in 1949. **Above:** Demonstration of mill carpentry to local farmers, Rank's of Limerick, 1948. (Mercier Collection, c/o Croom Mills)

its ability to invest in new facilities. Absence of new plant meant higher costs than industry average.

Though associated with Rank's/Hovis/McDougall (who had three non-executive members on the Board of the Irish Company), Rank's (Ireland) employed largely Irish capital, Irish employees and produced Irish-made products for the Irish market. It did not want to go under. Despite uncertainty in the industry, plans were drawn up to modernize Limerick and Dublin, in conjunction with the IDA. However, one of the major problems was that dramatically increasing flour imports in 1981–2 were being sold at a much lower price than Irish flour, resulting in Rank's being unable to implement price increases. This had a disastrous effect on the general outlook and prospects

Rank's Shannon Mills, Limerick, in the 1970s. (George Spillane)

for Rank's (Ireland), given all the other problems it was contending with. Any remaining optimism was slowly extinguished. The closure of the Limerick mills was announced for Friday, 4 February 1983. It was a sad and difficult end for Rank's Ireland Ltd and its employees. The closures did not go smoothly: fourteen employees of the Dublin mill staged an acrimonious sit-in over a three-month period, and a similar type of action took place in Limerick. Rank's did, however, salvage some goodwill within the trade with many bakeries. So by the end of 1983 they returned to the position they had started at in the 1920s as importers of flour into the Irish market with a separate company set up to facilitate this activity.

Wheat Industries Ltd[25]

While one major company made its exit from production in Ireland, another was planning to enter the industry. On 6 February 1981 the Irish Flour Millers'

Association held a meeting with the Industrial Development Authority to express concern at the development of a proposed new flour mill at Ringaskiddy, Co. Cork, by Fielder Gillespie Davis of Australia. The plan was that the mill would produce starch, protein and glucose from wheat, Fielder Gillespie being specialists in this field. Ceimici Teoranta was also involved and were already producing starch, glucose, alcohol, etc., at a number of plants in the state. The intention to largely mill Irish wheat was one of the major attractions to the government of the day. When the plant was brought into production in 1983 it was one of the largest integrated wheat-processing operations in the world.[26] Unfortunately, Irish wheat failed to give the necessary yield and protein content compared to hard Australian wheat. Recovery from the Irish plant was less than forecast. Eventually, Wheat Industries Ltd was sold to Cerestar. The Ringaskiddy plant closed in early 1990s and many of the products were supplied to the Irish market from their Manchester plant.[27]

Northern Ireland

After the Second World War, there were four flour mills operating in Northern Ireland: Rank's in Belfast; Morton's in Ballymena; Andrews of Belfast; and James Neill of Belfast. Robert Morton & Co. of Ballymena[28] was the only rural flour mill left in Northern Ireland at this point. The 25-sack (4 tons of wheat per hour) mill worked on two shifts with all the best equipment. The business was ultimately sold in 1989 to Andrews Milling, who discontinued production there in 1993. Morton's Early Riser Flour is still on the supermarket shelves, but produced by Andrews.

In 1962, James Neill Ltd came under the control of Allied Mills.[29] Mr Gordon Neill continued as managing director until retirement in 1977.[30] In 1987, they established a new fully automated mill installed by Buhler Switzerland, which was one of the early computer-controlled mills in Europe from wheat intake to finished flour production. The plant is designed to run continuously and, when in full production, runs straight through for two weeks night and day, including Saturday and Sunday, with only a four-hour shutdown for routine maintenance. Once the programme of production is set the mill starts up in sequence, selects the settings on the rollers, etc., to get the optimum flour extraction. Each wheat is conditioned and milled separately and the resultant flour stored in bins. These flours and any additives required are then blended to meet the customer's individual needs. The majority are delivered in bulk, with lesser amounts in standard 16-kg paper bags or 1-kg packets for the supermarket trade. When one bin is full, the computer selects the next until all are full and then the mill is closed down automatically. Today, Neill's Mills[31] are one of the most modern flour mills in the world.[32]

Rank's Pacific Mill in Belfast had been built in 1933 to a typical Rank design located directly on the quayside,[33] and was equipped with a 60-sack plant by Henry Simon Ltd. Rank's had purchased Messrs Hughes Dixon Flour Mills and Model Mills, Divas Street, some years earlier, which were closed down after the new Pacific Mill was built, but the Hughes Dixon brands of 'Democrat' and 'Magnificent' flours were continued. The mill was a traditional Rank Mill

Bulk flour tanker with Scottish flour at Mothers Pride Bakery, Belfast, 2003. (James Davidson)

of the period. During its lifetime only modest updating took place, and often with second-hand equipment.[34] The provender and maize plant closed in 1976. Rank's closed the Pacific Mills in 1982. However, having built up a significant flour trade, they were naturally not willing to let it go. They had also made some investment in baking (buying the Inglis Bakery in 1967, which was amalgamated into Mothers Pride). Part of the premises was used as a warehouse and distribution centre for Rank's flour from Glasgow, with a small warehouse/transport and administrative sales staff retained. Bulk flour for bakeries came directly from their Glasgow mill.[35] Later an outside transport and warehousing contractor took over this activity, with Rank's staff being reduced to a few sales personnel. Their Mothers Pride Bakery took over Ormo Bakery from Andrews in 2002, having originally sold it to Andrews for a nominal sum in 1975.

Since the Second World War, Andrews operations have been continuously updated to the highest efficiency and standards,[36] and the animal feed side has been as important as the flour side.[37] With John Thompson & Sons, they were the dominant companies in the market in Northern Ireland. Bolands of Dublin entered a technical/marketing agreement with Andrews, selling the same brand both sides of the border, with Bolands paying Andrews a royalty for their technical/nutritional advice. This was a much-acclaimed cross-border initiative for the 1960s. Andrews continued their policy of upgrading their flour mill to the highest standards; their capacity is now approximately 40 sacks per hour (160 tons of wheat per day). In 1980 a management buyout saw the Andrews family exiting from the company with the previous managing director, Dawson Moreland, becoming chairman and his son Michael taking over as MD. Andrews sell flour throughout Ireland.[38] The market in Northern Ireland was estimated in 2002 at approximately 85,000 tons, $2/_3$ of which is produced in the Belfast Mills – Andrews Milling and Allied Mills – with the balance being imported by Rank's.[39]

Epilogue

Despite the withdrawal of Rank's from Irish flour production in 1983, they still supplied 25 per cent of the market in the Republic by 1986, having therefore lost only 7–8 per cent of market share from their production days. In addition, flour was being imported from other UK mills, so the industry's capacity problems remained. In April 1983, the Industrial Development Authority commissioned a study of Irish flour milling, which noted:

The existing milling companies in Ireland have in total sufficient milling capacity available to supply the domestic market (including the present imported element) even after Rank's have closed down their milling operation in Limerick. New capacity, or a re-opening of the Limerick mill is not necessary in this context.

Unlike the popular image of the industry, we do not believe that the existing milling companies or their mills are inefficient. Associated with the withdrawal of Rank's from the market, and because of the impact of imported flour being sold in the market the millers' cartel market sharing arrangements no longer exist and companies are free to allow individual pricing and marketing policies. A 'free' market now exists.

… We do think that the present industry may well operate at some disadvantage to the GB industry – mainly in matters of scale, and certain costs – but we have formed the impression that, in the main, the now existing milling operations are far from being incompetent and outmoded.[40]

The fate of some of the surviving Independents is worth tracing during the period that the industry became ever more concentrated. In 1978, for example, Roma Foods Ltd acquired a controlling interest in the Anna Liffey Mill of George Shackleton & Sons Ltd in Lucan. This firm manufactured pasta products made from semolina and had been one of the mill's main customers since the mid-1970s. The mill was modified so that its principal product was semolina rather than flour. A small amount of flour and bran continued to be produced, along with wheatmeal, pre-mixers and rice flour. The workforce was reduced to about a dozen employees and by the early 1980s the mill was returning a healthy profit. In 1991, Roma was taken over by the Allegro Group, a Dublin-based food distribution company. Richard Shackleton (the sole representative of the old milling family associated with the company), was retained as manager until his retirement on 31 December of that year. Operations continued until November 1998, when the mill processed its last batch of durum wheat and closed. Another small survivor, the Milford Flour

Mills[41] in Donegal, was still producing 8 per cent of the industry's capacity in the Republic by 1983–4.[42] They exported flour into the Northern Irish market successfully, being nearer to counties Londonderry and Tyrone than the Belfast Mills – much to the annoyance of the latter. Milford Mills ceased production in 1990. While the number of flour mills in Ireland had already begun to contract from the second half of the nineteenth century, the survival of some of these Independents until the last decades of the twentieth century is a surprising feature of the sector, given the wider developments within the industry.

Flour milling in the Republic became more concentrated in the last decades of the twentieth century as a consequence of a number of mergers.[43] The IAWS bought Bolands Mills in 1984 when the parent company was liquidated; merging Bolands, The Dock Milling Co. and Davis in 1987, and subsequently purchasing Howard's Wheatenmeal Millers of Cookstown, Co. Cork in 1988. In the same year, IAWS Plc was established. 1989 saw investment in the First National Bakery Company, which launched the Irish Pride brand in 1990. In the latter year R. & H. Hall Ltd, the major grain dealers in Ireland, were also purchased, and the Davis mill in Enniscorthy finally ceased production. In 1994 the Dock Mill also ceased production but carried out packing for Bolands until 1999. Bolands installed an additional milling plant by Golfetto of Italy – capacity 180 tons per day (40 sacks) – and this came on-stream coinciding with the closure of the Dock Mill milling operation. IAWS Plc also acquired the highly successful Cuisine de France hot goods operation in 1997 and they have now expanded internationally. An important figure in these transition years was Philip Lynch, who had joined the IAWS as chief executive in 1983. With experience working in the Odlum Group and the largest grain merchants in Ireland, R. & H. Hall, he had a good working knowledge of the industry.

Odlums was sold to Greencore (the holding company of the Irish Sugar Company), with half the shares being purchased in 1989 and the balance in 1991. Members of the Odlum family continue to play a major role in the management of the organization. At the close of the '80s, with only two groups surviving, the need for the Irish Flour Millers' Association diminished and it was finally disbanded in 1989. When Bolands Mills were closed in 2001, the IAWS took a 50 per cent shareholding in the Odlum Group. So the flour-milling industry in the Republic has effectively been consolidated into a single company, Odlums, operating on only three strategic sites, thus ensuring excellent economies of scale and a good distribution network. Two groups (Greencore and IAWS) jointly own this company, each of which has multinational interests in a range of agri/food sector activities.

As of 2003, Odlums owns and operates three modern flour mills and an oatmeal mill, and its products are sold nationwide. Although the bulk of the flour sold in the Irish Republic is produced by the Odlum Group, approximately 20 per cent of requirements were imported in 2002, including some from France. Much of these imports came from Rank's, and some came from the two mills operating in Belfast (Andrews Milling and Allied [James Neill Ltd]).[44] As of 2003, Odlum Mills have a capacity to supply 80 per cent of the Republic's flour market. The mills are located at Dublin,[45] with a capacity of 70 sacks (300 tons per day of wheat); Portarlington,[46] with a capacity of 40 sacks (160 tons per day of wheat); and Cork,[47] with a capacity of 60 sacks (240 tons per day of wheat). It also has an oatmeal mill at Sallins.[48]

The Portarlington Mill makes most of the household flour and there is a subsidiary packing plant at Mulhuddart, Co. Dublin (ex-Bolands). All of the flour mills are in excellent condition and with the modern compact plants in them it is likely that capacity could be increased at a reasonable cost. With over 75 per cent of the population living east and south of the Shannon, the three mills are well placed for the effective distribution of products. In 2002, estimated total flour consumption in the Republic was 265,000 tons, of which 35 per cent was imported. The industry also exported 10,000 tons. With a population of 3,917,336, that represents 67 kg or 147 lbs per head, compared to 128 kg or 270 lbs in 1952. It is evident that flour consumption per head has fallen dramatically in the intervening years.

The revival of the Irish flour-milling industry in the 1930s was an important chapter in the industrial history of the Republic, helping the country through the Emergency without the rationing of flour and bread. The policy of self-sufficiency and support for the growth of native wheat production in the 1930s contributed to this development. Ireland in the 1950s and '60s still had a diverse and widely dispersed milling industry, supplying even remote areas from local flour and feed mills. Since then, consolidation inevitably followed, and new technologies and equipment were adopted, which required new investment, reorganization and the utilization of concepts and methods that originated elsewhere. The development of better road transport facilitated a wider distribution of products from mills, which also contributed to the process of consolidation.

The investment in the development of improved wheat varieties led by the Irish Flour Millers' Association in conjunction with University College Dublin in the 1960s, '70s and early '80s is still paying off today. More wheat is grown now than ever before, total wheat production rising from 273,000 tons in 1980 to 883,000 tons in 2002. The flour-milling industry used a total of 260,000 tons in 2002 – 40 per cent of which was Irish wheat and the balance imported. However no new mills were built from 1935 until 1978, when Odlums erected one in Portarlington, and subsequently another in Cork in 1981–2. In many respects it was the capacity of Odlums to build these new plants, and historically their more favourable locations relative to population growth centres than their major competitors historically, that explains why its mills remain the survivors in the Republic. Andrews and Neill's in Belfast have survived as major players for the same reasons. These mills continue to provide the bulk of flour for the Irish market.

As in brewing, distilling, tobacco and the other branches of food processing, flour milling has been transformed since the mid-eighteenth century, when the industry relied on a large number of small producers. Many impressive ruins of old flour mills still survive in urban contexts and in far flung rural locations, dating back to the nineteenth century when the industry became more concentrated in larger and more technically sophisticated mills. Today only a few highly modern mills service most of the market, indicating that the Irish industry has made the necessary transition that has enabled it to compete on the international market. The Irish flour-milling industry now has a larger share of the Irish market for flour than it had at the beginning of the twentieth century. This book has provided some insight into the long history of an industry that has been obscured to a large degree from the mainstream of Irish industrial history. Yet, despite their concentration, flour milling and the food and drink sector have survived, and Ireland's agri-industries now compete globally. Many of Ireland's major staple industries at the beginning of the twentieth century, such as linen and shipbuilding, have passed away in the meantime, while large new industries such as electronics and pharmaceuticals have emerged, further transforming the social and economic landscape. This book has clearly demonstrated that the survival and development of flour milling in particular, and the food and drink industries in general, are critically important features of Ireland's social, economic and cultural history, and they have sadly been neglected by historians for far too long.[49]

Appendix

Presidents of Irish Flour Millers' Association, 1902–1989

1902–3 Charles J. Furlong	1932–3 Thomas D. Hallinan	1962–3 Henry G. Glynn
1903–4 Charles J. Furlong	1933–4 Thomas D. Hallinan	1963–4 J. Stanley Mosse
1904–5 J. Perry Goodbody	1934–5 Thomas D. Hallinan	1964–5 J. W. Macmullen
1905–6 William H. Going	1935–6 Thomas D. Hallinan	1965–6 D.C. Crowley
1906–7 Ebenezer Shackleton	1936–7 Thomas D. Hallinan	1966–7 G. Maurice Goodbody
1907–8 Charles A. Webb	1937–8 Thomas D. Hallinan	1967–8 Peter D. Odlum
1908–9 J. Ellis Goodbody	1938–9 Thomas D. Hallinan	1968–9 M.G. Shiels
1909–10 William Pilsworth	1939–40 Algernon A. Odlum	1969–70 W. Hastings Brown
1910–11 Charles S. Neill	1940–1 Algernon A. Odlum	1970–1 Peter L. Greenwood
1911–12 Joshua Fowler	1941–2 Pierce Higgins	1971–2 J.H. Scott
1912–13 Joshua Fowler	1942–3 Francis P. Hallinan	1972–3 J.H. Scott
1913–14 Edward Hallinan	1943–4 Francis P. Hallinan	1973–4 P.J. Murphy
1914–15 Edward Hallinan	1944–5 Francis P. Hallinan	1974–5 R.C. Loombe
1915–16 John Andrews	1945–6 William J. Pilsworth	1975–6 A.J. Fleming
1916–17 John Andrews	1946–7 Henry Golden	1976–7 Peter D. Odlum
1917–18 James P. Goodbody	1947–8 George Shackleton Jnr	1977–8 D.C. Crowey
1918–19 James P. Goodbody	1948–9 George Shackleton Jnr	1978–9 C.A. Odlum
1919–20 William E. Shackleton	1949–50 G. Maurice Goodbody	1979–80 G.W. Bull
1920–1 Ernest W. Andrews	1950–1 Edward A. Spratt	1980–1 M.G. Shiels
1921–2 Algernon A. Odlum	1951–2 David H. Brown	1981–2 C.A. Odlum
1922–3 William E. Shackleton	1952–3 Henry G. Glynn	1982–3 G.W. Bull
1923–4 Ebenezer Shackleton	1953–4 Peter D. Odlum	1983–4 F.H. Poff
1924–5 Reginald M. Goodbody	1954–5 H.P. Goodbody	1984–5 J. Furlong
1925–6 William R. Moore	1955–6 J. F. Mahony	1985–6 J. Furlong
1926–7 Gerald E. Goodbody	1956–7 A.G. Smith	1986–7 J. Furlong
1927–8 Gerald E. Goodbody	1957–8 W. Bryan Nichols	1987–8 N.D. Odlum
1928–9 William E. Shackleton	1958–9 W. Bryan Nichols	1988–9 N.D. Odlum
1929–30 Charles S. Neill	1959–60 George Shackleton	
1930–1 Charles S. Neil	1960–1 G. Maurice Goodbody	
1931–2 Thomas D. Hallinan	1961–2 Peter D. Odlum	

Note: A name-board listing all the presidents was displayed at the Association's offices and is now accommodated at Shackleton's mills, Lucan (2003). This mill of 1930s vintage was bought by Fingal Co. Council in 2000 (at the behest of the Industrial Heritage Association of Ireland), as part of their community heritage facilities.

Abbreviations

BPP	British Parliamentary Papers
CSO	Central Statistics Office
DATI	Department of Agriculture and Technical Instruction
DFHL	Dublin Friends Historical Library
EHR	*Economic History Review*
H. of C. Journal (Ire.)	*House of Commons Journal (Ireland)*
IAWS	Irish Agricultural Wholesale Society
IFMA	Irish Flour Millers' Association
IHAI	Industrial Heritage Association of Ireland
JCHAS	*Journal of the Cork Historical and Archaeological Society*
JLAHS	*Journal of the County Louth Archaeological and Historical Society*
JWHS	*Journal of the Wexford Historical Society*
JFHS	*Journal of the Friends Historical Society*
NABIM	National Association of British and Irish Millers
NAI	National Archives of Ireland
NLI	National Library of Ireland
Parl. Gaz.	*Parliamentary Gazeteer*
PDDE	Dáil Debates
PDSE	Seanad Debates
PRO	Public Record Office, London
PRONI	Public Record Office of Northern Ireland
ROD	Registry of Deeds, Dublin
TCD	Trinity College Dublin

Notes

1. ## The Development of Milling Technology in Ireland, *c.* 600-1875
   COLIN RYNNE

1. H.E. Wulff, *The Traditional Crafts of Persia* (London, 1966). J. Ryan, 'Rotary Querns', *Old Kilkenny Review*, 24 (1972), 68.
2. P. Joyce, *The Social History of Ancient Ireland*, vol. 2 (London, 1903), p. 346.
3. D. Ó Corráin, *Ireland before the Normans* (Dublin, 1972), p. 46.
4. P. Rahtz and D. Bullough, 'The Parts of the Anglo Saxon Mill' in *Anglo Saxon England*, vol. 6 (1977), pp. 15–39.
5. C. Rynne, 'The Introduction of the Vertical Waterwheel into Ireland: Some Recent Archaeological Evidence', *Medieval Archaeology*, 33 (1989), 21–31.
6. M. Monk, 'Post-Roman Drying Kilns and the Problem of Function: A Preliminary Statement' in D. Ó Corráin (ed.), *Irish Antiquity: Essays and Studies Presented to Prof. M.J. O'Kelly* (Cork, 1982), pp. 227–8.
7. E.M. Fahy, 'A Horizontal Mill at Mashanaglass, Co. Cork', *JCHAS*, 61 (1956), 13–57. C. Rynne, 'Some Observations on the Production of Flour and Meal in the Early Historic Period', *JCHAS*, 95 (1990), 20–9.
8. Rynne, 'The Introduction of the Vertical Waterwheel', (1989), 21–31; 'Milling in the Seventh Century: Europe's Earliest Tide Mills', *Archaeology Ireland*, 6, no. 2, (Summer, 1992), 22–4; 'Early Medieval Mill Penstocks from County Cork', *JCHAS*, 97 (1992), 54–68; T. McErlean and N. Crothers, 'The Early Medieval Tide Mills at Nendrum: An Interim Statement' in T. McErlean, R. McConkey and W. Forsythe (eds), *Strangford Lough: An Archaeological Survey of a Maritime Landscape* (Belfast, 2002), pp. 200–11.
9. M.G.L. Baillie, *Tree-Ring Dating and Archaeology* (London, 1982).
10. C. Rynne, 'Discussion' in R. Cleary, 'A Vertical-Wheeled Water-Mill at Ardcloyne, Co. Cork', *JCHAS*, 104 (1999), 51–6.
11. C. Rynne, 'The Craft of the Mill Wright in Early Medieval Munster' in M. Monk and J. Sheehan (eds), *Early Medieval Munster* (Cork, 1998), pp. 87–101.
12. C. Rynne, *Technological Change in Anglo-Norman Munster*, Barryscourt Lecture Series, Gandon Editions (Kinsale, 1998).
13. M. Moore, *Archaeological Inventory of County Meath* (Dublin, 1987).
14. J. Tierney and M. Hannon, 'Plant Remains' in M.F. Hurley, O.M.B. Scully and W. McCutcheon, *Late Viking Age and Medieval Waterford: Excavations 1986–1992* (Dublin, 1997), p. 892.
15. M. Walsh, 'A Watermill at Ballyine, Co. Limerick', *JCHAS*, 70 (1965), 14–25.
16. D.W. Crossley, *The Bewl Valley Ironworks, Kent, c. 1300–1730*, Royal Archaeological Institute Monographs (Leeds, 1975), fig. 9c; G.G. Astill, *A Medieval Industrial Complex and its Landscape: The Metalworking Watermills and Workshops of Bordesley Abbey*, CBA

research report 92 (York, 1993), pp. 214–16.

17. J. Lydon, 'The Mills at Ardee in 1304', *JLAHS*, 14, no. 4 (1980), 259–63.

18. P. MacCotter and K. Nicholls (eds), *The Pipe Roll of Cloyne* (Rotulis Pipae Clonensis), Cloyne Literary and Historical Society (Cork, 1996), p. 73.

19. R.J. Hunter, 'A Seventeenth-Century Mill in Tyrhugh', *Donegal Annual*, 9, no. 2 (1970), 238–40.

20. *The Pipe Roll of Cloyne*, p. 73.

21. Lydon, *art. cit.* p. 262.

22. R. Bennett and J. Elton, *A History of Cornmilling*, vol. 3 (London, 1900), p. 199.

23. J. Muendel, 'The Distribution of Mills in the Florentine Countryside During the Late Middle Ages' in J.A. Raftis (ed.), *Pathways to Medieval Peasants* (Toronto, 1981), pp. 83–115.

24. J. Muendel, 'The Horizontal Mills of Medieval Pistoia', *Technology and Culture*, 15 (1974), 194–225.

25. J.A. Claffey, 'Rindoon Windmill Tower' in H. Murtagh (ed.), *Irish Midland Studies: Essays in Commemoration of N.W. English* (Athlone, 1980), pp. 84–8.

26. A. O'Sullivan, 'Tacumshin Windmill – Its History and Mode of Operation', *JWHS*, 9 (1983–4), 66–73.

27. F. Hamond, 'The North Wind Doth Blow: Windmill Evolution in Ulster' in R. Schofield (ed.), *The History of Technology, Science and Society 1750–1914* (Jordanstown, 1989), pp. 134–50; 'Power Generation' in F.H.A. Aalen, K. Whelan and M. Stout (eds), *Atlas of the Irish Rural Landscape* (Cork, 1997), pp. 225–33.

28. Hamond (1997), pp. 225–33.

29. A. Calladine and J. Fricker, *East Cheshire Textile Mills*. Royal Commission on the Historical Monuments of England (London, 1993).

30. C. Smith, *The Ancient and Present State of the County and City of Cork*, vol. 1 (Cork, 1750, repr. 1815), p. 167; L.M. Cullen, 'Eighteenth-Century Flour Milling in Ireland', *Irish Economic and Social History Review*, 4 (1977), 10.

31. Cullen (1977), 11.

32. *Ibid.* p. 10.

33. M. Watts, *Water and Wind Power* (Princes Risborough, 2000), pp. 43–4.

34. Cullen (1977), 13. C. Elleson, *The Waters of the Boyne and the Blackwater* (Dublin, 1993).

35. A. Bielenberg, *Cork's Industrial Revolution 1780–1880: Development or Decline?* (Cork, 1991), p. 43.

36. C. Rynne, *The Industrial Archaeology of Cork City and its Environs* (Dublin, 1999), p. 89.

37. *Ibid.* p. 75.

38. J. Kemmy and L. Walsh, *Limerick in Old Picture Postcards* (Zaltbommel, 1997), p. 114.

39. H.D. Inglis, *Ireland in 1834: A Journey Throughout Ireland During the Spring, Summer and Autumn of 1834*, vol. 1 (London, 1834), p. 190.

40. National Library of Scotland; MS 19816, Henry Walker to John Rennie, 22 May 1814. I am indebted to Dr Andy Bielenberg for this reference.

41. CSO Cork; Agricultural Statistics (Ireland), 1891.

2. Eighteenth-Century Flour Milling in Ireland
   L.M. Cullen

1. S.D. Chapman, 'Fixed Capital Formation in the British Cotton Industry 1770–1815', *EHR*, 2nd series, 23 (1970), 237.

2. G. O'Brien (ed.), *Advertisements for Ireland, being a Description of the State of Ireland in the Reign of James I* (Dublin, 1923), p. 35.

3. R.C. Simington (ed.), *The Civil Survey A.D. 1654–1656* (Irish Manuscripts Commission, 1931–53), I, II, V, VIII, IX.

4. TCD, MS 1209, nos 22, 24, 33.

5. NLI, MS 392, p. 83: Thomas Dineley, 'Observations on a Voyage through the Kingdom of Ireland, 1680'. This sketch has been reproduced in L.M. Cullen, *Life in Ireland* (London, 1968), p. 63.

6. *Ibid.* p. 147 (reproduced in Cullen, *op. cit.* p. 52).

7. TCD, MS 1209, nos. 22, 24, 33.

8. Mr and Mrs S.C. Hall, *Ireland, its Scenery, Character etc.*, vol. 3 (London, 1843), p. 283.

9. Armagh Public Museum; Isaac Butler's journal (1744), f. 96.

10. *H. of C. Journals (Ire.)*, VIII, app. cccxxxix.

11. H. Dutton, *Statistical and Agricultural Survey of the County of Galway* (Dublin, 1824), p. 433. According to Dutton, the first flour mill in Galway was erected by a Mr Waddlesworth: 'he was opposed by all the bakers, and at length they burned his mill, and from the injuries and insults he received, was obliged to quit Galway'.

12. *H. of C. Journals (Ire.)*, VIII, p. 230.

13. *H. of C. Journals (Ire.)*, VII, p. 213.

14. 'The corn upon being unloaded, is hoisted through doors in the floors to the upper storey of the building, by a very simple contrivance, being worked by the water-wheel, and discharged into spacious granaries which hold 5000 barrels. From thence it is conveyed, during seven months of the year, to the kiln for drying, the mill containing two, which will dry 80 barrels in 24 hours. From the kiln it is hoisted again to the upper storey, from thence to a fanning machine for redressing, to get out dirt, soil, etc. And from thence, by a small sifting machine, into the hoppers, to be ground, and is again hoisted into the bolting mills, to be dressed into flour, different sorts of pollard and bran. In all which progress, the machinery is contrived to do the business with the least labour possible'. Young, *Tour in Ireland*, vol. 1 (London, 1780), p. 33.

15. H. Townsend, *A General and Statistical Survey of the County of Cork*, vol. 1 (Dublin, 1815), p. 30.

16. The bounties are described in K.H. Connell, *The Population of Ireland 1750–1845* (Oxford, 1950), pp. 270–1.

17. Details of bounty flour carried to Dublin for year ended 1 August 1759 and years ended 25 March 1762, 1763, 1764, 1765 in *H. of C. Journals (Ire.)*, VI, app. cclxxiv; VIII, app. xxxiii–xxxvi, ccxi–ccxii.

18. *H. of C. Journals (Ire.)*, VIII, app. cccxxxix. The data for individual mills are available

only from 1768. Also, apart from data for the year ended 1 January 1769, they are available only for years ending 24 June. Quantities on a county basis without differentiating between individual mills are also given for years ending 25 March.

19. Year ended 1 August 1759: *H. of C. Journals (Ire.)*, VI, app. cclxxiv.

20. *Ibid.* VIII, app. cccxxxix.

21. *Ibid.* VII, p. 213.

22. *Ibid.* VI, app. cclxxiv; VIII, app. xxxii–xxxvi, ccxi–ccxiii. No figures are available for the interval from 1 August 1759 to 25 March 1761.

23. *Dublin Newsletter, 14–18 March, 1737–8.*

24. C. Smith, *The Ancient and Present State of the County of Cork*, vol. 1 (Dublin, 1750), p. 167. A letter in the *Hibernian Chronicle* of 3 March 1774 suggests that a Cork man was the first to build a flour mill in the Kingdom. I am indebted to Prof. David Dickson for these references and for that in the preceding footnote.

25. NAI, Prim Collection, William Colles to Rt. Hon. Thomas Carter, Kilkenny, 14 October, 1747 (copy).

26. The claim that a Cork man, reported to have built the first flour mill, had applied to parliament for aid is not borne out in the Commons' *Journals*, as the first reference to Cork mills is in a petition from the Mayor and Common Council of Cork read on 9 December 1773 (IX, p. 63).

27. *H. of C. Journals (Ire.)*, VII, app. lviii. See also *ibid.* VII, p. 24, app. ccxxxix; VIII, p. 230. Judged by the output capacity claimed for the mill, it was very small compared with the great mill at Slane erected within a few years whose through-put capacity was said to be 120 barrels a day (Young, *Tour in Ireland*, vol. I, p. 33). Naul village is in Co. Dublin; the mill was on the Meath bank of the stream.

28. Details of supply in 1761 from *H. of C. Journals (Ire.)*, VII; and from George III, cap. 1, section 14. None of the many other mills that submitted claims in support of financial assistance in the 1760s seems to have succeeded in its object, though parliamentary committees favoured such assistance. Rowley Heyland's mill in Co. Antrim is said to have received a grant of £200 (S. Andrews, *Nine Generations, History of the Andrews family, Millers of Comber* [Belfast, 1958], p. 40), but details of supply in the Commons' *Journals* or in the statutes seem to afford no evidence of a direct grant.

29. M. Leadbetter, *Leadbetter Papers*, vol. 1 (London, 1862), p. 110, p. 111 note.

30. *H. of C. Journals (Ire.)*, VIII, pp. 30–1.

31. *Ibid.* pp. 29–30.

32. *Ibid.* pp. 36–7.

33. *Ibid.* p. 37.

34. *Ibid.* p. 37. Patterson's petition sets out at some length the processes in a flour mill.

35. *Ibid.* p. 27. See also *ibid.* VII, p. 200, app. ccli–cclii.

36. Andrews, *op. cit.* pp. 40–4. In 1772 the Andrews opened a new flour mill (*Ibid.* pp. 46–7).

37. *H. of C. Journals (Ire.)*, VIII, p. 30. See also pp. 113–4.

38. Date quoted by Young, *op. cit.* vol. 1, p. 33. This is confirmed by details in NLI, MS

9589, Slane wheat book, where wheat purchases go back to September 1766 but only become large in 1767.

39. *H. of C. Journals (Ire.)*, VIII, p. 230.

40. NLI, MS 10,273, 'The state of the Slane Co., 1 January 1773'.

41. *H. of C. Journals (Ire.)*, VIII, app. cccxxxix.

42. *Ibid.* app. cccxl.

43. *Ibid.* app. xxxiv, ccclvi–ccclvii.

44. Young, *op. cit.* vol. I, p. 324; *H. of C. Journals (Ire.)*, VIII, app. ccccxliv.

45. *Ibid.* IX, p. 102.

46. *Ibid.* IX, p. 63.

47. *Ibid.* VIII, app. ccccxliii–ccccxliv.

48. *Ibid.* XIV, app. cclxxxviii–ccxci. The heading of the list seems to suggest that it includes all the flour mills in Ireland. It is in fact a list of mills which consigned flour to Dublin under bounty. Most flour mills, especially those adjacent to urban centres, had a local market. The fact that the bounty on flour was higher than the costs of transport meant that carriage to Dublin was an attractive speculative proposition for most mills, and the list is likely to be comprehensive of nearly all mills in Ireland. This is less likely to be true of the north, where there were relatively fewer flour mills than in the rest of the island. In addition, the list seems to have a few omissions even in the case of mills from which bounty flour was consigned to Dublin.

49. *Ibid.* VIII, app. cccclviii–lix; XII, app. ccclxxxi–ccclxxxiii.

50. Leadbetter, *op. cit.* vol. I, p. 206.

51. Dutton, *op. cit.* p. 432.

52. Dutton, *loc. cit.*

53. *H. of C. Journals (Ire.)*, XIV, app. cclxxxviii–ccxci.

54. Hall, *op. cit.* vol. I, pp. 404–7.

55. NAI, Valuation Office Collection, House Book OL 50010 – parish of Cloydagh, barony of Idronewest, Co. Carlow. The house book has a sketch of the mills with the dimensions of the three main structures and offices. The layout can be seen also in the Ordnance Survey – Carlow, sheet 12, surveyed 1839.

56. The oatmeal mill is derelict, although the walls are well preserved, suggesting that its abandonment is comparatively recent. Some mill shafting is still within the mill. Mr O'Brien of Messrs Kennedy O'Brien & Sons (Milford) Ltd told me that an early turbine installed in this mill supplied current for the town of Carlow. The maltings and offices constituted in the 1970s the tannery of O'Brien & Sons.

57. Dutton, *op. cit.* pp. 432–3. The Nuns Island mills referred to by Dutton can be identified in the background of Bartlett's view up the Corrib, and in modified form the structures still survive (see illustration p. 50).

58. The Anner Mills, belonging to the Grubb family, were erected in 1765 (Olive C. Goodbody, *Guide to Irish Quaker Records, 1654–1860* [I.M.C., 1967], p. 87). See also W.P. Burke, *History of Clonmel* (Waterford, 1907), pp. 129–31.

59. A. Marmion, *The Ancient and Modern History of the Maritime Ports of Ireland* (London,

1855), p. 559. See also Burke, *op. cit.* pp. 129–31, 182–84.

60. Marmion, *op. cit.* p. 560.

61. Young, *op. cit.* vol. I, p. 33.

62. In the sketch in the Halls' *Ireland, its Scenery, Character etc.*, I, p. 405, the flour mill seems to be a storey higher than the maltings. It would therefore have been a six-storey mill, a likelihood confirmed by the fact that the oatmeal mill, which still stands in ruins beside the bridge across the river Barrow, is a six-storey structure. The mill's proportions are from NAI, Valuation Office Collection, House Book OL 50010.

63. *H. of C. Journals (Ire.)*, XI, pp. 51–2.

64. *Walker's Hibernian Magazine*, 1788, 279.

65. See note 1.

66. PRONI, Foster Papers, D/562/5910B. I am indebted to Prof. David Dickson for this reference. A modified structure still stood in the late 1960s as part of the premises of Waterproofs Ltd, Glansilagh Mills, Glanmire.

67. *H. of C. Journals (Ire.)*, VIII, pp. 30–1.

68. *Ibid.* p. 37.

69. *Ibid.* p. 30.

70. *Ibid.* VII, pp. 200, 229–30; VIII, p. 27.

71. *Ibid.* IX, p. 102.

72. Young, *op. cit.* vol. I, p. 324. See also Burke, *op. cit.* pp. 130–1, 183–4.

73. Dutton, *op. cit.* p. 433.

74. Chapman, *op. cit.* 238–41.

75. Marketing methods in milling can be studied from *H. of C. Journals (Ire.)*, IX, app. cccxviii–cccxxv; and from NLI Shaw MSS.

76. Historical Library of the Society of Friends, 6 Eustace Street, Dublin, Deeds and other legal documents, no. 87, Policy from Royal Exchange Assurance Co., no. 94090, Dublin, 1 August 1788.

77. *H. of C. Journals (Ire.)*, VIII, pp. 27, 30.

78. *Ibid.* p. 31.

79. *Ibid.* p. 25.

80. NLI, MS 10,273, 'The State of the Slane Co. 1 January, 1773'.

81. NLI, MS 9577.

82. *H. of C. Journals (Ire.)*, VIII, app. ccccxliii–ccccxliv.

83. Jefferys, landlord of Blarney, is an apposite example, investing heavily in the erection of industrial structures but letting them to others. His investments included 'a large bolting mill, just finished; and let for £132 a year' (Young, *op. cit.* vol. I, pp. 259–61). At Newtownmountkennedy in 1801 there was an 'excellent flour and bolting mill, built by lord Rossmore' (R. Fraser, *General View of the Agriculture ... of the County Wicklow* [Dublin, 1801], p. 265). The letting of a mill, even where the owner was not a landlord, was quite common. At Ballitore, for instance, the Shackletons leased their mill for much of the time (*Leadbetter Papers*, vol. I, pp. 80–1, 187–8). Their new bolting mill, erected in 1792, was leased the following year to 'Peter Delany, the son of a rich

neighbouring farmer' (*ibid.* p. 206).

84. ROD, 223/581/149353; 223/582/149354; 243/76/158559.

85. *Ibid.* 234/51/151053, Memorial of an Indenture dated 18 May 1764. The actual amount put up by each partner was £1250 according to various references in NLI, MS 10,273.

86. NLI, MS 10,273.

87. The amount owing had been reduced to £10,000 in the early 1780s. See a very interesting note in Jebb's hand relating to the financial and general situation of the mill, undated but from the early 1780s in MS 10,273.

88. NLI, Shaw MSS; L.M. Cullen, *Anglo-Irish Trade, 1660–1800* (Manchester, 1968), p. 203.

89. One of the partners in the Belmont mill was Thomas L'Estrange, 'late a merchant of Dublin' (*H. of C. Journals [Ire.]*, IX, p. 102).

90. R.B. McDowell, 'The Personnel of the Dublin Society of United Irishmen, 1791–4', *Irish Historical Studies*, 2 (1940–1), 36.

91. P. Lynch and J. Vaizey, *Guinness's Brewery in the Irish Economy 1759–1876* (Cambridge, 1960), pp. 72, 120–2. The cost of the mill in 1789 and 1790 had been between £4000 and £5000. It required a working capital of about £3000.

92. There is still a mill building on the site, now disused. I am indebted to the late Dr Raymond G. Cross of Brackenstown House for information and assistance.

93. J. Archer, *Statistical Survey of County of Dublin* (Dublin, 1801), pp. 203–7.

94. Irish Parliamentary Register, vol. 2, p. 347.

95. BPP, 1837–8, XXXV, *Second Report of the Commissioners appointed to consider and recommend a General System of Railways for Ireland*, pp. 112–3.

96. *H. of C. Journals (Ire.)*, VIII, p. 25.

97. *Ibid.* p. 230.

98. Young, *op. cit.* vol. 1, p. 33.

99. According to the 1843 valuation of the Milford flour mill, it was capable of grinding 150,000 barrels of wheat a year, but did not in practice grind at the time of the survey more than 50,000 barrels. The Slane mill could grind 120 barrels of wheat a day. In a year of 300 working days, its capacity would therefore amount to only 36,000 barrels. In fact, as the mill records show, it milled less than 20,000 barrels a year.

100. NAI, Valuation Office Collection, House Book OL 50010.

101. NLI, MS 10,273, 'Estimate of the Cost of Guard Lock at Slane Bridge'.

102. NAI, Prerogative Grant Book 1748–51, f. 231, 27 November 1751.

103. ROD, 223/581/149353; 234/51/151053.

104. *H. of C. Journals (Ire.)*, VIII, p. 25.

105. *Ibid.* VIII, pp. 25, 230.

106. NLI, MS 9521, Letter-book, 1780–98, 15 March 1793.

107. In the early nineteenth century apparently, Jebb determined to draw out of his Irish investment. Some lands on the north side of the Boyne of which Jebb held a lease were conveyed to Robert Colello in 1803 (ROD, 785/121/531056) – presumably the Robert Colello who in or around 1781 had established a cotton manufactory at Slane, *H. of C. Journals (Ire.)*, XI, pp. 44, 314. In 1810 Jebb sold his one-third share in

the mill to his partners (NLI, MS 10,273). In April of the same year he sublet his interest in land adjoining the mill to Blayney Balfour, and in 1823 sold for a capital payment his income from the subletting (ROD, 785/121/531056). David Jebb's marriage settlement is dated October 1773 (NAI; M5603[5], 16 October 1773). In 1786 his sons John and Richard, entered as lives in a lease, were aged two years, and six months respectively (lease quoted in ROD, 785/121/531056). According to his will – dated in 1826 – his surviving children were David, William, Susanna, Letitia, John and Richard. (NAI, T. 13,422). Among the property that the first four inherited was some land in Queen's County from his wife's settlement, the occasion later in the century of litigation. At the time of his will, David Jebb lived at Sanreme Lodge in the city of Worcester.

108. PRO, Colchester Papers, MS 30/9/1 pt. 1/3, 6 November 1801. I am indebted to Dr Anthony Malcomson for this reference.

109. There are several letters in the Foster papers in PRONI from Jebb.

110. Archer, *op. cit.* pp. 203–4.

111. BPP, 1837–8, XXXV, *Report of the Railway Commissioners*, pp. 112–3.

112. On the decay of Clonmel and of its flour mills, 'nearly all idle', see C.J. Kickham, *Knocknagow* (Dublin, 1952), pp. 619–20.

3. A Survey of Irish Flour Milling 1801–1922
ANDY BIELENBERG

1. By 1835, there were 1882 corn mills in operation in Ireland according to the Railway Commissioners, although this is an underestimate since it excludes Dublin city and counties Limerick and Clare. Hogg's book lists over 2100, which is also almost certainly an underestimate; his figure for the province of Ulster (over 700) can be compared to Gribbon's estimate of 790, while his estimate of Co. Kilkenny of 116 can be compared to Gulliver and Silvermann's count of 129 based on Griffith's *Valuation*, and a scan of Griffith's for Co. Cork, would raise Hogg's estimate of only 128 grain mills in the county to well over 200. Assuming some upward correction is needed in all provinces, there were probably in the region of 2500 grain mills operating in Ireland between the mid-1830s and the mid-1850s, of which roughly less than a sixth were flour mills (which on average had higher output, productivity and value). BPP, 1837–8, XXXV, *Report of the Railway Commissioners*, app. B. no. 14, p. 97. W. Hogg, *The Millers and the Mills of Ireland of about 1850* (Dublin, 1997). M. Silverman and P.H. Gulliver, *In the Valley of the Nore* (Dublin, 1986), p. 61. H. Gribbon, *The History of Waterpower in Ulster* (New York, 1969), p. 44. NAI, Griffith's *Valuation*. Millbooks are a useful source when complete, but they need to be interpreted with care since they are very incomplete in some counties and non-existent in others.

2. BPP, 1912–13, CIX, First Census of Production (UK), p. 492. Agricultural Statistics Ireland (1906).

3. W. McCutcheon, 'The Corn Mill in Ulster', *Ulster Folklife*, 15 (1970). J. Burls (ed.), *Nine Generations: A History of the Andrews Family, Millers of Comber* (Liverpool, 1958).

W. Scott, *A Hundred Years A Milling* (Dundalk, 1951). R. Green, 'The History of the Belfast Grain Trade', *Belfast Natural History Society Proceedings*, 7 (1967). Also see Gribbon (1969), which contains a chapter on grain milling. For a survey of Cork city and its hinterland see chapter 5 in A. Bielenberg, *Cork's Industrial Revolution* (Cork, 1991).

4. K. Connell, *The Population of Ireland 1750–1845* (Oxford, 1950), pp. 86–120. K. Connell, 'The Colonization of Wasteland in Ireland, 1780–1845', *Economic History Review*, 3 (1950), 44–52.

5. C. Ó Gráda, 'Poverty, Population and Agriculture 1801–45', in W. Vaughan (ed.), *A New History of Ireland: 1801–1870*, vol. 5 (Oxford, 1989), p. 130.

6. E. Wakefield, *An Account of Ireland*, vol. 1 (London, 1812), pp. 363–416, 746.

7. C. Ó Gráda, 'Industry and Communications 1801–45' in Vaughan (ed.), (1989), p. 146. P.M.A. Bourke, 'The Irish Grain Trade 1839–48', *Irish Historical Studies*, 20 (1976–7), 159.

8. BPP, 1836, VIII, *Second Report on Agriculture*, p. 81, Q. 6003–4, 6008–9. It was in this period of expansion (around 1834) that William Odlum first entered the flour milling business of his uncle, William Kelly at Meelick; the Odlum family name was to become the most enduring in the southern industry.

9. BPP, 1837, XXX, *Report of the Railway Commisioners*. G.L. Smyth, *Ireland, Historical and Statistical*, vol. 3 (London, 1849), pp. 306–10. McCutcheon's survey of the Ulster grain-milling industry concludes that many were rebuilt or expanded between 1780 and 1830, incorporating improved waterwheels and internal machinery. McCutcheon (1970), p. 73.

10. BPP, 1836, VIII, *Third Report on Agriculture*, p. 286, Q. 14781.

11. For Indian Corn see BPP, 1852–3, XCIX, *Grain and Flour Imported into Ireland*. For wheat see appendix. On 30 April 1847, McAdam, the Belfast iron-founder, noted in his diary that distress had increased their trade 'as it has caused a demand for machinery to grind Indian corn which is imported now in large quantities to feed the poor.' PRONI, D/2930/7/6, Diary of James McAdam; entry 30 April 1847.

12. Griffith's *General Valuation of Rateable Property in Ireland*, Borough of Cork (Dublin, 1852). C. Rynne, *The Industrial Archaeology of Cork City and its Environs* (Dublin, 1999), pp. 88, 92.

13. A. Marmion, *History of the Maritime Ports of Ireland* (London, 1860), p. 460. Andrews in Comber were 'still making a fair profit grinding wheat' by 1847, in which year they also set up rollers for Indian corn; see Burls (1958), pp. 140–1.

14. M. Crawford, 'Diet and the Labouring Classes in the Nineteenth Century', *Saothar*, vol. 15 (1990), p. 88.

15. PRONI, D/1854/4/19, Croker to Earl of Annesley (1803): Letter re. corn and flour trade in Dublin. In 1790, eighty-two flour mills from all over Ireland were listed sending flour to Dublin. *H. of C. Journals (Ire.)*, XIV, 'Account of Number of Corn Mills at Present in Ireland'.

16. L. Clarkson and M. Crawford, 'Dietary Directions: A Topographical Survey of Irish Diet, 1836', in R. Mitchison and P. Roebuck (eds), *Economy and Society in Scotland and*

Ireland 1500–1939 (Edinburgh, 1989), pp. 171–92.

17. L. Clarkson and M. Crawford, *Feast or Famine: A History of Food and Nutrition in Ireland 1500–1920* (Oxford, 2001), pp. 34, 41, 57, 67–70, 76, 80, 83. They have also demonstrated that for upper- and middle-class families expenditure on cereal consumption (including flour and wheat meal) was considerable after the 1750s.

18. Collins has suggested a more conservative figure of 88 per cent for England and Wales in 1850 and 44 per cent for Scotland in the same year, and going back in time he tentatively suggests 66 per cent for England and Wales at the beginning of the nineteenth century and 10 per cent for Scotland. E. Collins, 'Dietary Change and Cereal Consumption in Britain in the Nineteenth Century', *Agricultural History Review*, 29 (1975), 110, 114.

19. This is assuming a harvest of 6,750,000 cwt after 10 per cent has been deducted for seed, stock feed, waste, etc., then deducting net wheat exports of 249,000 cwt leaving 6,501,000 cwt, which with an extraction rate of 80 per cent produces 5,201,000 cwt of flour from which 636,000 cwt deducted for net flour exports, leaving Irish flour consumption at 4,565,000 cwt (or 62 lbs per capita). P. Solar, 'The Great Famine Was No Ordinary Subsistence Crisis' in M. Crawford (ed.), *Famine: The Irish Experience 900–1900* (Edinburgh, 1989), pp. 132–3. C. Ó Gráda, 'Irish Agricultural Output Before and After the Famine', *Journal of European Economic History*, 13 (1984), 149–65.

20. Census (1831). This only records males aged twenty or more, which accounts for most bakers. L. Clarkson, M. Crawford and M. Litvack, *Occupations of Ireland 1841* (Belfast, 1995).

21. J. Magee, *Bernard Hughes of Belfast 1808–1878* (Belfast, 2001), pp. 1–44. It was also in this period (1823) that Patrick Boland first established a bakery in Dublin on Capel Street.

22. L. Cullen, *The Emergence of Modern Ireland 1600–1900* (London, 1981), pp. 144, 150.

23. Clarkson and Crawford (1989), p. 189; and (2001), pp. 69–70, 83. BPP, 1837–8, XXXV, *Second Report of the Railway Commissioners*, app. B, p. 26.

24. NLI, MS 5219, Mill account book of Mullins, Thomastown, Co. Kilkenny, 1815–62. MS 12150, Mill records in Wilson Slator Papers for 1839–46.

25. NLI, MS 10379, MS 10273, Townley Hall Papers (records relating to Slane Flour Mills).

26. BPP, 1837–8, XXXV, *Second Report of the Railway Commissioners*, app. B, p. 26.

27. B. Mahon, *Land of Milk and Honey: the Story of Traditional Irish Food* (Cork, 1998), pp. 7, 74. E. Estyn Evans, *Irish Folk Ways* (London, 1957), pp. 77–80. C. O'Danachair, 'Bread', *Ulster Folklife*, 4 (1958).

28. Solar (1989), p. 123.

29. Ó Gráda (1984), pp. 149–65. Three-fifths of oatmeal in Ó Gráda's estimate was consumed on farms, and this would have been milled locally.

30. Bourke (1976–7), p. 165.

31. C. Ó Gráda, *Ireland Before and After the Famine* (Manchester, 1988), p. 32.

32. P. Solar, 'The Agricultural Trade of the Port of Waterford 1809–1909' in W. Nolan

and P. Power (eds), *Waterford: History and Society* (Dublin, 1992), pp. 506, 511, 514.

33. Bielenberg (1991), pp. 41–9. Cullen (1977), p. 24.

34. W. Burke, *History of Clonmel* (Clonmel, 1907), pp. 183–4. Also see Cullen's essay in this volume.

35. BPP, 1884–5, IX, *Select Committee on Industries (Ireland, 1885)* Q. 7331.

36. G. Bowie, 'Corn Drying Kilns, Meal Milling and Flour in Ireland', *Ulster folklife*, 17 (1979), 12.

37. Green (1967), p. 42. PRONI, D/1905/2/185a/1b records that the the Steam Flour Mill in Steam Lane, Donegal Quay, Belfast in 1854 belonged to Robert Austen, flour miller and baker who was declared bankrupt, and the mills were sold to John Milford.

38. Magee (2001), pp. 226–31. Also see Jones's essay in this volume.

39. NAI, DUB 10, 1/1, Memorandum of Association of Dublin North City Milling Co. Ltd DUB 10, 2/4 Shareholders Minutebook 1874–1945.

40. J. Tann and G. Jones, 'Technology and Transformation: The Diffusion of the Roller Mill in the British Flour Milling Industry 1870–1907', *Technology and Culture*, 37, no. 1 (1996), 53. *The Miller*, 2 December 1889, 5 February 1894.

41. Cork Archives; Hall Collection B 501/55/5, Hall's outgoing letter-book 1849–50, Hall to Kingsford 21 July 1849, Hall to Sargent 23 October 1849.

42. Cork Archives; Hall Collection B 501/55/6, Letter-book 1850–1, Hall to Pollans Ferguson 22 May 1850. According to Rynne (1999), pp. 89–91, most of the flour mills in the city and its immediate hinterland already had auxiliary steam engines by the end of the 1840s.

43. Cork Archives; Hall Collection B 37/87, Cargo Ledger 1866–73 and 1874–6.

44. McCutcheon (1970), p. 76. Solar (1987), pp. 233–4.

45. R. Green, 'Industrial Decline in the Nineteenth Century', in L. Cullen (ed.), *The Formation of the Irish Economy* (Cork, 1969), p. 100.

46. R. Perren, 'Structural Change and Market Growth in the Food Industry: Flour Milling in Britain, Europe, and America, 1850–1914', *Economic History Review*, 43 (1990), 423–4.

47. BPP, 1884–5, IX, *Select Committee on Industries (Ireland, 1885)*, Q. 342, Q 2245–2252, Q. 5518, Q. 6612, Q. 7379, Q. 9243. For the poor condition of a number of Galway mills in 1880, see PRO Kew; T 1/17314, and the more prosperous state of flour milling in Galway on the eve of the Famine see Marmion (1860), p. 460.

48. *The Miller*, 7 May 1883, 7 April 1884.

49. P. Solar, 'Growth and Distribution in Irish Agriculture Before the Famine' (Unpublished PhD, Stanford, 1987). DATI trade figures.

50. W.L. Micks, *An Account of the Congested Districts Board for Ireland* (Dublin, 1925), app. 3.

51. NLI, MS 10380 (3), Townley Hall Papers, Lamont to Balfour, 7 July 1845.

52. *Thom's Directory of Manufacturers and Shippers of Ireland* (Dublin, 1908), p. 440.

53. *The Miller*, 4 February 1878, 4 December 1893. Bielenberg (1991), p. 47. Scott (1951), p. 153.

54. Bielenberg (1991), p. 47. BPP, 1884–5, IX, *Select Committee on Industries (Ireland, 1885)*,

Q. 5641, Q. 7353. Green (1967), p. 43. James Neill Ltd was also remodelled for roller milling in the 1880s.

55. Burls (1958), pp. 159–66. *Milling*, 16 December 1933. The firm also innovated and benefited from advances in bleaching flour, which reduced American competition.

56. However, after the turn of the century, flour milling in the port began to recover and expand down to 1910, falling off a little before rising to a similar level again in 1920. Green (1967), pp. 41–4.

57. *The Miller*, 4 December 1893, 5 February 1894. William Stringer (of Black Lion, Co. Carlow) had been in charge of Shackleton's mill in Carlow when it was converted, ultimately becoming one of the major engineers and innovators in Simon's service in England. Simon's equipment increasingly dominated the Irish milling industry in the following decades. By 1936, Simon Ltd claimed that over 75 per cent of the flour produced in the Irish Free State was produced by Simon plants: *Milling*, 25 April 1936.

58. Tann and Jones (1996), pp. 64–5.

59. Cork Archives; Hall Collection, B. 501, private letter-book 1874–98, Halls to Anderson Cooper 16 March 1886.

60. Cork Archives; Hall Collection, Private letter-book 1887–1910; Hall to Barlow 14 March 1893. This was one of a few years when the company turned in a loss, see B. 501 Profit and Loss Account. Hall's dominated the Waterford grain trade, from where corn could be forwarded to mills in counties Waterford, Carlow and Kilkenny.

61. Cork Archives; Hall Collection, B 501/85/1, Yearly Summary Book 1901–12, and List of Shareholders 1901. The nominal capital of the company remained low (at £226,000) given its huge turnover. Other than the extensive Hall family interest, there were a number of millers (usually customers) on the shareholders' register.

62. *Irish Free State Census of Industrial Production* (1926 and 1929), (Dublin, Stationary Office, 1933), p. 47.

63. Bielenberg (1991), pp. 47–9. *Cork's Past and Present: A Handbook for the Irish Convention on its Visit to Cork* (Cork, 1917), pp. 48–9.

64. *Milling*, 17 December 1910. *Cork's Past and Present* (1917), p. 49. Notes on the Hallinan family from Edward Hallinan.

65. Perren (1990), p. 433.

66. NAI, LIM 2 Croom Mills and CL 4, Glynn & Sons, Kilrush. Glynn was also manager/owner of a steamship company trading between Limerick and Kilrush, and as such gained preferential rates with the Great Southern and Western Railway Company on all goods, including grain, passing between Dublin and Limerick (in return for confining his trade to the GSWR). Glynn could get grain for 3s. a ton from Dublin to Limerick, while Bannatyne paid 9s. a ton, which was deemed by the court to be undue preference. T.H. Maxwell, *The Irish Digest 1894–1918* (Dublin, 1921), p. 2160.

67. NAI, LIM 21 Deed Box no. 4, O'Mara v. Bannatyne (statement of defence 1886).

68. Russell's ground over £409,000 worth of wheat in the year between August 1921–August 1922, and over £140,000 worth of maize. Both these Limerick concerns

linked well with their jute factory (which made sacks) at Clara and their milling interests there, which could be supplied with grain from Limerick. NAI, LIM 21, Rank's Deed Boxes, no. 1 and 4. *Stratten's Dublin, Cork and the South of Ireland* (London, 1892), p. 288. D.B. Quinn, 'Clara: A Midland Industrial Town 1900–1923', in W. Nolan and T.P. O'Neill (eds), *Offaly: History and Society* (Dublin, 1998).

69. *Milling*, April 25 1936.

70. NAI, LIM 21, Deed Box no. 1, Rank's Collection, Bannatyne's Minutebook 1894–.

71. NAI, DUB 115, Prospectus Johnston, Mooney & O'Brien Ltd, Minutebook 1890–1956.

72. *Irish Builder*, 1 January 1888 (supplement). NAI, DUB 115, Johnston, Mooney & O'Brien, Minutebook 1890–1956, contains Bolands' Prospectus. DUB 69, Bolands' Secretary Dept. Abstract Account, Ringsend Rd Mills 1889–. This shows more sacks of flour produced in the mills than were used in their three bakeries.

73. Burls (1958), p. 162.

74. *Free State Farmer*, December 1928.

75. NAI, OFF 9/3/17, Robert Perry & Co. letter-book 1892–4. NAI, KLD 8/2/1, Ledger Manor Mills Maynooth, 1854–66, which also undertook the production of oatmeal, Indian meal and flour. In addition to a local trade, it was selling to customers in the greater Dublin area, Carlow and Kilkenny.

76. Silverman and Gulliver (1986), pp. 76–8. Some firms, like Mosse Ltd at Bennettsbridge, Co. Kilkenny, survived almost entirely on local trade even after independence.

77. NAI, WICK 3/2, notebook, 1 August 1867. WICK 3/5, Wheat Purchase Book. *Milling*, 25 April 1936.

78. NAI, DUB 128/B/2/1, 1904 AGM Irish Flour Millers' Association, p. 7. Scott (1951), p. 160.

79. NAI, DUB 128/b/2/7, Irish Flour Millers' Association; and 128a/4/2/1, Odlum and Pemberton's Leinster Steam and Water Roller Mills, Irish wheat book 1881–1920. Also see NAI, Hoey and Denning Box 38 (1a-37–38).

80. *Milling*, 25 April 1936, 43, 54. Kennedy's had six Dublin bakeries, *Milling*, 25 October 1924. NAI, D/2448, Dock Milling Co. In 1923, the company was valued at £24,606.

81. For some valuable insights into these networks among Quaker milling families see Harrison's contribution to this volume.

82. Cork Archives; Hall Collection, B. 37, Yearly Summary, 1901–12.

83. Cork Archives; Hall Collection, private letter-book, 1910–17, letters dated 7 October 1910 and 18 December 1913.

84. K. Laffin, 'A South Kilkenny Mill', *Decies*, no. 4 (1977), 14. Silverman and Gulliver (1986), p. 78.

85. *Application for a Tariff on Flour*, Tariff Commission, R36/3 (Dublin, 1923). *Prices Commission Report on Wheaten Flour* (Dublin, 1934). *Milling*, 25 October 1924. *Irish Trade Journal*, April 1926. A.J.H. Latham and L. Neal, 'The International Market in Rice and Wheat 1868–1914', *Economic History Review*, 36 (1983), 274. M. Daly, *Industrial Development and Irish National Identity* (Syracuse, 1992), p. 44.

86. Those who assume Ireland had an extremely limited wheat-eating population include B. Thomas, 'Food Supply in the United Kingdom During the Industrial Revolution', in J. Mokyr (ed.), *The Economics of the Industrial Revolution* (London, 1985). S. Fairlie, 'The Corn Laws and British Wheat Production 1829–76', *Economic History Review*, 22, no. 1 (1969). Thomas (p. 140) cites average annual wheat production for 1851–5 for Ireland at 4,532,000 cwt as an indicator of wheat consumption. This does not take into account net imports of wheat, which averaged 3,122,000 in these years, and the higher level of native wheat production in the pre-Famine era.

87. McCutcheon (1970), p. 75.

88. *Ibid.*

89. G. O'Brien, *Economic History of Ireland from the Union to the Famine* (London, 1921), p. 206.

90. J. Mokyr, *Why Ireland Starved* (London, 1983), p. 14.

91. J. Swift, *History of the Dublin Bakers* (Dublin, 1949), pp. 226–7.

92. H. Gribbon, 'Economic and Social History 1850–1921', in W. Vaughan (ed.), *A New History of Ireland*, vol. 6 (Oxford, 1996), p. 292.

93. Fairlie (1969), p. 102.

94. C. Knick Harley, 'Transportation, the World Wheat Trade, and the Kuznets Cycle, 1850–1913', *Explorations in Economic History*, 17 (1980), 219.

95. E. Riordan, *Modern Irish Trade and Industry* (London, 1920), pp. 61, 88–92.

96. *The Board of Trade Journal*, 2 February 1928 (Preliminary Reports of the Third Census of Production, 1924, no. 2, grain milling).

97. This rough estimate is achieved by adding the 1924 figure for the 6 counties of Northern Ireland (see note 96) to the 1926 figure for the 26 counties. *Irish Free State Census of Industrial Production 1926 and 1929* (Dublin, 1933), p. 38. BPP, 1912–13, CIX, *First Census of Production* (UK).

98. E. O'Malley, 'The Decline of Irish Industry in the Nineteenth Century', *The Economic and Social Review*, 13 (1981).

4. Irish Quakers in Flour Milling

RICHARD S. HARRISON

1. A. Raistrick, *Quakers in Science and Industry* (Newton Abbott, 1968). W.H. Crawford, 'Drapers in the Early Ulster Linen Industry' in L.M. Cullen and P. Butel (eds), *Négoce et Industrie en France aux XVIIIe et XIXe siècles* (Paris, 1980), pp. 113–9. For Thomas Phelps, check under Wilcocks Phelps, in R.S. Harrison, *A Biographical Dictionary of Irish Quakers* (Dublin, 1997).

2. L.M. Cullen, 'Eighteenth-Century Flour Milling in Ireland' in *Irish Economic and Social History*, 4 (1977), 21.

3. *H. of C. Journals (Ire.)* 1789–90, XIII, app. cclviii–cclx and cclxi–cclxii.

4. See for example, ROD, 654/457/449/250, Deed of Release between Samuel Watson Fayle and John Boardman Fayle of Waterford, and Richard and Elizabeth Davis of

Waterford and their daughter Elizabeth Davis, 15–16 September 1812. This deed formed part of a marriage settlement and involved a demise of Thomas Fayle's Strang's Mill, Kilkenny, at a rent charge of £200 per annum.

5. John Barcroft Haughton was originally from Carlow. His brother Benjamin Haughton was an exporter of bay-yarn. See Harrison (1997), p. 61, under Benjamin Haughton.

6. ROD, 590/495/403/286, Marriage Settlement, Richard Grubb to Susanna Haughton (involving Richard Grubb of Clogheen, John B. Haughton and Susanna Haughton, Benjamin Haughton and J. Pike Haughton Grubb), 18 September 1807.

7. ROD, 610/78/416/292, Marriage Settlement, Archibald Christy Shaw and Helena Haughton, 8 March 1809. Such settlements brought in respected relatives or Friends who would guarantee the arrangements. In this settlement, James Pike Haughton oversaw for the Haughtons and, for Shaw, it was James Nicholson Richardson of Lisburn.

8. ROD, 755/71/513/006, Marriage Settlement, Thomas Samuel Grubb and Elizabeth Haughton (John Barcroft Haughton, Abraham Grubb and Richard Grubb), 1819, and registered 30 September 1820.

9. This could grind about two and a half sacks of flour per day. George Shackleton, Memoirs, pp. 1–2 (Item in keeping of Mary Shackleton, Lucan).

10. M. Leadbeater, *The Leadbeater Papers*, vol. 1 (London, 1861), p. 206. See also Harrison (1997), pp. 91–2, under Abraham Shackleton II.

11. Thomas Gibbins & Son were at 12 Meath Street, Dublin. For an account of flour factorage see E. Wakefield, *An Account of Ireland, Statistical and Political*, vol. 1 (London, 1812), p. 746.

12. Ballitore Museum, Co. Kildare; Ledger (1807–10), donated by Mary Shackleton. I have appreciated help from Mary Malone the librarian, and from Mary Fitzpatrick, archivist, County Archives, Newbridge, Co. Kildare. As appears from the ledger, subsidiary to their milling enterprise the Shackletons operated a foundry, acquiring iron from Quaker merchants in Waterford.

13. Sarah Grubb was a sister of John, Joseph and Joshua Pim, for whom, see entries in Harrison (1997), pp. 55, 83–4.

14. NLI, p. 6935, Notes on the Malcomson Family.

15. NAI, WAT 8/1, Ledger of Malcomson's Mill (1795–8). This provides evidence for his early partnership with Richard Sparrow.

16. DFHL, Dr II b 10 d 101. Conveyance of Corporation Mills to trustees of John Howell and sold by him to John Malcomson, merchant. Also, see Indenture 21 Fourth-Month 1808 (DFHL, Dr II b 103). The mill had been bought by John Howell from the Quakers Isaac Jacob, Thomas Taylor, Joseph Grubb Benjamin and Robert Dudley of Suir Mills.

17. 'Annual Inventories' and 'David Malcomson's Business Career up to 1837' in 'Notes on the Malcomson Family'.

18. Little Island Mill had ten pairs of stones, for which see W.P. Burke, *The History of Clonmel* (Waterford, 1907), p. 184.

19. L.M. Cullen, *An Economic History of Ireland since 1660* (London, 1972), pp. 101–2.

20. ROD, 786/III/531/647, Indented Deed of Conveyance, Thomas Samuel Grubb and Isaac Bell, assignees, John Barcroft Haughton (bankrupt), and Joshua Carroll, assignee, 25–30 August 1823.

21. R.S. Harrison, 'The Carroll Family: A Cork Quaker Business Dynasty' in *JFHS*, 57, no. 1 (1994). Joshua Carroll put up the £800 purchase price for the Glen Mills which were then reassigned to Haughton. See *Cork Constitution*, 30 April 1823.

22. See Burke (1907), pp. 181–2.

23. DFHL, AR Cup Pam Box 23/1, J.F. Bennis, *Friends and Former Irish Industries* (n.d.).

24. I. Grubb, *J. Ernest Grubb of Carrick on Suir* (Dublin, 1928), p. 39, where she states there were fourteen Quaker-owned mills.

25. M.T. Fogarty, 'The Malcomsons and the Economic Development of the Lower Suir Valley, 1782–1877' (unpublished M.Econ.Sc., UCC, 1968), p. 32. R.L. Sheil, *Sketches Legal and Political*, vol. 2 (London, 1855), p. 356.

26. Sheil, vol. 2 (1855), p. 356.

27. Ledgers in the possession of Jonathan Shackleton of Mullagh, Co. Cavan.

28. Information supplied by Jonathan Shackleton of Mullagh from his 'Shackleton Register, November 1999', and from a Deed, James Wiley and Bryan Cogan to Ebenezer Shackleton, 24 July 1824 (from ROD, 817/512/550/447).

29. D. Walsh, *Family Industry in Enniscorthy* (Enniscorthy, n.d.), p. 9.

30. In notes in a letter from Michael Goodbody to Richard S. Harrison, 12 February 2002. I gratefully acknowledge Michael Goodbody's assistance. See Harrison (1997), under Robert Goodbody, pp. 49–50.

31. R.S. Harrison, 'Dublin Quakers in Business, 1800–50' (unpublished M.Litt., TCD, 1980) chapters 3 and 4. For James Pim, see Harrison (1997), p. 83.

32. *Thom's Directory* (1894), p. 704.

33. S. Lewis, *Topographical Dictionary of Ireland*, vol. 2 (London, 1837), p. 587.

34. H. Inglis, *A Journey through Ireland during Spring, Summer and Autumn of 1834*, vol. 1, 2nd edn (London, 1835), pp. 131, 190.

35. Lewis, vol. 2 (1837), p. 605. (Tullahortin.)

36. Lewis, vol. 1 (1837), pp. 355–8; Clonmel, vol. 1, p. 355–8. BPP, 1837–8, XXXV, *Second Report of the Commissioners on a General System of Railways for Ireland*, app. B, pp. 17, 112–3. The Commissioners commonly known as the 'Drummond Commission' note two mills having a 30 h.p. engine at Clonmel and another one at Suirville of 25 h.p., both used for manufacturing flour and installed in 1834 and 1837 respectively.

37. *Parl. Gaz.* (Dublin, 1845), 293, states that perhaps eighty attended the Quaker meeting-house in Cahir. See also, Inglis, vol. 1 (1835), p. 127.

38. ROD, 786/575/532/III/28, Ellis to Grubb, 28 April 1823, states that Joshua Fennell had built two 'boulting mills' in Cahir. For Richard Grubb and the Abbey Mills, see W. Grubb, *The Grubbs of Tipperary* (Cork, 1972), pp. 127–8.

39. Ellison Smith, 'The Goings of Munster', *Irish Ancestor*, 1 (1977), 39. Hannah Clendennan was a daughter of John and Elizabeth (née Walpole) Clendennan, and the Walpole family was also associated with flour milling.

40. ROD, (1837) 2/III, Mortgage Assignment, George Walpole and Joseph Walpole to the Agricultural Bank, 1837. Also see ROD, (1840) 20/218, George Walpole and others and James Doyle. Branches of the Walpole family were extensive farmers and had been involved in cloth maufacture. George Walpole owned 3000 paid-up shares in the ill-fated Agricultural & Commercial Bank (set up in 1834), and in 1837 assigned his mill to it for £1476. Difficulties in meeting obligations led to the Drumakeena mill being let for £230 p.a. to the Dowds; also see NAI, Mill Books, Offaly. The Dowds had another mill in the nearby parish of Ettagh. See Harrison (1997), pp. 40–41 under Dowd. See ROD, (1841) 19/273, Walpole and another to Dowd.

41. *Parl. Gaz.*, 328, under Maryborough.

42. Lewis, vol. I (1837), p. 328, under Clara. Samuel Robinson, another Clara miller, a Quaker, owned one mill insured for £2400 in the 1840s. See C. Ó Gráda, *Ireland, A New Economic History 1780–1939* (Oxford, 1994), p. 351. John Dugdale owned the Erry Mill that passed into the hands of the Perrys and later to the Goodbodys.

43. For further detail, see NAI, Mill Books, Offaly, and also VO House Books, Clara (NAI, 5.3190/91, 2a.17.28).

44. Goodbody: Letter (see footnote 30).

45. *Parl. Gaz.*, 315.

46. *Ibid.* 315.

47. *Industrial Yearbook* (Dublin, 1963). NAI, 5.2949/50 Dest 2a.17.16, VO House Books, Town of Graigue (Offaly), pp. 56–7, which describes the mills as they were in 1848. The mill was then leased by Benjamin Haughton at £180 from the representatives of John Haughton. It had six pairs of flour millstones, one pair for shelling wheat. It had four dressing machines, one screen, one separator, two fans, and three sets of elevators all driven by a water wheel 20:0:12:0. John Haughton was a brother of James and Wilfred Haughton, flour and commission merchants of City Quay, Dublin, and nephew of John Barcroft Haughton of Cork. See Harrison (1997), pp. 61–2, under James Haughton.

48. Lewis, vol. I (1837), p. 315, under Carlow.

49. *Ibid.*

50. *The Miller*, 5 July 1886. I thank Norman Campion for this reference.

51. Shackleton Ledger for the 1830s for Anna Liffey Mills. George Shackleton was also investing in the City of Dublin Steampacket Company, in the Steamship Building Company and in the National Insurance Company.

52. T.A.B. Corley, *Quaker Enterprise in Biscuits: Huntley and Palmers of Reading 1822–1972* (London, 1972), p. 39, and see Séamas Ó Maitiú, *W & R. Jacob: Celebrating 150 Years of Irish Biscuit Making* (Dublin, 2001).

53. Harrison (1997), p. 26, under George Baker.

54. R. Goodbody, *A Suitable Channel: Quaker Relief in the Great Famine* (Bray, 1995), and also *Transactions of the Central Relief Committee of the Society of Friends during the Famine in Ireland 1846 and 1847* (Dublin, 1852).

55. *Thom's Directory* (1849).

56. P. Solar, 'The Agricultural Trade of the Port of Waterford, 1809–1909' in *Waterford, History and Society* (Dublin, 1992), p. 502.

57. *Slater's Royal National and Commercial Directory of Ireland*, part 2 (London, 1856), pp. 198–203.

58. T. Hunt, *Portlaw, County Waterford 1825–1876* (Dublin, 2000). *Dublin Gazette*, 23 May 1848, 553. Grubb (1928), p. 39, notes the changeover to corn-milling and the Grubb steam-mill at Carrick.

59. *Parl. Gaz.* (Tullamore).

60. W.E. Hogg, *The Mills and Millers of Ireland of about 1850* (Dublin, 1997). The valuation material for Laois and Offaly obtained from Griffith's *Primary Valuation* for the various Unions in those counties which were published in different years, 1850–4.

61. The ledger in which this information appears seems to be Ballinagore NAI, OFF 9/1/12, Perry Ledger 1843–50.

62. NAI, OL 5.3442, VO House Book (Towns) Ballinagore. Par. Newtown, Barony Moycashel.

63. Lewis, vol. I (1837), under Ballinagore, and *Slater's Directory*, part 2 (1856), pp. 57–8. See also above footnote. The mill was driven by a breast-shot waterwheel, which kept six pairs of millstones in operation for twelve hours a day throughout the year.

64. NAI, 9/4/1, Conveyance from LEC of mills, house and property at Ferbane to Henry Robert Perry, 1854 and, for references to Captain John Collin's mill, see also VO House Book, Bar. of Tissaran, King's County, and Bar. of Garrycastle, Belmont NAI, OL 1379 and OL 51380.

65. Henry Robert Perry was perhaps the son of Robert Perry (1791–1855) of Rathdowney, who was a brother of John Perry of Ballinagore Mills.

66. NAI, OFF 9/1/72, 'Estimate of Rebuilding and Lengthening Dugdale's Mill 11 August 1849' in miscellaneous unlisted correspondence (1830–1885). Thomas Roberts was a Welshman who set up business in Mountmellick, for whom see Lewis, vol. 2 (1837), p. 357, under Mountmellick. As well as being responsible for much of the machine and metalwork at Belmont, he undertook much of the millwork on the Goodbody Clashawaun jute concern. See M. Stewart, *The Goodbodys of Clara* (Clara, 1965), p. 7. *Slater's Directory*, part 2 (1856), p. 32, describes Robert Perry's mill as having a 30-ft-diameter wheel of 80 h.p. and turning nine pairs of stones.

67. William Perry (1804–74) was married to Ann, a daughter of John Dugdale Snr. NAI, Mill Books King's County, indicate that John Dugdale & Co. operated the Erry Mill.

68. M.I.A. Goodbody, *The Goodbody Family of Ireland* (Halstead, 1976), and also Goodbody: Letter (see note 30). An entry in Lydia (Clibborn) Goodbody's (1809–86) diary at 24 Tenth-Month 1865 (DFHL), records, 'John Dugdale [Junior] came to lodge and gave up possession of the Erry mill.'

69. See Grubb (1972), p. 124.

70. *Ibid.* p. 140.

71. See for example NAI, OFF 9/172, Robert Perry to Haughton & Livingstone, Liverpool, 10 January 1876 (Perry, unlisted miscellaneous correspondence).

72. ROD, 1856, 5/35/6, Deed, Davis to Davis, 6 Fourth-Month 1855. Also see, Davis Brothers to Bank of Ireland, ROD, 1856, 18/17. William Fisher had set St John's Mill to Francis Davis at a rent of £80 p.a. in 1827 and Fairfield Mills had been let to him at £200 p.a. in 1845.

73. Shackleton: Short Account, p. 3. There sometimes appear to be slight disparities in the dates in Shackleton's different accounts. Anna Liffey Mills had six pairs of stones.

74. Goodbody: Letter (see note 30). The dates for ownership of this mill were 1871–3. See also, Ó Maitiú (2002), p. 84.

75. But all the metalwork was made locally, for which see NAI, OFF 9.172, 'Estimate of fitting machinery in the mill of Messrs. Robert Perry, Belmont', Thomas Roberts (Mountmellick), 26 November 1859. (See note 67.)

76. NAI, OFF 9/172, see letters addressed to Henry Perry, Belmont Mills, Clara [sic] 10 September 1863 and 21 September 1863.

77. DFHL, Newscutting, 6 August 1867 in Perry Family Album.

78. DFHL, Newscutting n.d. (c. 1870) and letter from Ballinagore Mills addressed to 'My dear father', dated 26 Eleventh-Month 1870 in Perry Family Album. Also, see Stewart (1965), p. 11.

79. NAI, OFF 9/172, J.W. Throop, Cork, to Robert Perry & Sons, Belmont, 28 December 1877.

80. *Cork Examiner*, 9 May 1875. I am grateful to Colman O' Mahony for this reference. For British Corn Millers League, see the *Times*, 25 March 1851. There was co-operation between Irish and British interests in the Anti-Corn Law agitation.

81. *Cork Constitution*, 3 August 1877.

82. *Cork Constitution*, 20 April 1881. Reuben Harvey Jackson emigrated for a while to Australia. See 'Cork Monthly Meeting Membership List' (1886, in keeping of Cork Monthly Meeting, Friends Meeting House, Summerhill South, Cork City).

83. Brackets within a name contain the name of the person's father, e.g. Richard, son of Ebenezer.

84. *Slater's Directory*, part 2 (1856), pp. 23–6, lists Benjamin Haughton (1825–95) as a miller at Graigue. He concentrated on building up a business as a civil engineer and emigrated to England. See 'Memoirs of the Family of Haughton in Ireland' (unpublished manuscript in private hands). The Shackletons rented the mill in 1871 at £190 10s. p.a. This information is from Jonathan Shackleton.

85. Information from Mary Shackleton and see also P.N. Gale, 'George Shackleton & Sons, An Anglo-Irish Family and Business 1900–50', p. 5 (an unpublished item in possession of Mary Shackleton, Lucan).

86. Shackleton: Memoirs, p.7, and Shackleton: Short Account.

87. Shackleton: Memoirs, p. 7.

88. *Southern Industry*, September 1889, 12.

89. Ellison Smith (1977), p. 40.

90. R.G. Jones, 'The Diffusion of Technology in Flour Milling and the Emergence of the Modern British Milling Industry, 1789–1914' (M.Phil thesis, Aston University), p. 408.

91. *Ibid.* pp. 413–4.
92. *The Echo*, 11 August 1962.
93. *List of Members and Attenders of Munster Quarterly Meeting* (1895), Cork Monthly Meeting, and Stratten, *Dublin, Cork and the South of Ireland* (London, 1892), p. 237.
94. NAI, OFF 9/4/20, *Application for Shares in Robert Perry & Co. Ltd*, and see also OFF 9/4/28, Lease by Thomas Perry of Belmont to Robert Perry & Co. Ltd.
95. Goodbody: Letter (see note 30). James Ellis Goodbody (1864–1914) was a son of Lewis Frederick Goodbody (1819–87) of Clara.
96. *Ibid.*
97. NAI, LIM 21 V.18, *James Bannatyne & Co.*, 15 August 1894.
98. Part of the Russell enterprise, which dated back to 1810, was Plassy Mills, which they took over in 1861 from the Limerick Quaker Reuben Harvey. (Not to be confused with the several, but related, 'Reuben Harveys' of Cork.) ROD, (1861) 37/223, Reuben Harvey to Francis William Russell MP, Thompson Russell, Richard Russell, Arthur Russell, 9 December 1861.
99. *Stratten* (1892), p. 228.
100. *Freeman's Journal*, 31 May 1912.
101. Shackleton: Memoirs, p. 17. 'The first offices of the Association were in two rooms on the top floor of 102, Grafton Street … the Secretary [was] John Brown, one of a number of that Irish milling family, a tall man with a beard, who employed … as typist Miss Claire Mitchell *c.* 1919'.
102. Miscellaneous notes on Shackleton's mills (in possession of Mary Shackleton, Lucan). These notes are unattributed, but probably by George Shackleton. See also note 51.
103. Shackleton: Memoirs, p. 6.
104. *Ibid.*
105. P.N. Gale, 'George Shackleton & Sons, an Anglo-Irish Family and Business, 1900–50' (unpublished manuscript in possession of Mary Shackleton, Lucan), p. 6.
106. Shackleton: Memoirs, pp. 12, 18, and information from conversations with Mary Shackleton, Lucan, whose generous assistance towards this essay I gratefully acknowledge.

5. **The Introduction and Establishment of Roller Milling in Ireland, 1875–1925**
   GLYN JONES

1. *The Miller*, December 1894, 785–86.
2. NABIM lists of members.
3. *The Miller*, January 1881, 802.
4. Royal Commission on supply of food and raw material in time of war, BPP, 1905, III, table A1 (1).
5. Glyn Jones, *The Millers* (Lancaster, 2001), p. 36.
6. *The Miller*, May 1884, 213.
7. Proceedings of the Institution of Mechanical Engineers (1872), p. 238.

8. *Thom's Directory* (Dublin, 1908), p. 440.

9. *The Miller*, August 1882, 411.

10. Jones (2001), chapters 2 and 3.

11. Proceedings of the Institution of Civil Engineers (1882), pp. 240–2.

12. B. Simon, *In Search of a Grandfather* (Leicester, 1997), p. 109.

13. *Milling*, April 1906, 361.

14. A. Simon, *The Simon Engineering Group* (Stockport, 1953), chapters 1 and 2.

15. Henry Simon, *Occasional Letter XLIX*, October 1898.

16. *The Miller*, January 1880, 831.

17. *The Miller*, June 1886, 130–5.

18. *The Miller*, April 1882, 116–20, 129–30.

19. *The Miller*, December 1882, 791–2.

20. *The Miller*, June 1882, 271–2.

21. Jones (2001), pp. 123–30.

22. *The Miller*, April 1884, 108–9; September 1884, 544; September 1886, 348; October 1886, 387.

23. BPP, 1884–5, IX, *Select Committee on Industries (Ireland, 1885)*, pp. 995–6.

24. *The Miller*, June 1886, 162: Carter's largest plant in Ireland.

25. *The Irish Builder*, November 1884: brief impression of exterior.

26. *The Miller*, February 1876, 775–6.

27. *The Miller*, November 1893, 373–4.

28. H. Simon, *Roller Flour Milling* (1886), pp. 65–8; *The Miller*, September 1885.

29. Jones (2001), chapter 5.

30. *The Miller*, February 1882, 896.

31. *The Miller*, July 1886, 185–7.

32. *The Miller*, June 1886, 129–36.

33. *The Miller*, July 1886, 213.

34. NABIM *Transactions* (1887), pp. 112–9.

35. Jones (2001), pp. 115–18.

36. *The Miller*, December 1889, pp. 421–2.

37. 'Trade items' in *The Miller*: short statements of various dates.

38. At the start of a new era of mill photography.

39. *Proceedings of the Institution of Mechanical Engineers* (1889), Simon's map series, seventh edition, accompanying his paper.

40. *The Miller*, August 1893, 257.

41. H. Simon, *Occasional Letter XLI*, May 1897.

42. *The Miller*, June 1894, 281–2; September 1897, 524.

43. *The Miller*, August 1894, 428.

44. Jones (2001), pp. 215, 226–31.

45. H. Simon, *Circular XVII*, August 1894.

46. *Ibid.* July 1894.

47. *The Miller*, August 1900, 354.

48. *The Miller*, March 1886, 21: rules and regulations.
49. *The Miller*, December 1902, 557–8.
50. *Milling*, October 1924.
51. Jones, (2001), 253–6.
52. R. Bennett and J. Elton, *History of Corn Milling*, vol. 3 (Liverpool, 1898), pp. 308–14.
53. Joseph Rank Ltd, *The Master Millers* (1955), p. 47; *Milling*, April 1914, 401–2.
54. *Milling*, January 1903, 73–6.
55. *Milling*, December 1911, 668.
56. J. Burls, (ed.), *Nine Generations: A History of the Andrews Family, Millers of Comber* (Liverpool, 1958), pp. 164–6; D.W. Kent-Jones and A.J. Amos, *Modern Cereal Chemistry* (1950), pp. 240–2.
57. *Milling*, October 1905, 307–8.
58. *Milling*, July 1907, 56.
59. *Milling*, September 1910, 260.
60. *Milling*, December 1910, 538–67; December 1911, 614–5; May 1914, 248–50.
61. H. Simon, *Occasional Letter LXXXX*, February 1912; *Milling*, December 1911, 618–9.
62. *Milling*, December 1911, 680–4.
63. H. Simon, *Occasional Letter LXXXXII*, June 1912.
64. Jones (2001), chapter 14.
65. Rank (1955), pp. 27–39; *The Miller*, April 1891, 44–6; November 1895, 716.
66. *The Miller*, August 1916, 345.
67. *The Miller*, December 1917, 529–30; June 1918, 164.
68. *The Miller*, June 1914, 233.
69. *Milling*, October 1924, xv.
70. Jones (2001), p. 282.
71. 'The Whitley Report', Ministry of Labour 1917, and Reconstruction Committee report on joint standing industrial Councils, BPP, 1917–18, XVIII, were the initiating documents. Preliminaries in Britain described in Jones (2001), pp. 274–5.
72. *Milling*, June 1922, 653–4.
73. *Milling*, June 1922, 598.
74. *Milling*, February 1923, p. 144; October 1924, vii.
75. *Milling*, October 1924, xxxix–lv; April 1936, 42–3.
76. *Milling*, October 1924, lxxxvii, x respectively.
77. *Milling*, June 1925, 745–7; December 1925, 786–7; February 1925, 206, 265.
78. *The Miller*, January 1925, 992.
79. Rank (1995), pp. 64, 79; *Milling*, March 1934, 312–18.
80. *Milling*, April 1936, pp. 52–3.
81. E. Bowen, *The Shelbourne* (1951), p. 71.

6. The Political Economy of the Irish Flour-Milling Industry, 1922–1945
AKIHIRO TAKEI

1. *Milling*, 8 September 1923, 28, 16 September 1939, 340–1; *Irish Trade Journal*, 1926, 137; J. Burls, (ed.), *Nine Generations: A History of the Andrews Family, Millers of Comber* (Liverpool, 1958), pp. 166–7.

2. E.J. Riordan, *Modern Irish Trade and Industry* (London, 1920), p. 91.

3. *Milling*, 17 December 1921, 691.

4. *Ibid.* 21 January 1922, 75; 3 June 1922, 572; 10 June 1922, 653–4; 28 October 1922, 505; 16 December 1922, 692–3, 697; 24 February 1923, 195; 21 July 1923, 63–4.

5. *Ibid.* 21 July 1923, 63–4.

6. These figures must be treated with caution as they possibly excluded idle mills and partially included non-wheat products. NAI, Department of Agriculture, G76/1943. C.A. Mitchell to Department of Agriculture, 6 April 1926; Comparative Statement of Flour Requirements and Milling Capacity of Irish Free State; Irish Flour Milling Trade, pp. 1, 5.

7. NAI, Department of Agriculture, G76/1943. *Irish Flour Milling Trade*, p. 1.

8. *Census of Industrial Production* (1926–9), p. 37; (1932–5), p. 31; A. Takei, 'Business and Government in the Irish Free State: The Case of the Irish Flour Milling Industry 1922–1945' (Unpublished Ph.D., TCD, 1998), p. 25.

9. Fiscal Inquiry Committee Reports, 1923: R20, pp. 13, 47, 50–2.

10. NAI, Department of Agriculture, G76/1943, C.A. Mitchell to P. Hogan, 13 February 1926; Irish Flour Milling Trade, pp. 4, 6–7.

11. File on 'Wheat and Flour, Observations', NAI, Department of Agriculture, G76/1943. M.E. Daly, *The First Department: A History of the Department of Agriculture* (Dublin, 2002), pp. 148–150.

12. PDDE, vol. 21, 3 November 1927, 787.

13. Tariff Commission, *Report on Application for a Tariff on Flour* (1928), R36/3 [hereafter, *Tariff Commission's Report*], pp. 48–9.

14. *Ibid.* p. 26.

15. A. O'Rahilly, *Flour, Wheat and Tariffs* (Dublin, 1928), pp. 31–4.

16. *Tariff Commission's Report*, pp. 24, 26–9; S. Ó Maitiú, *W & R Jacob: Celebrating 150 Years of Irish Biscuit Making* (Dublin, 2002).

17. *Tariff Commission's Report*, p. 5.

18. *Tariff Commission's Report*, pp. 4–6; Takei, *op. cit.* pp. 45, 99–100, 110–11, 170.

19. J. Haughton, 'The Historical Background' in J.W. O'Hagan (ed.), *The Economy of Ireland: Policy and Performance of a Small European Country* (Dublin, 1995), pp. 27–8.

20. G. O'Brien, 'Patrick Hogan: Minister for Agriculture 1922–1932', *Studies* (1936).

21. *Tariff Commission's Report*, pp. 51–8.

22. M.E. Daly, *Industrial Development and Irish National Identity 1922–1939* (Dublin, 1992), pp. 27–8, 44.

23. *Ibid.* pp. 24–5, 29, 33, 35, 43; PDDE, vol. 1, 19 September 1922, 422; 22 September 1922, 592; Daly (2002), pp. 146–7.

24. Economic Committee., *Second Interim Report on the Question of a Tariff on Flour, 1928*: R42 [*hereafter, Second Interim Report*]. PDDE, vol. 23, 30 May 1928, 2270–2328; vol. 3, 23 May 1929, 174–332.

25. Takei, *op. cit.* pp. 122–31.

26. Daly (1992), p. 49.

27. PDSE, vol. 14, 3 December 1930, 83.

28. H.F. Gospel, 'Product Markets, Labour Markets, and Industrial Relations: the Case of Flour Milling', *Business History*, (1989), vol. 31, no.2, pp. 86–7.

29. *Irish Times*, 6 March 1930.

30. PDDE, vol. 38, 14 May 1931, 1246–7; *Milling*, 25 April 1931, 455.

31. *Census of Industrial Production* (1931), pp. 39–40.

32. NAI, DUB 128 A/6/7/15, 18, The Dublin Port Milling Co., Statement of Account, 1930–1.

33. P. Hogan, *Tariffs and the Farmer* (Dublin, 1931), p. 16.

34. *Irish Times*, 25 April 1931.

35. Economic Committee, *First Interim Reports on Wheat Growing, 1929*: R42; *Second Interim Reports.*

36. *Irish Times*, 25 May 1932.

37. NAI, Department of Taoiseach, S6045, Extracts from Cabinet Minutes, Cab.6/8, 24 March 1932, item no. 7, Cab. 6/5, 18 March 1932, item no. 2; PDDE, vol. 45, 23 November 1932, 123–4.

38. *Irish Industrial Year Book* (1936), p. 89, 393; Daly (1992), pp. 100–1.

39. *Public General Acts passed by the Oireachtas of Saorstat Eireann 1932* [hereafter *Public General Acts*], pp. 446–9.

40. Lemass wrote to P.F. Higgins on 20 December 1932, 'I have to inform you that the Executive Council is unable to accept the view that there is any obligation on the State to provide compensation for any adverse effects which the changed circumstances may have had on the firms concerned. The Executive Council is of the opinion that those who invested capital in the business of distributing foreign goods in the Saorstat took the ordinary risk associated with any commercial enterprise.' I would like to thank Mr N.P. Higgins for this information.

41. Public General Acts 1933, pp. 28–161.

42. PDDE, vol. 45, 23 November 1932, 120.

43. Public General Acts 1933, pp. 28–161.

44. PDDE, vol. 45, 24 November 1932, 239–40.

45. NAI, DUB 128 A/6/7/20, The Dublin Port Milling Co., Detailed Statement of Accounts, 1932.

46. PDDE, vol. 45, 24 November 1932, 240.

47. Takei, *op. cit.* chapter 6.

48. *Milling*, 5 November 1932, 502.

49. *Ibid.* 25 April 1936, 14.

50. *Census of Industrial Production* (1932–5), pp. 26–7; (1936), pp. 46–8, 51; *Irish Industrial Year Book* (1937), p. 99.

51. NAI, Department of Industry and Commerce, OC/14 Memorandum to Sullivan.

52. *Milling,* 17 March 1934, p. 283.

53. *Report of the Survey Team Established by the Minister of Agriculture on the Flour Milling Industry* (1965), A53/5 [hereafter, *Report of the Survey Team*], p. 15.

54. Statistical Abstract 1936, p. 32.

55. NAI, Department of Taoiseach, S69175 December 1934, Memorandum of the Minister for Agriculture for the Amendment of the Agricultural Produce (Cereals) Acts, 1933 and 1934.

56. *Ibid.* Public General Acts, 1935, pp. 672–709.

57. *Census of Industrial Production* (1932–5), p. 28.

58. *Census of Industrial Production* (1936), p. 53.

59. NAI, LIM 21 (unlisted) Cork Milling Co. Ltd, Finance Statements and Reports, 1932–39; Rank's Financial Statement and Reports, 1934–45; H.F. Gospel, *Markets, Firms, and the Management of Labour in Modern Britain* (Cambridge, 1992), pp. 45–6.

60. Spillars used to export 400,000 sacks of flour to Ireland, which was the equivalent to nearly half of the total export from Britain, but they also had markets in Finland, Lithuania, Estonia, Sweden, Norway and the west coast of Africa. P.F. Higgins & Sons to Lemass 10 May 1933. I am grateful to Mr N.P. Higgins for this information.

61. J. Horgan, *Seán Lemass: The Enigmatic Patriot* (Dublin, 1997), pp. 75–6.

62. Takei, *op. cit.* pp. 183–92.

63. *Census of Industrial Production* (1936), p. 53.

64. Takei, *op. cit.* pp. 183–91.

65. *Census of Industrial Production* (1932–5), p. 26; (1937), p. 46; (1938–44), p. 80.

66. NAI, LIM 21 (unlisted) Minutes of Cork and District Flour Millers; Takei, *op. cit.* chapter 5.

67. NAI, Department of Industry and Commerce, OC/47 For Supplementaries; *Prices Commission Report,* pp. 33–5.

68. *Census of Industrial Production* (1932–5), pp. 26–9.

69. NAI, Department of Industry and Commerce, OC/136, Note for the Information of the Minister.

70. PDDE, vol. 66, 15 April 1937, 991.

71. *Flour and Bread Commission of Inquiry Report* (1951), R81, p. 28; *Report of the Survey Team,* p. 76.

72. Takei, *op. cit.* pp. 194–7.

73. PDDE, vol. 45, 24 November 1932, 240.

74. NAI, Department of Industry and Commerce, OC/122, Memorandum for Government on Flour Prices; Takei, *op. cit.* pp. 218–20.

75. *Ibid.* NAI, Department of Industry and Commerce, OC/136, Note for the Information of the Minister.

76. NAI, DUB 128 B/1/120 September 1938, 12 September 1939, Minutes of General Meeting of Irish Flour Millers' Association; *Milling*, 2 December 1939, 558; 9 December, 1939, 578. F. Forde, *The Long Watch: The History of the Mercantile Marine in World War Two* (Dublin, 1981), p. 64.

77. Statistical Abstract 1946, p. 40.

78. NAI, Department of Taoiseach, S12331, Report of Interdepartmental Committee Appointed by the Minister for Supplies on 11th November 1943 to Consider Matters Relating to Increased Cost of Living and Stabilisation of Prices [hereafter *Report on Cost of Living*], app. 4.

79. *Irish Press*, 8 September 1939.

80. NAI, DUB 128/B/2/21, Irish Flour Millers' Association, *Annual Report and Statement of Accounts for Year 1941/2, 1943/4*; NAI, Department of Taoiseach, S12335A 23 September 1943, Department of Supplies, Memorandum for the Government.

81. NAI, Department of Industry and Commerce, 2000/12/266/CF/525/70. Memorandum. Flour Subsidy. C. Flour, p. 5.

82. NAI, DUB 128/B/1/1–2, 11 September 1940, 22 July 1942, Minutes of General Meeting of Irish Flour Millers' Association; Takei, *op. cit.* pp. 347–50, 366–72.

83. NAI, DUB 128/B/2/21, Irish Flour Millers' Association, *Annual Report and Statement of Accounts for Year, 1941/2*; B. Girvin, 'Industrialisation and the Irish Working Class since 1922', *Saothar*, 10 (1984), 34.

84. D. Nevin, 'Industry and Labour' in K.B. Nowlan and T.D. Williams (eds), *Ireland in the War Years and After 1939–51* (Dublin, 1969), p. 96.

85. NAI, DUB 128 C/1/1, 3 July 1941, 6 November 1942, 5 September 1945, Minutes of Joint Industrial Council: *Some Statistics of Wages and Hours of Work in 1949*, p. 97.

86. C. Ó Gráda, *A Rocky Road: the Irish Economy since the 1920s* (Manchester, 1998), p. 17.

87. NAI, Department of Taoiseach, S12331, *Report on Cost of Living*, Appendix 10.

88. NAI, Department of Industry and Commerce, EHR3/23, History of Flour and Bread Rationing; *Trade and Shipping Statistics 1945–47*, p. 28.

7. **Irish Flour Milling Since the Second World War**
NORMAN CAMPION

1. *Milling*, 25 August 1924.

2. NAI, DUB 128/B/1/3 Annual Report of IFMA, 1953.

3. Loose cutting in Bolands Files (1964), in IHAI, check with author for these. NAI, DUB 128/B; IFMA summary period 1936–65 and population figures from CSO.

4. NAI, DUB 128/B/1/1–14, IFMA Minutebooks and Annual Reports 1953–61.

5. A useful appraisal of the structure and location of the industry in the Irish Free State at this point can be found in Department of Agriculture and Fisheries *Report of the Survey Team Established by the Minister for Agriculture on the Flour Milling Industry* (Dublin, 1965), pp. 64–9. For a full return of Irish flour millers in 1963 see PDDE vol. 205, 1963, 525–5. Following this return, twelve wheatmeal millers with quotas in excess of

1000 barrels were listed and a further forty with the same for less than 1000 barrels.

6. Unpublished article on the miller bakers by Peter Lyons, in IHAI files.

7. Interview, Neill Higgins, 2002.

8. Odlums, who transferred the license to their Dublin Port Mill, bought the company.

9. IHAI Files; Papers of Hastings Brown, Enniscorthy.

10. The Shackleton family had previously owned it. It was taken over by a bank-financed group in 1973, who used this public company to carry out other acquisitions, notably Bolands in 1976.

11. The eight-sack mill had been re-equipped by Miag in 1936. They also had grain facilities at nearby Grange Mills on the Grand Canal.

12. Interview, Stewart Freeman, 2002.

13. *The Derry Journal*, 11 November 1965.

14. The Milford bakery closed but the Ballyshannon bakery survives.

15. Interviews, Patrick J. Murphy, Dan O'Donoghue, John Flynn, Joe Humphries, John McInerney, David Carroll, Freda McGrane, 2002.

16. In 1977, the company's name was changed to Odlum Group Ltd. Information comes from interviews with Loftus Odlum, Stephen Odlum, Tim Odlum, Norman Odlum, John Flynn, 2002. Also see NAI, DUB 128/A/1–4, Records of the Odlum Group and within this DUB 128/A/5 for Pollexfen material, and DUB 128/A/6–7, for records of the Dublin Port Milling Co.

17. Towards the end of its days, this mill with a capacity of eight sacks concentrated on long runs of flour for Irish biscuits and wheatmeal.

18. This mill has had a continuous programme of modernization ever since Henry Simon converted it to roller milling in the 1880s, with the Millers Supply Company of Liverpool re-modelling it in the 1930s.

19. Rowe's of Wexford would have been one of a number of specialist wheatmeal millers and a large list of those with the requisite milling license was published in 1963 under the Agricultural Produce (Cereals) Acts. In addition to these firms, who are licensed to mill wheat, the owners of 536 other mills hold Milling (Homegrown Wheat) permits under the Agricultural Produce (Cereals) Acts, which authorize them to engage in the milling of homegrown wheat. As these permit holders were not normally authorized to purchase wheat, their milling was confined in practice to the milling of wheat on commission for local farmers.

20. Odlums also engaged in the production of animal feeds, establishing a nationwide market for their Bestock animal feed range in the 1960s, which was manufactured adjacent to most of their flour mills. However, in the late '70s and '80s as the co-ops and commercial feed millers built larger mills, flour millers like Odlums exited from this trade.

21. One of the contributions to Odlums' profit margin is their oatmeal facility at Sallins. The sale of tinned Pinhead Oatmeal under the McCann brand to the USA is significant (McCann and Hills of Drogheda were the originators of the market; they closed in the 1970s). Odlums established an oat-milling plant at Sallins on the banks

of the Grand Canal in 1915. This was remodelled in 1930, but a disastrous fire in 1960 necessitated building a whole new mill. In 1984 it was totally re-equipped by Buhlers. During all these periods it was constantly updated with new equipment including a Buhler PLC controlled kiln. It has nine operatives plus administration staff. W. P. & R. Odlum decided in 1955 to form a separate company from their flour-milling activities so the company of Odlums (Sallins) Ltd was established. However, it was dropped when the Odlum Group was formed.

22. The Records of Rank's Ireland are held in Rank's Archive. I would like to thank Gordon Bull who made his private papers available, copies in IHAI Files. Interviews, Declan Wallace, Edward Hallinan, Canice Kelly, Arthur Jones, Seamus Funge, George Spillane, Ken Brislane. Also David Mercier Diaries 1920–58, Rank's mill superintendent, c/o Croom Mills, Co. Limerick.

23. In the early 1970s serious discussions took place between Odlums and Rank's over a possible merger. This would have given a possible two-thirds combined share of the market. However, these efforts were abandoned in 1974.

24. The bakery side of the operation was also going badly. Eventually Kilcock was restructured successfully, but the Dublin and Cork bakeries were closed in May and September of 1982 respectively.

25. Interview, Declan Wallace, 2002.

26. The 10,000-square-metre premises occupied a four-hectare (ten-acre) site. The market for their products was wide and varied: starches from food products to industrial-pharmaceutical cosmetic; glucose and dextrose syrups were even more varied. They did, however, compete with Irish Sugar products in some markets. A number of ex-Rank's personnel provided Wheat Industries with a fully trained milling staff under the direction of Declan Wallace, who had been Milling Superintendent for Rank's, which had recently closed down.

27. In 2002, Cargill, the giant international grain and milling operation, bought Cerestar.

28. *Milling*, 6 January 1961.

29. Associated British Foods (ABF) is a Garfield Weston Company, operating Sunblest and a chain of mills in Britain, plus numerous bakeries, etc.

30. Interview, Bill Cleland, 2002.

31. Allied Mills operated nine mills in the UK including James Neill Ltd, Belfast. In 2003 they have sold six of these to A.D.M. Milling Ltd (A.D.M. own Southern Milling Cork, one of the largest feed-milling operations and a citric acid plant at Ringaskiddy). Allied Mills have retained Neill's and two other mills sufficient to supply their Associated British Foods Bakery and other requirements, plus some free-market flour sales. The managing director, Bill Cleland, came from the engineering industry.

32. They were the first to achieve ISO 9002/EN 299002. It was also the first food company in Northern Ireland to achieve the Quality Management Award BS5750.

33. Interview, Bill Anton, 2002.

34. Indeed it was the only Northern Ireland mill still using bucket elevators instead of pneumatic conveying in the process by the 1970s (pneumatic conveying being more

hygienic). The same prevailed in all the Rank's Mills in the Republic.

35. One of the problems of operating a flour-importing business is the disruption of ferries by bad weather. Bag flour can be stocked, but bulk direct to bakeries is a different matter. Bakery bulk storage is usually of limited capacity. On more than one occasion Rank's have had to buy flour from competitors to keep their bakery clients happy, even buying from Bolands in Dublin. This situation was eventually overcome by holding a reserve flour stock in a special container system in an Irish warehouse, which could be tipped directly into the bulk delivery lorry when required.

36. Interviews, Dawson Morland, Maurice Faquhart, Michael Taylor, Michael Clarke, Ed Neill, 2002.

37. By 1960 these were producing 2500–3000 tons of balanced feed per week.

38. In 2001 they ceased animal feed production at their Percy Street site and joined forces with United Feeds (a farming co-operative) in feed production at Belfast Docks. They also sold the Ormo Bakery in 2002.

39. With a population of 1,675,000, this gives a per capita consumption of 112 lbs (50.7 kg) per annum.

40. Industrial Development Authority, Report on Flour Milling (internal report for Rank's, *c.* 1983)

41. Interviews, Alan Keegan, Jeromy Shiels.

42. S.A.R.A. associated with Halal Meats, Ballyhaunis, who purchased the operation in 1988.

43. IAWS, *Quest for Quality* (1997).

44. Even the Northern Ireland market was partially supplied from Britain.

45. Ex-Dublin Port Milling Company.

46. Ex-W. P. & R. Odlum.

47. Ex-National Flour Mills.

48. Ex-W. P. & R. Odlum. One of only three oatmeal millers in Ireland in 2003 (the others are Flahavan's, Kilmacthomas, Co. Waterford, White's Speedicook, Tandragee, Co Armagh, part of Fane Valley Co-op). Of the 130,000 tons of oats grown in Ireland in 2002, less than 10 per cent was used for human consumption.

49. As this book was going to the printers it was discovered that M. J. &L. Goodbody's, Erry Mills, Clara, still had most of its early 1900s equipment in place, in spite of the fact that Rank's had closed it in 1969. (Industrial Heritage Association, 15 October 2003).

This book has demonstrated that in the case of flour milling, a surprising amount of old business records have survived for many old mills across the country, in libraries, archives and in private hands. Others survive as part of the heritage of companies, which have taken over older mills. These invaluable sources provide one of the avenues to building additional and better case studies of the history of many flour mills by local historians, business historians, industrial archaeologists, social and economic historians or, last but not least, molinoligists.

Appendix A

Some Terminology Used in the Milling Industry

Sacks: 1 sack = 280 lbs of flour
8 sack = imperial ton of 2,240 lbs

Mill capacity was usually expressed in sacks per hour of flour produced at 70 per cent extraction rate.

Now mill capacity is expressed in tons of wheat milled per 24-hour day, e.g. a 50-sack mill = approx. 215 tons of wheat per 24 hours.

Extraction rate, or yield: the per cent of flour obtained from wheat (usually 70–72 per cent, but during WWII 80–85 and 90 per cent was the requirement)

Bushel weight: an imperial bushel is a volumetric measure equal to 8 gallons

The quality of wheat was expressed in lbs per bushel. Good wheat weighs more than poorer wheat, good wheat averaging 60 lbs (barley 56 lbs and oats 39 lbs). The Corn Returns Act of 1882 fixed this bushel weight. Bushel weight has now been replaced by kilos per hectolitre.

Barrel: 280 lbs (20 stone) of wheat
Quarter: 8 bushels – UK standard weight 480 lbs. US markets, etc., used various other weights.

Other measurements were:
1 central = 100 lbs
1 cwt = 112 lbs
1 windle = 220 lbs
1 boll = 240 lbs

All measurements are now, in 2003, in metric tonnes, though the USA still uses bushels internally. US bushels are approximately 3 per cent smaller than imperial bushels.

Pneumatic conveying: material conveyed in an air stream, as opposed to mechanical conveyors.

Appendix B

Members of Irish Flour Millers' Association, 1918

Andrews & Sons, Isaac, Belfast Mills, Belfast
Ardagh, R., Portlaw, Waterford
Bannatyne & Sons, J., Ltd, Limerick
Bennett & Co., Clonakilty
Bolands Ltd, Ringsend Mills, Dublin
Brown & Crosthwait, Lodge Mills, Bagnalstown
Brown & Co., Walter, Hanover Street Mills, Dublin
Comerford & Sons, J., Rathdrum
Dublin North City Milling Co., Ltd
Davis, S. & A. G., Ltd, St John's Mill, Enniscorthy
Dock Milling Co. Ltd, Barrow Street, Dublin
Furlong & Sons, C. J., Ltd, Lapps Quay and Marina Mills, Cork
Fogarty, Owen, Aughrim
Gilliland & Sons, S., Rock Mills, Londonderry
Glynn & Sons, M., Kilrush
Going & Smith, Cahir
Goodbody, M. J. & L., Clara
Hallinan & Sons, T., Ltd, Midleton and Clondulane, Co. Cork
Hannon & Sons, Henry, Ardreigh Mills, Athy
Howard Bros., Crookstown, Co. Cork
Hughes, Dickson & Co. Ltd, Belfast
Halligan, John, City Flour Mills, Dublin
Johnston, Mooney & O'Brien Ltd, Clonliffe Flour Mills, Dublin
Maguire, Martin, Limerick
Morton, R. & Co., Ballymena
MacMullen & Sons, J. W., George's Quay, Cork
Mosse, W. H., Bennettsbridge
Neill, James, Ltd, Reliable Flour Mills, Belfast
Odlum & Odlum, Naas
Odlum, W. P. & R., Portarlington, Maryborough, and St Mullin's
Oliver, W. R., Buttevant, Co. Cork
Palmer, R. & Co., Galway
Pollexfen & Co., W. G. & T., Ltd, Sligo
Pilsworth, Robert, Grennan Mills, Thomastown
Perry & Co., R., Ltd, Belmont
Rowe, Howard & Son, Wexford
Russell & Son, J. N., Ltd, Limerick

Shackleton & Sons, E., Moone and Barrow Mills, Carlow
Shackleton & Sons, George, Ltd, Anna Liffey Mills, Lucan
Shaw & Sons, George, St John's Mills, Cork
Spicer & Co., John, Ltd, Boyne and Blackwater Mills, Navan
Thomas, T. D., Ltd, Bridge Mills, Castletownroche
Victoria Milling Co., Londonderry
Webb, J. & R., Ltd, Mallow

Source: As returned in NAI: AGM Irish Flour Millers' Association, 1918.

Appendix C

Principal Flour-Milling Firms in the Irish Free State, 1926

Bannatyne (James) and Sons, Limerick

Bennett and Co., Clonakilty, Co. Cork

Bolands Ltd, Ringsend Road, Dublin

Brown (Walter) and Co., Hanover Street, Dublin

Brown and Crosthwaite, Bagenalstown, Co. Carlow

Comerford (J.) and Sons, Rathdrum, Co. Wicklow

Davis, S. and A. G., Enniscorthy, Co. Wexford

Dock Milling Co. Ltd, Barrow Street, Dublin

Dublin Port Milling Co. Ltd, Alexandra Wharf, Dublin

Fogarty, Owen, Aughrim, Co. Wicklow

Furlong (John) and Sons Ltd, Lapp's Quay and Marina Mills, Cork

Glynn (M.) and Son, Kilrush, Co. Clare

Going and Smith Ltd, Cahir, Co. Tipperary

Goodbody, M. J. and L., Clara, Offaly

Halligan, John, Usher's Island, Dublin

Hallinan (T.) and Sons Ltd, Midleton, Co. Cork, and Fermoy, Co. Cork

Hannon (H.) and Sons, Athy, Co. Kildare

Howard Brothers, Crookstown, Co. Cork

Johnston, Mooney and O'Brien Ltd, Clonliffe Mills, Dublin

McDonagh (Thomas) and Sons, Galway

MacMullan (W. J.) and Sons Ltd, George's Quay, Cork

Mosse, W. (representatives of), Bennett's Bridge, Co. Kilkenny

North City Mills, Glasnevin, Dublin

Odlum, W. P. and R., Maryborough and Portarlington, Leix; and St Mullin's, Graigue, Co. Carlow

Odlum and Odlum, Naas, Co. Kildare

Oliver, W. R., Buttevant, and Mallow, Co. Cork

Palmer (Thomas) and Co., Galway

Pilsworth, Robert, Thomastown, Co. Kilkenny

Pollexfen (W. and G. T.) and Co. Ltd, Sligo

Russell (John) and Sons, Newtown Perry Mills, and Mallow Street Mills, Limerick

Shackleton (E.) and Son, Moone, and Barrow Mills, Carlow

Shackleton (G.) and Sons Ltd, Lucan, Co. Dublin, and Straffan, Co. Kildare

Shaw (George) and Sons, John Street, Cork

Webb, J. and R., Ltd, Mallow, Co. Cork

Source: As returned in the *Irish Trade Journal*, May 1926.

Appendix D

Flour Millers in 1963 who were Holders of Wheat-Milling Licenses under the Agricultural Produce (Cereals) Acts

Ballina Flour Mills Ltd, Ballina Flour Mills, Ardnaree, Ballina, Co. Mayo

The Barrow Milling Co. Ltd, Barrow Mills, Leighlin Road, Carlow

*Bennett & Co. Ltd, Shannon Vale Mills, Clonakilty, Co. Cork

Bolands Ltd, Bolands Flour Mills, Ringsend Road and Barrow Street, Dublin

Davis, S. & A. G. Ltd, St John's Mills, Enniscorthy, Co. Wexford

The Dock Milling Co. Ltd, Dock Mills, 38/39 Barrow Street, Dublin

Dublin North City Milling Co. Ltd, The North City Mills, 113 Phibsboro Road, Dublin

Dublin Port Milling Co. Ltd, The Dublin Port Mill, Alexandra Wharf, Dublin

Furlong, John & Sons (1920) Ltd, Marina Mill, Victoria Quay, Cork

Glynn, M. & Sons Ltd, Co. Clare Flour & Meal Mills, Merchant's Quay, Kilrush, Co. Clare

Going & Smith Ltd, Cahir Mills, Bridge Street, Cahir, Co. Tipperary

*McDonagh Milling & Trading Co. Ltd, Nun's Island Flour Mills, Nun's Island, Galway

Milford (Donegal) Bakery & Flour Mills Ltd, Milford, Co. Donegal

Mosse, W. H. Ltd, Bennett's Bridge Mills, Bennett's Bridge, Co. Kilkenny

The National Flour Mills Ltd, The National Flour Mills, Victoria Quay, Cork

Odlum, W. P. & R. Ltd, Leinster Mills, Naas, Co. Kildare

Odlum, W. P. & R. Ltd, Maryborough Mills, Portlaoighise, Leix

Odlum, W. P. & R. Ltd, Portarlington Mills, Portarlington, Leix

Odlum, W. P. & R. Ltd, St Mullins Mill, St Mullins, Graiguenamanagh, Co. Kilkenny

Pollexfen, W. & G. T. & Co. Ltd, Avena Mills, Ballysadare, Co. Sligo

Ranks (Ireland) Ltd, Erry Mill, Clara, Offaly (formerly M. J. & L. Goodbody)

Ranks (Ireland) Ltd, Shannon Mills, The Docks, Limerick

Shackleton, George & Sons Ltd, Anna Liffey Mills, Lucan, Co. Dublin

Waterford Flour Mills Ltd, Waterford Flour Mills, Ferrybank, Waterford

---

*Closed but milling license not yet revoked.

Following this return, twelve wheatmeal millers with quotas in excess of 1000 barrels were listed and a further forty with the same for less than 1000 barrels.

Source: As returned in Dáil Éireann Parliamentary Debates, vol. 205 (1963), 525–6.

Appendix E

Mills to Visit

A number of mills and places of milling interest are open from time to time. The following list is not comprehensive, but can be used as a guide.

Co. Antrim	Bushmill's Distillery	028 20732134	All year
Co. Armagh	Miltown		
Co. Cavan	Cavan town, The Mill Rock (temporarily closed) contact Boyne Valley Foods	041 987300	
Co. Cork	Macroom	087 2662192	April–September
	Midleton Distillery	021 4613594	All year
Co. Donegal	Newmills near Letterkenny (corn and flax mill)	074 25115	June–September
Co. Down	Annalong Corn Mill	028 43768736	All year
	Ballycopeland windmill, near Millisle	028 90543033	July–August
	Ballyduggan Mill near Downpatrick	028 44613654	Now a hotel
	Castleward, The National Trust	028 44881204	
	Ulster Folk and Transport Museum Centre	028 90428428	
Co. Dublin	Shackletons' near Lucan (1930s roller mills) Special interest groups – contact conservation officer	01 8905000	
	Skerries (restored water and windmills)	01 8495208	All year
Co. Fermanagh	Mullyvovet (restored corn mill), near Belcoo		
Co. Galway	Tuam Little Mill (oat mill)	093 25486	
Co. Kerry	Blennerville windmill	066 7121064	April–October
Co. Limerick	Croom Mills (exhibition and restaurant)	061 397130	All year
Co. Louth	White River Mill, Dunleer	041 6851141	By arrangement
Co. Tyrone	Coalisland Heritage Centre	028 87748532	All year

	Dyan Mill near Caledon	028 388771238	
	McBready's Mill, Aughnacloy		
Co. Wexford	Craanford Mill near Gorey	055 28125	Easter–September
	Garrylough Mill near Castlebridge		Restaurant
	Tacumshin (restored windmill)		
Co. Westmeath	Locke's Distillery, Kilbeggan		All year

For updated information please write to:

The Industrial Heritage Association of Ireland,
c/o The National Trust for Ireland,
The Tailors Hall,
Blacklane,
Dublin 8

or

The Mills & Millers of Ireland Association,
c/o Mentrim Mills,
Drumcondra,
Co. Meath